MUSIC IN THE RENAISSANCE

MUSIC IN THE RENAISSANCE

Richard Freedman

Haverford College

W. W. NORTON AND COMPANY

NEW YORK • LONDON

Editor: Maribeth Payne
Associate Editor: Justin Hoffman
Assistant Editor: Ariella Foss
Developmental Editor: Harry Haskell
Manuscript Editor: Bonnie Blackburn
Project Editor: Jack Borrebach
Electronic Media Editor: Steve Hoge
Marketing Manager, Music: Amy Parkin
Production Manager: Ashley Horna
Photo Editor: Stephanie Romeo
Permissions Manager: Megan Jackson
Text Design: Jillian Burr
Composition: CM Preparé
Manufacturing: Quad/Graphics-Fairfield, PA

A catalogue record is available from the Library of Congress
ISBN 978-0-393-92916-4

W. W. Norton & Company, Inc., 500 Fifth Avenue, New York, NY 10110-0017
wwnorton.com
W. W. Norton & Company, Ltd., Castle House, 75/76 Wells Street, London W1T3QT

In memory of my parents—my first teachers

CONTENTS IN BRIEF

CONTENTS

ANTHOLOGY REPERTOIRE

SERIES EDITOR'S PREFACE

Western Music in Context: A Norton History starts from the premise that music consists of far more than the notes on a page or the sound heard on a recording. Music is a product of its time and place, of the people and institutions that bring it into being.

Many music history texts focus on musical style and on individual composers. These approaches have been a valuable part of writing about music since the beginnings of modern scholarship in the later nineteenth century. But in the past few decades, scholars have widened their scope in imaginative and illuminating ways to explore the cultural, social, intellectual, and historical contexts for music. This new perspective is reflected in the volumes of Western Music in Context. Among the themes treated across the series are:

- The ways in which music has been commissioned, created, and consumed in public and private spheres
- The role of technology in the creation and transmission of music, from the advent of notation to the digital age
- The role of women as composers, performers, and patrons
- The relationships between music and national or ethnic identity
- The training and education of musicians in both private and institutional settings

All of these topics—and more—animate the pages of Western Music in Context. Written in an engaging style by recognized experts, the series paints vivid pictures of moments, activities, locales, works, and individuals:

- A fourth-century eyewitness report on musical practices in the Holy Land, from a European nun on a pilgrimage
- A lavish wedding at the court of Savoy in the mid-fifteenth century, with Music by Guillaume Du Fay

- Broadside ballads sung on the streets of London or pasted onto walls, and enjoyed by people from all levels of society
- A choral Magnificat performed at a church in colonial Brazil in the 1770s, accompanied by an organ sent by ship and mule from Portugal
- The barely literate impresario Domenico Barbaia making a tidy fortune at Italian opera houses by simultaneously managing gambling tables and promoting Gioachino Rossini
- A "radio teaching piece" from 1930 by Kurt Weill celebrating the transatlantic flight of Charles Lindbergh

Each volume of Western Music in Context is accompanied by a concise anthology of carefully chosen works. The anthologies offer representative examples of a wide variety of musical genres, styles, and national traditions. Included are excerpts from well-known works like Aaron Copland's *Billy the Kid*, as well as lesser-known gems like Ignacio de Jerusalem's *Matins for the Virgin of Guadalupe*. Commentaries within the anthologies not only provide concise analyses of every work from both formal and stylistic points of view, but also address issues of sources and performance practice.

StudySpace, Norton's online resource for students, features links to recordings of anthology selections that can be streamed from the Naxos Music Library (individual or institutional subscription required), as well as the option to purchase and download recordings from Amazon and iTunes. In addition, students can purchase access to, and instructors can request a free DVD of, the Norton Opera Sampler, which features over two hours of video excerpts from fourteen Metropolitan Opera productions. Finally, for readers wanting to do further research or find more specialized books, articles, or web-based resources, StudySpace offers lists of further readings that supplement those at the end of each chapter in the texts.

Because the books of the Western Music in Context series are relatively compact and reasonably priced, instructors and students might use one or more volumes in a single semester, or several across an academic year. Instructors have the flexibility to supplement the books and the accompanying anthologies with other resources, including Norton Critical Scores and *Strunk's Source Readings in Music History*, as well as other readings, illustrations, scores, films, and recordings.

The contextual approach to music history offers limitless possibilities: an instructor, student, or general reader can extend the context as widely as he or she wishes. Well before the advent of the World Wide Web, the renowned anthropologist Clifford Geertz likened culture to a spider's web of interconnected meanings that humans have spun. Music has been a vital part of such webs throughout the history of the West. Western Music in Context has as its goal to highlight such connections and to invite the instructors and students to continue that exploration on their own.

Walter Frisch
Columbia University

"I am always more affected by the causes of events than by the events themselves." These words, from the writings of the Roman statesman, philosopher, and orator Marcus Tullius Cicero, are an ideal starting point for this volume, and an ideal entry point into the Renaissance as a historical period. Cicero's letters and speeches were models of eloquence for those who aspired to be persuasive speakers and writers. His writings were copied, printed, taught, and emulated in the original Latin, and later in vernacular languages like Italian, French, and English.

It was from classical authorities like Cicero that Renaissance statesmen, preachers, and gentlemen learned to write and speak, swaying their readers and listeners to their point of view. But Cicero's influence was more than stylistic. His writings on history in particular instilled in Renaissance historians a new self-consciousness about the past and prompted new efforts to explain what happened, in addition to chronicling it. Indeed, it was through this new perspective on the historian's craft that Italian writers of the fifteenth century first declared themselves the true heirs to classical Greek and Roman civilization, dismissing the previous centuries as "Middle Ages" between antique culture and the "Renaissance" of their own day.

Throughout this book we will try to explain *why* music developed in the ways it did, even as we chart its changing forms and techniques. We will look at who made music, who sponsored it, who preserved and owned it—and above all what composers, performers, and listeners wanted from music, and what purposes it served. We will encounter many types of music: sacred (such as masses and motets), secular (chansons and madrigals), and instrumental (variations, fantasias, and other improvisatory genres). It is important to understand the stylistic hallmarks of each of these genres as they developed during the fifteenth and sixteenth centuries. But it is no less important to explain the course of these developments as cultural practices. The pieces considered in these pages are beautiful, poignant, complex, and even fun to listen to. But we can significantly deepen our appreciation of them by exploring the training of the musicians who made them, the institutions that fostered them, and the values they helped to enact. Musical genres are not just formal or technical categories; they are also social practices in constant transformation.

The chapters that follow will always be historical—in Cicero's sense of probing for meaning and explanation—even when they are not strictly chronological in their organization. The core of the narrative divides into three spans. The first deals with enduring musical practices of the fifteenth century. From here we pause to consider transformative ideas about music that emerged around the year 1500. Finally, we explore the rapid expansion of expressive means heard over the course of the sixteenth century in secular and sacred vocal music, and in instrumental practice too. As prelude to these three parts, I offer a pair of introductory chapters that put the broad trajectory of the text in sharp relief, first with a few carefully chosen examples, documents, and testimonies about the Renaissance as a period in music history and then by exploring transformations in the content and purposes of a musical education (for amateurs and professionals alike) in the Renaissance. The ideas offered in these chapters will serve us well as we explore the place of music in the courts, churches, and private spaces of Renaissance Europe.

Like other volumes in the series, *Music in the Renaissance* is relatively concise, providing a selective overview of the period. The book makes no pretense of covering all of the composers, genres, and techniques of the fifteenth and sixteenth centuries. Such information can readily be found in any of the excellent scholarly and reference works about the period on which this text builds. At times I quote directly from these sources; still others are referenced in the suggestions for further reading that can be found at the conclusion of each chapter and in an expanded bibliography on StudySpace, Norton's online resource for students. In addition, I maintain a website (linked from books.wwnorton.com/books/Music-in-the-Renaissance) that lists numerous online resources, such as facsimiles, for the study of Renaissance music and gathers musicians and terms encountered in each chapter. All of these materials have been selected in the interest of stimulating further discussion, study, and reaction.

The text is sparing in its use of musical examples and analytical remarks. For those who want to delve deeper into individual works, twenty-seven full musical scores, each with detailed commentary, are included in the accompanying *Anthology for Music in the Renaissance*. Links to recordings of anthology repertoire are available on StudySpace. The selections favor pieces that are available in excellent modern recorded performances through electronic vendors like iTunes and the Naxos Music Library, as well as on CD. (Specifically recommended performances are listed on StudySpace.)

ACKNOWLEDGMENTS

I would like to offer my thanks to the many friends, colleagues, and students who offered advice and help throughout the gestation of this book. Among them Lawrence F. Bernstein deserves pride of place. Everything I know of this field (and much else) is thanks to him. Many others took time to offer interesting examples, test chapters with students, unpack my prose, and save me from clumsy errors, including John Griffiths, David Crook, Patrick Macey, Yossi Maurey, Grantley McDonald, Stefano Mengozzi, Stephanie Schlagel, Pamela Starr, John Thompson, Emily Zazulia, and Carla Zecher. Marcia S. Tacconi, Honey Meconi, Pamela F. Starr, and Blake Wilson reviewed the manuscript for W. W. Norton; I am grateful for their suggestions of ways to improve the book. Harry Haskell brought focus and clarity to the whole. Bonnie Blackburn did far more than copyedit the book. There are no words to describe her skill and professionalism. Leofranc Holford-Strevens was generous with his translations.

I would also like to acknowledge the support of Haverford College, for a sabbatical during 2007–2008 when the first draft was written, and to John C. Whitehead, whose gift to the College provides generous support for my research. I am also grateful to the staff of our John B. Hurford '60 Center for the Arts and Humanities, which provided a summer research stipend for Ariella Foss, then a Haverford student, now assistant editor at Norton, who has been invaluable from start to finish. Walker Anderson VII benefited from the same stipend in the summer of 2011 and helped greatly with reading lists for the book. Finally, my thanks to Walter Frisch, Maribeth Payne, and the entire team of series authors—Margot Fassler, Wendy Heller, John Rice, and Joe Auner—for many stimulating conversations on music, history, and ideas.

Richard Freedman

MUSIC IN THE
RENAISSANCE

PART I

Beginnings

By the Renaissance, historians generally mean a series of cultural trans-formations that took place across Europe during the fifteenth and six-teenth centuries. For some the period is framed by political events, like the Battle of Agincourt in 1415 and the beginning of the Thirty Years' War in 1618, each of which inaugurated a series of radically destabilizing alliances and conflicts that literally redrew the map of Europe.

These were not the only watershed events of our period. The capture of Constantinople in 1453 by the Ottoman Turks (who renamed it Istanbul) sent westward a wave of Greek scholars, whose precious manuscripts exerted a pro-found influence on their colleagues in the Italian peninsula and helped give rise to the intellectual movement known as humanism. In the private academies sustained by influential patrons in places like Florence, Rome, and Mantua, the cultivation of ancient learning transformed scholarly method, philosophy, and the study of history.

These new ideas and methods spread thanks in part to the advent of an equally transformative technology: the printing press. Johannes Gutenberg's Bible, produced between 1452 and 1456, was the first European book prepared from movable type. Others followed, many in vernacular languages rather than Latin, including William Caxton's *History of Troy* (1473), Niccolò Machiavelli's *Il principe* (The Prince, 1513), Baldassare Castiglione's *Il libro del cortegiano* (The Book of the Courtier, 1528). Through these and other books, speakers of lo-cal tongues found new models of speech and behavior. Literary expression in French, Italian, and English also flourished during this period, first in courts and scholarly academies, and later among the ever-widening circle of literate city dwellers.

The press was also an important agent of religious change and debate, as when Martin Luther issued his German translation of the New Testament in 1522, or when Roman Catholic authorities began a book-by-book investigation and cen-sorship of heretical teachings, the *Index librorum prohibitorum* (List of Forbidden Books) in the 1540s. The Protestant Reformation, and the subsequent Catholic Counter-Reformation, did not merely involve personal belief; they embroiled nearly every aspect of life, from politics to the arts. Meanwhile, European ex-plorers fanned out to Africa, Asia, and the New World, carrying their political and religious agendas to alien places and peoples. Columbus's voyage of 1492 was neither the first nor the last of these encounters, which were as destructive as they were transformative for all concerned.

Music was actively enlisted in, and shaped by, each of these transformative processes. In Chapter 1, we consider a pair of works from the extreme limits of our period. A motet by Johannes Ciconia from about 1400 features three differ-ent Latin texts at once, all organized around a slow-moving melody drawn from the sacred plainsong repertory. Melding political with sacred imagery, the work reminds us of the weight of tradition. In both sound and method of composition, it is in many ways indistinguishable from similar motets crafted during the fourteenth century, as detailed in Margot Fassler's *Music in the Medieval West*.

Against this we pit an Italian madrigal of the 1580s by Luca Marenzio, a setting of an intensely passionate poem of the sort that was fashionable across musical Europe among cultivated courtiers and urbane amateurs. As Wendy Heller shows in *Music in the Baroque*, this kind of polyphonic expression of inner sensibilities was in the early seventeenth century rapidly abandoned in favor of an idiom founded on solo expression to the accompaniment of instruments. But in its orientation around its literary text, and especially in its free treatment of contrapuntal dissonance, Marenzio's madrigal has much in common with later musical forms.

Framing this pair of pieces is a corresponding set of testimonies from contemporary theorists, whose advice to aspiring composers reveals a lot about the methods by which these sorts of pieces were crafted, the purposes they served, and the mentalities they represent. From these close-ups we zoom out to establish a wider context, filling in the main stylistic developments and the changing modes of musical expression that span the gulf between the twin anchoring points of our narrative.

In Chapter 2 we turn to another kind of beginning, in this case of musical education. We will learn about the basic scale, or gamut; how singers were taught to navigate their way around it with mnemonic hexachords; and what happened as new chromatic intervals (*musica ficta*, or "false music") were added. We will see how the medieval melodic modes were adapted to modern practice. We will also learn about various techniques by which church singers were taught to harmonize with plainsong melodies (like fauxbourdon), and to create counterpoint on the spot against a preexisting tune known as a cantus firmus (literally, fixed melody). All of this, in turn, is considered in the context of the changing purposes of musical education for choirboys of the fifteenth century and aspiring gentlemen of the sixteenth century.

CHAPTER ONE

Music and the Cultures
of the Renaissance

How did musicians of the fifteenth and sixteenth centuries understand their craft? And how did music-making, in all its varied forms, take its place among the practices, ideas, and beliefs that we understand collectively as the Renaissance? In this book we will seek to answer these questions by considering treatises, sacred and secular texts, chronicles, and other documents of the day for what they can reveal about changing approaches to music during this important period in European history. But reversing the perspective is often no less productive, for through music we can also take time to gauge aspects of daily life—from religious debates to the intimate experiences of the passions—that are not easily accessible to us through other historical sources. Musicians of the fifteenth and sixteenth centuries can teach us much about their age. They can also teach us much about the present, a period of technological, social, and philosophical changes no less far-ranging than those experienced during the Renaissance.

THE CRAFT OF COMPOSITION: TWO VIEWS

Consider, for instance, two pieces of practical advice to would-be composers, one from the years around 1350, the other from about 1600. In his *Tractatus cantus mensurabilis* (Treatise on Measured Song), the French cleric Egidius of Murino (active mid-fourteenth century) offers succinct instructions on how to put together a motet for several voices. His model is a conservative one, reflecting compositional methods in use since the mid-1300s. (In music, theory typically lags a generation or two behind practice.) "First take for your tenor [fundamental voice] any antiphon or responsory or any other chant from the book of Office chants; and its words should accord with the theme or occasion for which the motet is being made." After arranging the tones of the tenor melody in rhythm, Egidius suggests adding up to three additional parts in succession, adjusting musical counterpoint for suitable consonances and subtle syncopations, like an elaborate musical gloss of a basic idea. Now for the words, Latin or French verses for each of the upper voices of the motet:

> Divide them into four segments; and divide the music into four corresponding segments; and put the first segment of the words over the first segment of the music as best you can, and proceed in this way all the way to the end. Sometimes it will be necessary to stretch many notes over few words in order to make the setting come out right, and sometimes many words must be squeezed into a small amount of time. Just fit it together any way you can.

Egidius's do-it-yourself approach makes a number of assumptions that are worth pausing to consider. On one hand, he presumes on the part of his readers a considerable knowledge of musical notation and counterpoint—hardly as simple as his step-by-step formula implies. On the other hand, he finds no embarrassment in advocating that these sophisticated musicians would simply "fit it together any way you can" when it comes to the text. If, as he suggests, the words of the tenor melody are supposed to accord with the occasion to be marked by the motet, it is certainly strange that the words of the other voices matter so little, like a piece of upholstery casually stapled over a sturdy frame!

A Plaine and Easie Introduction to Practicall Musicke (1597), by Thomas Morley (1557/58–1602), in contrast, takes the careful representation of texts as the highest aim of musical composition. Borrowing heavily from the Venetian music theorist Gioseffo Zarlino, whom we'll meet in Chapter 2, he details various ways the musician might "dispose your musicke according to the nature of the words which you are therein to expresse, as whatsoever matter it be which you have in hand, such a kind of musicke must you frame to it." Morley's suggestions for various ways to do this cover the entire range of polyphonic practice, from the selection of harmonies (now "somwhat harsh and hard," now "sad and doleful") to rhythmic motion (light subjects imply "quicknesse of time," lamentable ones call for "slow and heavie motions"), melodic direction (allusions to heaven call for ascent), and even accent and phrasing suited to the declamation of the text. The result, for musicians who follow these guidelines, will be "a perfect agreement . . . betwixt the matter and the musicke."

Morley's insistence on the close connection between text and tone contrasts strikingly with Egidius's successive layers of casual alignment and ceremonial purpose. For those familiar with the intimate alliance of poetry and music in the nineteenth-century lieder of Franz Schubert and Robert Schumann, for example, Morley's model seems self-evidently logical in a way that Egidius's can never be. But there is more: Morley also suggests that in order to succeed in this enterprise, aspiring composers ought to engage in a bit of make-believe, temporarily participating in the subject matter being represented. Such imaginative musical role-playing was especially important for madrigals—settings of secular poetry in Italian (and later English) that were wildly fashionable in Morley's England. "If therefore you will compose in this kind," he continues, "you must possess your selfe with an amorus humor (for in no composition shal you prove admirable except you put on, and possesse your selfe wholly with that vaine wherein you compose)."

It is tempting to read in Morley's manifesto a mirror of our own ideas about individual expression through music. His ideas certainly stand in stark contrast to Egidius's advice, which passes over the notion of self-expression in silence. Morley's aspiring composer, after all, is not advised to "express your selfe" but instead to "put on, and possesse your selfe." The composer of a madrigal, by this measure, is a temporary self, undertaken as part of a theater of expression through words and tones. This dynamic interplay between the rival claims of music as ceremony or ritual (as Egidius's model clearly advocates) and music as a force for self-presentation and expression (as in Morley's) will return often throughout this book.

What is it like to listen to and study pieces written according to the ideals set out two centuries apart by Egidius and Morley? The musical engagement of varied images and passions seems to be the main business of the five-voice madrigal *Liquide perle* (Liquid Pearls, 1580) by Morley's Italian contemporary Luca Marenzio (1553/54–1599). In this compact piece, we hear a series of striking combinations, each designed to capture the meaning or mood of the text. It opens with a cascade of intertwining ornaments for the upper voices, patterns that cast before our ears something of the visual abundance of the erotic "liquid pearls" that emanate from the eyes of the beloved. But Marenzio also captures ideas that are better felt than seen, particularly the evocative sighing figures and dissonant combinations at the word "ohimè" (alas; Ex. 1.1). Spoken language normally has an important *denotative* function, whereby words are understood to signify concepts. But exclamations like "alas" are chiefly *connotative*—they imitate gestures or feelings rather than embody an idea. Music meets the needs of such exclamations nicely, for it fills in the aesthetic space with sounds more meaningful than any words. Morley's pupils would have done well to imitate such a model, which presumes a composer ready to take on the temporary trappings of the human passions, and a set of performers and listeners ready to participate in them. (For further discussion of Marenzio's piece, see Anthology 1 and Chapter 10.)

If the music of Morley's and Marenzio's day was filled with a dynamic sense of "becoming," works from Egidius's world seem to have been largely concerned

Example 1.1: *Luca Marenzio,* Liquide perle, *mm. 20–27. From Luca Marenzio, Il Primo libro de madrigali a cinque voci* (Venice: Angelo Gardano, 1580), p. 1.

But alas, my heart

with the hierarchical structures and symbolic forms that we'll examine in Chapter 5. *Doctorum principem* (Prince of Teachers), a four-voice polytextual motet by Johannes Ciconia (ca. 1370–1412), exemplifies this tradition. The work is exceedingly complex to hear. The upper voices trade rapid fusillades of words and music, while the comparatively slow-moving tenor and contratenor create a continuous foundation of sound (Anthology 2). As taught by Egidius and generations of music theorists of the fifteenth and sixteenth centuries, cantus-firmus structures like these (so called on account of the borrowed liturgical or secular tunes stretched out in long notes in the tenor) were the basis of much Latin-texted music of the period. The prevailing contrapuntal ideal favors perfect intervals such as fifths and octaves as the main points of articulation and stress, but on account of the rhythmic complexity we can also hear many other combinations in passing. Things become a little clearer once we turn to the Latin texts—one each for the two upper voices, plus a fragment of text for the plainsong tenor—which present the words in a welter of verbal as well as musical counterpoint. This was apparently a ceremonial piece, written in honor of Francesco Zabarella, archpriest of Padua Cathedral and one of Ciconia's patrons, who is praised in a torrent of florid fanfares as the "prince of teachers" and "true father of the commonweal," thus joining occasion and musical movement in a clockwork of symbolic commemoration (Ex. 1.2). Egidius probably would have approved, for this work coordinates many of the practical suggestions offered in the *Tractatus* in a sophisticated way.

Example 1.2: *Johannes Ciconia,* Doctorum principem, *mm. 52–57. From Johannes Ciconia,* The Works of Johannes Ciconia, *ed. Margaret Bent and Anne Hallmark, Polyphonic Music of the Fourteenth Century, 24 (Monaco: Editions de L'Oiseau-Lyre, 1985), p. 91.*

O Francesco Zabarella, glory, teacher
O Francesco Zabarella, glory, protector

CHANGING STYLES AND CONTEXTS

The changes framed by these two examples are profound. Between them, we can trace the development of a number of related musical innovations, notably:

- The transition from a hierarchical, successive system of composition to one in which all parts carry equal weight and were conceived at once, frequently around points of imitative counterpoint.

- The development of a contrapuntal ideal that gave increasing prominence to long successions of imperfect consonances (thirds and sixths). Such vertical intervals had certainly been a part of older idioms, especially in their capacity to draw the listener firmly to a perfect consonance (unison, octave, or fifth) at a cadence. But now composers favored long chains of imperfect consonances well before the cadence. These new preferences were explained partly through appeals to reason and mathematics, but also increasingly on the basis of what was observable through sensation and experience.

- Alongside the expanding universe of acceptable concords, a newly expanded chromatic musical palette, dictated in part by requirements of counterpoint. This new musical range also served to undermine the distinctiveness of the old church modes (see Figs. 2.5 and 2.6) that were conceived as a framework for plainsong melodies of the Catholic liturgy.

- The emergence of melodic gestures organized around the stylized patterns of dance and speech. The first comes with a growing sense of linear time aimed at climax and resolution; the second with the recognition that musical discourse could be allied to the time-bound arts of rhetoric and oratory. These new ways of organizing musical time both complemented and expanded the kinds of musical time heard under the old mensural system of musical rhythm, with its hierarchical levels of duple and triple time and its abstract notational schemes used both to organize tenor melodies and to engender all sorts of contrapuntal motion among different voices. (The system is also considered in Chapter 2.)

- The persistent interplay between written and unwritten modes of musical expression. Traditions of solo delivery and embellishment once known mainly to singers and instrumentalists were newly taught, notated, and even borrowed by composers for written works, which in turn yielded new opportunities for interpretation and variation.

The pathways among these developments are complex. Indeed, during the fifteenth and sixteenth centuries, as in any period, many contradictory impulses were at work in European music. Given all of these competing trends, we would be hard pressed to imagine them as unified by any but the broadest of similarities. For instance, the elaborate cantus-firmus motets of the fifteenth-century English composer Leonel Power have much more in common with Ciconia's *Doctorum principem* in terms of design and function than with Marenzio's madrigal. And the urge to imitate the affective, even dramatic, character of Marenzio's literary texts anticipates Claudio Monteverdi's *seconda prattica* (second practice) of composition (see Chapter 14), itself an important avatar of new currents in the seventeenth century, which Wendy Heller describes in her volume in this series, *Music in the Baroque*.

These stylistic changes were encouraged and enabled by a series of cultural, social, and technological developments, including:

- New technologies of music printing that permitted composers to put text in tight alignment with tone, making possible a new level of fixity for their works not possible in a musical culture transmitted by manuscript or unwritten tradition.

- New mobility of both music and musicians across boundaries of class, religious belief, and geography, in part aided by the new printing technologies, which also made it possible for more people to own musical works as well as to hear or perform them.

- Detachment of polyphonic music from its ritual and political moorings, which were now joined by new aesthetic or recreational purposes. Increasingly, music was valued for its expressive and representational qualities no less than its ceremonial or ritual ones.

- New roles for singers and instrumentalists, leading to new and specialized genres for particular combinations of forces. New literacies implied by the widening availability of printed music and music instruction manuals transformed the role and purpose of embellishment and variation in performance, amateur and professional alike.

- A new kind of self-conscious speculation about the purposes and status of music—whether it works upon listeners for good or bad, and how to control its power, both secular and sacred.

- A new sense of musical works as more than symbolic systems; they are also something to be performed and heard, vital acts of communication from author to listener, and perhaps among listeners, too.

The task of measuring the changing purposes and meanings of music against these broad developments raises its own challenges, as we'll discover. Before exploring this cultural history and the musical men and women who made it happen, we should pause to consider two key concepts, Renaissance and humanism, and their echoes in the process of religious reform, in the world of music printing, and in the emergence of the courtier ideal.

MUSIC AND THE RENAISSANCE: SOME PROBLEMS

Was there some set of ideals or aspirations that bound this remarkable series of developments together? To some extent, the answer depends on how we understand music in relation to the idea of the Renaissance itself. One of the first and most influential scholars to apply the term as a historical label was the great Swiss scholar Jacob Burckhardt, who used it in *The Civilization of the Renaissance in Italy* (1860) to describe a "reborn" sense of individualism and universal ideals. Burckhardt (1818–1897) had good reason to highlight this trend, as in many respects Italian scholars, courtiers, and even generals began in the fourteenth, fifteenth, and sixteenth centuries to think of themselves as undertaking a rebirth of ideals that they understood as an inheritance of classical Greek and Roman civilization.

It was the Italian historian and philologist Flavio Biondo (1392–1463) who first characterized the preceding centuries as "Middle Ages" between the high points of classical culture and its rebirth in his own day. Over a century later, the Italian painter and biographer Giorgio Vasari (1511–1574), in his book on the lives of "the most excellent painters, sculptors, and architects," traced the rebirth of art from Tuscan painting of the mid-thirteenth century (as in the naturalistic works of Giotto di Bondone), through various discoveries of perspective and anatomy in the fifteenth century, to the "perfection" of Michelangelo, Raphael, and Leonardo. It would be naive to presume that these ideals of rebirth and progress were shared by all segments of European society. Where popular or peasant traditions are concerned, for instance, scholars rightly doubt that the concept "Renaissance" (in the narrow sense of a renewal of classical ideals and models) helps us understand the past in all its variety and richness.

The question of a specifically musical Renaissance presents its own riddles and problems. For some, the search for a musical counterpart to the rebirth of ancient civilization leads to an academy of literati that met in the home of Count Giovanni de' Bardi in Florence during the 1570s and 1580s. The so-called Florentine Camerata sought to reproduce the effects of ancient dramatic performances in current styles of solo singing. Vincenzo Galilei (1520s–1591), the father of the famous mathematician and astronomer Galileo, wrote about these questions in his *Dialogo della musica antica et della moderna* (Dialogue on Ancient and Modern Music, 1581). His ideas set the stage for the experimental music dramas subsequently created in this elite circle by the poet Ottavio Rinuccini in collaboration with the musicians Jacopo Peri and Giulio Caccini in their settings of *Euridice* (Eurydice, 1600), *Dafne* (Daphne, 1598), and other works on mythological subjects.

The aesthetic and musical basis of the solo, or monodic, idiom employed in these works was not entirely new to sixteenth-century musical culture; it was simply obscured by the relative dominance of polyphonic forms. Nor can this narrowly "classical" definition of the musical Renaissance sustain itself for long, unless we are willing to think about the arts as moving out of sync with each other. Instead, our search to understand music and its place in fifteenth- and sixteenth-century Europe should take a broader view of how cultures change, and how music might be at work within them. Perhaps it's here that our other key concept, humanism, can help us bring the manifest musical variety of our period into focus.

HUMANISM IN THOUGHT, WORD, AND BELIEF

In the modern imagination, humanism is identified with secularism, and above all with the idea that individual men and women are the measure of all things. It is thus often characterized as being opposed to religious faith, or at least with institutional religion. For thinkers of the fifteenth and sixteenth centuries, the discipline known as *studia humanitatis* (studies of humanity) meant something quite different. Humanism was certainly not incompatible with religious institutions and other forms of authority. Its beginnings can be traced to the seven liberal arts (Fig. 1.1) that had formed the core of the European university curriculum for centuries: arithmetic, geometry, music, and astronomy (the quadrivium), alongside logic, rhetoric, and grammar (the trivium).

New texts and modes of inquiry had continually been folded into this demanding intellectual world. But particularly during the fifteenth and sixteenth centuries, new emphasis was placed on the arts of language. They were put to use in the study of texts in Latin and Greek, and these texts in turn became models for new interests in persuasive writing and speaking in Italian, French, and other vernacular languages used in civic life, in private academies like the Florentine Camerata, and in literature. Plato, Plotinus, Cicero, Virgil, Ovid, and other ancient writers became models for generations of not only scholars, but also literate rulers and the men and women who advised them. Statesmen and gentlemen were glad to be counted as humanists. So were religious thinkers, from Desiderius Erasmus to Jean Calvin, who used new modes of inquiry and new texts to reexamine religious faith from within. Music, too, was drawn into this heady mix. It was increasingly seen as a rhetorical art that served the needs of statesmen and preachers alike. (As Wendy Heller discusses in *Music in the Baroque*, the tension between "ancients" and "moderns" produced in the course of this humanistic work was intrinsic to music and musical thought in the seventeenth and eighteenth centuries as well.)

Figure 1.1: *Allegorical personifications of the seven liberal arts: arithmetic, geometry, music, astronomy, logic, rhetoric, and grammar, by Domenico de Michelino, ca. 1460*

MUSIC AND THE SPIRIT OF RELIGIOUS REFORM

As theologians and political authorities questioned the character and conduct of faith, music was frequently enlisted in the fray. It remained a crucial part of worship, as it had been in the medieval era, but many religious thinkers were increasingly concerned about the seductive sway it seemed to exert on hearers. When Calvin addressed readers of the earliest printed edition of the Geneva Psalter (first published in 1542), which included monophonic melodies for use in congregational worship by members of his new Genevan church, he worried about the "secret and almost incredible power" of music (see Chapter 11). Fearing the possibility that music might give "free rein to dissoluteness" or make listeners "effeminate with disordered pleasures," he sought to rule it "in such a manner that it may be useful to us and in no way pernicious" (SR 57:366; 3/22:88).

Calvin's anxieties about the dangerous effects of music were not new, of course; he enlisted both Plato and patristic writers such as St. Augustine in support of his plan. But characteristic of his attempts to control music are the ways he called upon the equally powerful medium of language to pin down the elusive capacity of music to move human passions. In this respect Calvin's project can be framed by the same profound concern for language seen in the writings of Catholic theologians, who otherwise would seem to have little in common with Protestant reformers. As we have seen, alliances of text and tone also figured centrally in Thomas Morley's advice to aspiring composers: For both Calvin and Morley, music can complement texts, which give purpose and meaning to sound.

MUSIC AND THE CULTURES OF PRINT

Calvin's preface to the Geneva Psalter points to the ways in which Renaissance music was radically transformed by the printing press, by expanding patterns of literacy, and by the rise of vernacular languages as eloquent vehicles of expression alongside Latin and Greek. Through these interrelated developments, access to books—and the ideas contained in them—was extended to new communities of readers, much as electronic media have made ideas, sounds, and images available with unprecedented breadth in the last hundred years. For music, the effects of this social transformation were profound. By the middle of the sixteenth century a number of important cities, including Venice, Paris, Antwerp, Nuremberg, and Munich, hosted important publishing houses that issued music books of incredible variety and quality (see Chapter 9). The compositions offered to newly literate amateurs reflected a wide range of repertories, from pieces composed for church and state ceremony to chansons, madrigals, and instrumental music for domestic consumption. Political authorities encouaged such work. When King Francis I in 1531 issued an official privilege assuring Pierre Attaingnant of a monopoly to protect his investment in this comparative ly new technology, he balanced the private benefit that would accumulate to the printer against the general welfare of society: "in order to serve the churches, their ministers, and generally all people, and for the very great good, utility, and recreation of the general public" (SR 46:331; 3/11:53).

MUSIC AND THE RENAISSANCE GENTLEMAN

The sort of musical literacy implied by this agenda of public good was quickly taken up as essential to the education and the ethical formation of the ideal gentleman. *Il libro del cortegiano* (The Book of the Courtier, 1528) by Baldassare Castiglione (1478–1529) was the first and most influential of these "courtesy" manuals. As we'll see in Chapter 7, Castiglione's interlocutors frequently invoke musical performance as a measure of social skill. Praising those ready to sing and accompany themselves on the lute, they nevertheless encourage the would-be gentleman to attune himself to his audience: "If the Courtier be a righteous judge of himself, he shall apply himself well enough to the time and shall discern when the hearers' minds are disposed to give ear and when they are not" (SR 45:329; 3/10:51).

By this standard, musical performance is no less an act of persuasion than a form of self-expression or entertainment. As such it was increasingly associated with language by courtiers, bureaucrats, and merchants. No longer confined to its place in the old Scholastic quadrivium (where it was studied in alliance with geometry, astronomy, and mathematics), music was now associated with the *studia humanitatis*, especially rhetoric and oratory. These rival claims over the purposes and character of musical expression return us once again to the gulf with which we began—between the symbolic, functional order embodied in Egidius of Murino's musical handbook and the implicitly communicative, persuasive model advocated by Thomas Morley two centuries later. For Morley, the very idea of a composer who might take on an "amorus humor" only makes sense if we also imagine a listening subject to and upon whom such effects are represented in an effort to convince, move, or persuade.

A DIALOGUE WITH THE PAST

Whenever we encounter works from an earlier time or a distant place, we unavoidably unhinge them from their original cultural foundation. Such eavesdropping is characteristic of our contemporary musical landscape, with

its propensity to mingle styles and genres. To the extent that Renaissance humanists were concerned to understand themselves in relation to the past, it
seems a little ironic that music history per se was not chief among their projects. They heard only the music of their present, or at best what they imagined
to be the *effects* of ancient music refracted through modern means. Separated
from the music of the fifteenth and sixteenth centuries by a gulf of some 500
years, however, our encounter with the past ought to be a more deliberate process, attempting to recognize the past as much as possible in its own terms,
and not only in ours. We will thus pause to consider what musicians and musical thinkers of the day had to say about their art, even as we reflect on what it
might mean for us today.

Given this twin set of perspectives, our inquiry will necessarily be highly
selective. The names, careers, and ideas of a number of important men and
women will return throughout our study. We could hardly lay claim to a complete history of music during the years between 1400 and 1600 on the basis of a
limited survey of composers, theorists, performers, and arbiters of taste. But
without wishing to give the impression that history is best studied through the
achievements of illustrious figures, we can certainly gain through them a good
sense of the many roles that music played in their lives, and why it mattered.

According to the thematic logic of the chapters that follow, we will refrain from giving long lists of musicians, genres, forms, and technical terms.
Instead, we will use a relatively small number of examples, situations, and
case studies to highlight a number of persistent issues, both musical and cultural. We will often be concerned with music as a ceremonial and expressive
form, tracing the claims of ritual and representation in various sacred and
secular contexts. We will also dwell on the intersection of oral and written traditions, and in particular on the ways in which singers and instrumentalists
brought specialist skills to the realization of the works they performed. By the
end of our inquiry, we will come to understand the power of music as it was
understood in the old Scholastic tradition of order and number, and how it was
enlisted in the new humanist concerns for language, oratory, and persuasive
speech. We begin our exploration of these currents with a brief survey of the
changing profile of musical education, the story of which can be taken as a
measure of many of the themes noted above.

FOR FURTHER READING

Atlas, Allan, *Renaissance Music: Music in Western Europe, 1400–1600* (New York:
W. W. Norton, 1998)

Campbell, Gordon, *The Oxford Dictionary of the Renaissance* (Oxford: Oxford
University Press, 2003)

Haar, James, *European Music, 1520–1640* (Rochester, NY: Boydell Press, 2006)

Lowinsky, Edward E., "Music in the Culture of the Renaissance," *Journal of the History of Ideas* 15 (1954): 509–53; reprinted in *Music in the Culture of the Renaissance and Other Essays*, 2 vols., edited by Bonnie J. Blackburn, 1:19–39 (Chicago: University of Chicago Press, 1989)

Owens, Jessie Ann, "Music Historiography and the Definition of 'Renaissance,'" *Notes* 47 (1990): 305–30

Page, Christopher, *Discarding Images: Reflections on Music and Culture in Medieval France*, pp. xv–xxiv (Oxford: Oxford University Press, 1993)

Perkins, Leeman, *Music in the Age of the Renaissance* (New York: W. W. Norton, 1999)

Ⓢ Additional resources available at wwnorton.com/studyspace

CHAPTER TWO

Learning to Be a Musician

A s we saw in Chapter 1, Egidius of Murino and Thomas Morley articulated very different ideas about the relationship of words and music, the order and priorities of polyphonic lines, and the aims of composition itself. Their views give us insight into how musicians of the fourteenth and sixteenth centuries understood their craft. But how, exactly, did one go about acquiring musical knowledge to begin with? And where did an aspiring singer or player seek instruction?

As with many aspects of musical life during this period, few people took the time to systematize the prerequisites of an art that depended so heavily on aural sensibilities and first-hand instruction. But books like Morley's *A Plaine and Easie Introduction to Practicall Musicke* offer a wealth of information. They allow us to explore the basics of the Renaissance tone system, the role of duets in study, and the importance of counterpoint as a preliminary to any attempt at composition. We'll put these skills in a broader historical frame, tracing the social and professional changes that gradually took music education out of the old cathedral choir schools of the fifteenth century and into the private chambers of the men and women of the sixteenth century who wanted to demonstrate civility and good manners. Along the way we'll encounter other teachers and students, from the French choirboys in the charge of men like the theologian Jean Gerson to the royal princess tutored by Johannes Tinctoris and the Lutheran pupils of

Adrian Petit Coclico. Music instruction remained a conservative world, even as the uses of musical knowledge were changing.

A PLAIN AND EASY INTRODUCTION

Morley's *Plaine and Easie Introduction* seems a good place to begin. It is a self-help manual for musicians in the form of a dialogue between a young man about to go off to university, Philomathes ("lover of knowledge"), and his tutor Gnorimus ("wise one"). The student knows nothing of music except his need to acquire a command of it in order to take part in the colloquy of "excellent schollers, (both gentlemen and others)." At a banquet one evening, Philomathes found himself in an unenviable position, unable to take part in either a conversation about music or its performance:

> But I refusing and pretending ignorance, the whole companie condemned mee of discurtesie, being fully perswaded, that I had beene as skilfull in that art, as they tooke mee to be learned in others. But supper being ended, and Musicke bookes, according to the custome being brought to the table: the mistresse of the house presented mee with a part, earnestly requesting mee to sing.

The shame of ignorance brought him to Gnorimus: "Begin at the verie beginning," Philomathes pleads, "and teach mee as though I were a childe." Having set the scene, Morley now lets his eager pupil ask questions conveniently posed to prompt his fictive master to present information in an orderly way. The question-and-answer format is hardly unique to music textbooks, having been employed in philosophical, literary, and didactic texts since antiquity. In addition to practical knowledge, such books provided ready models for discourse and discussion, rhetorical skills that were central to humanist intellectual pursuits and to the ambitions of every Renaissance gentleman (see Chapter 7).

Morley's dialogue serves the twin goals of civility and practical knowledge perfectly. The conversation unfolds in three large sections: "Teaching to Sing," "Treating of Descant," and "Treating of Composing or Setting of Songes." We've already encountered some of the aesthetic and social priorities of the last part. In "Teaching to Sing," Gnorimus presents the basics as they were commonly understood by generations of musicians: the gamut, or steps of musical space as defined by the human vocal range; the various clefs, which allow us to locate ourselves among the steps of the scale; and the signs for notating the rhythm of measured music, in contrast to the flexible rhythm of plainsong. (Morley's English colleagues referred to measured music as "pricksong," while Continental writers sometimes called it "figured" music.)

For modern musicians, these ideas are at once distant and familiar. We still use the clefs, and it is not hard for us to recognize the symbols used for rhythmic notation. North American musicians call them by different names, but the basic Renaissance hierarchy of long, breve, semibreve, minim, and semiminim—or quadruple whole-note, double whole-note, whole-note, half-note, and quarter-note—is the same as the one we use today.

In other respects, however, the foundations of musical space and time in Morley's day seem decidedly strange to us. For instance, the notes used to represent durations could change their meaning according to the context. In triple (or "perfect") time, a breve consisted of three semibreves. Under duple (or "imperfect") time it consisted of only two semibreves. Thus the same series of note shapes could mean a quite different series of rhythmic values when preceded by signs that indicated duple and triple mensuration. Both mensurations, moreover, could operate independently at levels both smaller (called "prolation") and larger ("mood") than the one just described, with the result that semibreves could be divided into either two or three minims, and breves could be organized in patterns of two or three to make longs. Morley's Gnorimus provides a simplified chart to help his pupil visualize the whole (Fig. 2.1). It seems straightforward enough, with circles and dots used to indicate the prevailing meter at each level. In practice, however, the system was capable of great subtlety, as we will discover in the case of a mensuration canon by Josquin des Prez considered in Chapter 5. (Figure 2.1 shows how the various mensuration signs can give different meanings to the same series of note shapes.)

Where the staff, note names, and musical scales are concerned, Morley's world also seems both familiar and odd. The gamut extends from low G (more or less at the bottom of the baritone register) to e″ (more or less at the top of a choirboy's range). It is not a chromatic scale, however; instead, it consists only of what we would call the "white" tones of the modern keyboard, plus a pair of alternatives for B: the "hard" B (in Latin terminology "durum," corresponding to our B♮) and the "soft" B (in Latin "molle," corresponding to our B♭). These were all the tones needed for the performance of sacred plainsong. But understanding the order of the pitch names and their place on the staff was only the beginning. Gnorimus insists on a distinction between what he calls the "cliefe," meaning the position of a given note on the staff, and the "note," in this case meaning the syllable—ut, re, mi, fa, sol, la—by which a given tone could be identified relative to its place in one of a series of seven overlapping hexachords (Greek for "six strings"), each identically organized to follow the same intervallic structure. According to this system, an individual tone was not just C or A; it was potentially one of two or three musical "places" in a local hexachord. C could be ut, fa, or sol depending on whether it was in the first position of a hexachord on C, the fourth position of one built on G, or the fifth position of one built on F, these three being the only regular locations for such structures in the gamut. (See

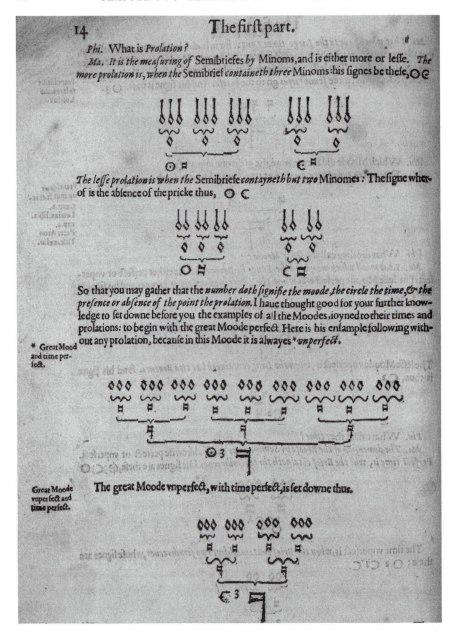

Figure 2.1: *Diagram of mensuration system, from Thomas Morley's* A Plaine and Easie Introduction to Practicall Musicke *(London, 1608 edition), p. 14*

Figures 2.2 and 2.3, which reproduce the gamut and hexachords as they were represented in a treatise by the fifteenth-century composer-theorist Johannes Tinctoris, and in Morley's *Plaine and Easie Introduction* nearly 150 years later.)

(a)

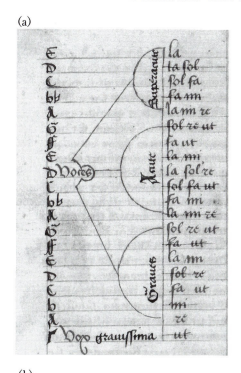

(b)

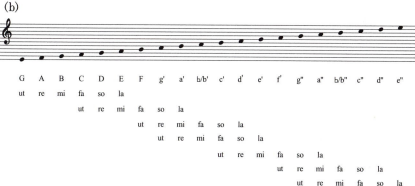

Figure 2.2: (a) *Diagram of the steps of the gamut on the left, ascending from lowest to highest tone. The overlapping hexachords rise at the right-hand side of the image in sequences of* ut, re, mi, fa, sol, la, *according to the positions in which they can occur within the gamut. From Johannes Tinctoris's* Expositio Manus. **(b)** *A representation of the same relationships in modern staff notation.*

The combination of the gamut and its overlapping hexachords was very old, having served as the basis of musical education since it was first proposed by the eleventh-century Benedictine monk Guido of Arezzo. Later writers elaborated and adapted it in various ways, perhaps most famously in the musical "hand" used as a didactic and mnemonic aid in treatises of the fourteenth, fifteenth, and

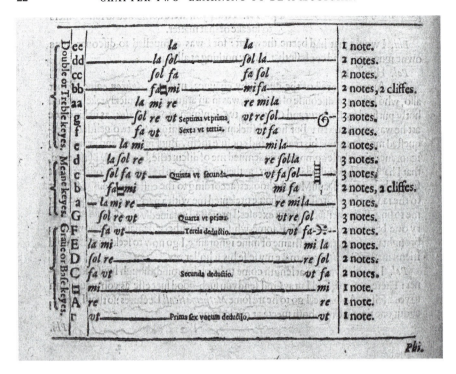

Figure 2.3: *Diagram of the steps of the gamut on the left, ascending from lowest to highest tone. The overlapping hexachords rise symmetrically toward the center of the page in sequences of* ut, re, mi, fa, sol, la, *according to the positions in which they can occur within the gamut. From Thomas Morley,* A Plaine and Easie Introduction to practicall Musicke *(London, 1608 edition), p. 2.*

sixteenth centuries (Fig. 2.4). Like our modern systems of movable solfege, the hexachordal system taught musicians to find their way through an unfamiliar melody by applying an aural grid that told them where to find the "narrow" adjacency of *mi–fa* (the crucial half step at the center of each hexachord) in any particular context. The identity of a particular tone was relative, not absolute; that is, it depended on local context for meaning, since there was no pitch standard at the time.

The hexachordal system was originally formulated for the teaching and study of monophonic plainsong melodies. Indeed, it could help a singer avoid certain forbidden leaps, like the tritone: in leaping up to B after F, the singer needed to use the "soft" form of the note (solmized as *fa*), while in leaping down to B after E, he needed to use the "hard" form (solmized as *mi*). As musicians began to make and notate polyphony, they found that these same rules helped them avoid forbidden intervals between voice parts. When this adjustment was confined to the inflection of B, all seemed well. But in other contexts they found it necessary to sing F as *mi* (or what we would call F♯), or E as *fa* (that is, E♭). These temporary or "false" tones (and the hexachords in which they were imagined)

(a)   (b)

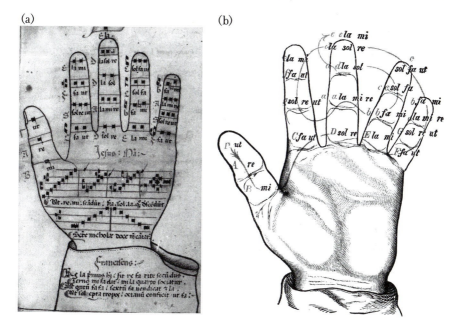

Figure 2.4: (a) *Guidonian hand with solmization syllables, as depicted in an Italian manuscript of the fifteenth century,* and **(b)** *diagram showing how it was used to trace the scale*

had a name, *musica ficta*, that musicians used to account for a whole series of "accidentals" that are essential to the realization of a work in sound, but were for various reasons slow to find their way onto the written page. The gamut retained an aura of visual correctness as *musica recta*. But particularly during the sixteenth century, composers began to deploy "fictive" tones like F♯, C♯, E♭, and A♭ in ways that made them no less "real" than the tones of *musica recta*, notating them in some cases, while leaving them to the educated judgment of performers in the case of others. Philomathes evidently had a lot to learn.

THE DUET AS TESTING GROUND

From here, it seems, it was all a matter of practice. Gnorimus sends his student off with some duets: "Here be some following of two parts, which I have made of purpose, that when you have any friend to sing with you, you may practise togither, which wil sooner make you perfect then if you should studie never so much by your selfe." Morley (through his proxy, Gnorimus) was hardly alone in advocating duos for the perfection of musical skills. Collections of duets, many with explicitly didactic intent, were issued in great numbers by the leading printing houses of sixteenth-century Venice, Nuremberg, Antwerp, Munich, and Paris.

Lutheran schoolmasters of the mid-1500s were particularly convinced of the utility of duets for the musical instruction of youngsters. An edition of the textbook *De arte canendi* (On the Art of Singing) by Sebald Heyden, issued in Nuremberg in 1540, relies mainly on duets drawn from larger works by Josquin and his contemporaries as vehicles for the study of solmization. "Through these examples," Heyden writes, "studied carefully on hexachords, young students will then compare all similar ones to them, and will not hesitate to sol-fa (*solmifandum*), as we usually say, in the very same order and manner in all other similar cases."

Protestant music printers of Heyden's world were quick to fill the need for practical books suited for boys and young men who studied in the civic schools of Lutheran Germany, where humanistic Latin was the principal language of instruction. Other books were directed at particular students, often aristocrats. When the Venetian printer Girolamo Scotto brought out a collection of duos to French and Italian texts assembled by the Flemish composer Jhan Gero in 1541, for instance, he dedicated the book to the young son of the wealthy Milanese ambassador and aristocrat Ottaviano Visconti. The collection, Scotto hoped, would support the practice of "art that is suited for princes and noblemen; art practiced by them when they are withdrawn from the hubbub of the crowd, enjoying, in the company of a few members of the household, melody that springs from the imagination of the finest composers." Hints of elitism in their dedications notwithstanding, these pieces circulated far and wide. Gero's duets were reprinted by various publishers at least two dozen times. The last edition known was issued when J. S. Bach was a toddler, in 1687! These were remarkably long-lived publications, testifying to their continued utility for musical instruction in schools and at home.

Morley, too, brought out a collection of vocal and instrumental duets, the *First Booke of Canzonets to Two Voyces* (1595). While he says nothing about the didactic value of the collection, it probably represents the sort of music Gnorimus would have offered Philomathes at the conclusion of his first book of lessons. *Miraculous love's wounding* certainly fits the need. It is a contrapuntal duo for two voices of equal range, thus allowing master and pupil or two friends to trade parts as needed (see Anthology 3 and Ex. 2.1, in which we have added syllables showing how singers might have solmized the various tones).

Even advanced musicians relied on duets to test out their ideas. In 1531 the Italian music theorist Pietro Aaron sent one of his four-voice compositions to his colleague Giovanni Spataro. The details of Spataro's critique need not concern us here, but the way he evaluated the piece is revealing: his approach was to check each of the four polyphonic parts by singing through them in pairs. "I have gone through your 'Letatus sum' (which we had already sung and praised) with a student of mine, singing two voices at a time, and I found certain passages that did not please me," he wrote. Clearly, duets were not just a way of building skill as a performer; they also served to "test" compositional practice. Even as style was changing toward an ideal founded on the equality of multiple voice

Example 2.1: *Thomas Morley,* Miraculous love's wounding, *mm. 1–8, with added solmization syllables. From Thomas Morley,* First Booke of Canzonets to Two Voyces *(London: Thomas Este, 1595), fols. 6ᵛ–7ʳ.*

parts, Spataro's "two at a time" dissection of Aaron's composition is a reminder that the cantus–tenor pairing so important to older styles remained a focal point for contrapuntal thought and criticism.

LEARNING ABOUT THE MODES

Editors organized their collections of didactic duets in various ways. The prolific composer Orlando di Lasso (1532–1594) brought out a book of 24 duos titled *Novae aliquot . . . ad duas voces cantiones* (Several New Songs . . . for Two Voice Parts, 1577) that were carefully arranged with an eye for musical symmetry and order. There are 12 pieces for voices, plus 12 more for instruments, representing various combinations of musical modes, ranges, and clefs. Like Bach's great *Well-Tempered Clavier* and similar cyclic sets, the collection stands as a great manifesto of musical possibilities. Lasso was acutely self-conscious about mode as an organizing principle, both within compositions and in anthologies. Morley's *Plaine and Easie Introduction*, in contrast, has relatively little to say about modality, either as a set of compositional priorities or as a fact of musical life for aspiring students. When, in the third part of the textbook, Gnorimus worries that Philomathes' latest attempt at composition has strayed from the usual limits of its given "key," his student clamors for guidelines: "Have you no generall rule to be given for an instruction for keeping of the key?" The master's answer is hardly satisfying: "No," he replies, for it must proceede only of the judgement of the composer, yet the church men for keeping their keyes have devised certaine notes commonlie called the eight tunes, so that according to the tune which is to be obserued, at that time if it beginne in such a key, it may end in such and such others, as you shall immediatly know. And these be (although not the true substance yet) some shadowe of the ancient modi whereof Boethius and Glareanus have written so much.

Perhaps Gnorimus was wise to say so little to his student about "ancient modi," for the topic could easily overwhelm any but the most patient reader. But the range of authorities he cites at least opens the door to further study, for between the writings on the Greek modes by the Roman statesman Severinus Boethius (ca. 480–ca. 524) and the proposals on polyphonic modality by the Swiss human-ist Heinrich Glarean (1488–1563) there was wide latitude of opinion. Debates on the subject were intense, with surprisingly little agreement among the advocates of various positions, both old and new. When Spataro wrote to another of his mu-sical acquaintances, Giovanni del Lago, about Aaron's treatise on the modes, he confessed his contempt for the work: "Just as I predicted," he complained, "it came out without order and truth." Spataro claimed to have written a 200-page rebuttal of the arguments found in Aaron's *Trattato della natura et cognitione di tutti gli tuoni di canto figurato* (Treatise on the Nature and Recognition of All the Modes of Figured Song, 1525; excerpts in SR 69:415–28; 3/34:137–50).

It is not clear what would have satisfied the acerbic Spataro, for in some important respects the challenge of reconciling modal categories codified to explain plainsong melodies with contemporary polyphonic practice was a daunting task. The eight ancient modes described by Boethius and adapted by churchmen of subsequent generations were conceived as ways of understand-ing the habits of monophonic melodies, which could be organized into various groupings of final tone, range, and characteristic patterns. An entire genre of plainsong manuscript, the tonary, was designed with exactly this purpose in mind.

How to integrate these modal families into polyphonic practice remained a persistent riddle for writers of the fifteenth and sixteenth centuries, for the fundamental reason that adjacent voice parts (in a duet for tenor and bassus, for instance) might share the same final tone, but occupy different ranges. According to the old system of monophonic modality, this would put a single composition in two modes at once: the "authentic," with the final tone at the bot-tom of the range, and the "plagal," with the final tone at the center of the range (Fig. 2.5). Aaron's solution was in some ways an avoidance of the problem: he identified the mode of the tenor as the mode of the rest of the polyphonic fab-ric: "The tenor being the firm and stable part, the part, that is, that holds and comprehends the whole concentus [combination of intervals] of the harmony, the singer must judge the tone by means of this part only" (SR 69:420; 3/34:142).

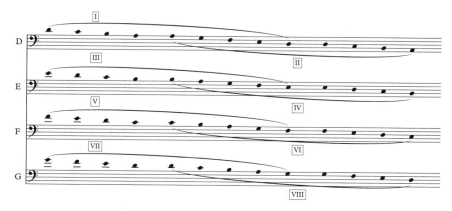

Figure 2.5: *Chart of the eight melodic modes, showing the four final tones (D, E, F, and G) and the eight authentic and plagal modes in pairs (I, II, III, etc.), following a diagram printed in Heinrich Glarean's* Dodecachordon *(Basel, 1547), p. 30*

In the middle of the sixteenth century, Glarean proposed a new system of modal classification that consisted of 12 rather than the traditional eight modes: authentic and plagal pairs on each of six principal tones, each labeled with suitably classicizing Greek terminology (Fig. 2.6). Soon the Venetian choirmaster Gioseffo Zarlino (1517–1590) proposed his own 12-mode system. Although the

Figure 2.6: *Chart of the 12 melodic modes, arranged in sets of authentic and plagal pairs, each with their Greek names, from Heinrich Glarean's* Dodecachordon *(Basel, 1547), p. 82*

two systems have some important differences, they both served to accommodate the growing corpus of compositions built around C and A, two tonal centers
absent from the old eight-mode system. The *sound* of these new compositions
was not at issue. What these composers, editors, and theorists were interested
in debating was how a work might belong to some normative category received as
part of a long tradition of musical thought.

The ancient claim that the individual modes had different expressive
and moral valences was something of an article of faith among fifteenth- and
sixteenth-century theorists. The trouble came in sorting out which mode went
with which affect, since even ancient authorities, from Aristotle to Aristoxenus,
were often at odds with each other, and sometimes with themselves. Glarean
noted the expressive properties of one mode after another, although he also allowed that compositions might mix affects as readily as they mixed modal inflections. (For an extended passage from Glarean's influential *Dodecachordon*
[The 12-String Lyre] of 1547, see SR 70:428–35; 3/35:150–57.) Zarlino, too,
repeated the truism that according to the ancients "each mode was capable of
inducing different passions in the souls of the listeners." While he dutifully re-
cites the many qualities attributed to each mode by various authorities, he also
admits that there is no easy way to make sense of their views as a whole, with
"some claiming one thing and others another."

As we will discover in Chapters 6 and 14, the moral and healing effects
of the modes, acting on individuals as well as social groups, were strongly
sensed throughout the Renaissance. Protecting his students from the swirling
controversies, Thomas Morley nevertheless had Gnorimus tell his pupil rather
less about mode than he might have.

THE LOST ART OF UNWRITTEN COUNTERPOINT

In the modern musical classroom, counterpoint is often regarded as the pinnacle of a curriculum organized around the repertory of the eighteenth and
nineteenth centuries. For music students of the fifteenth and sixteenth
centuries, it meant something different: a set of practices, partly improvised,
that depended on acute aural skills. Counterpoint was not only a prelude to good
composition, but also a worthy musical practice in its own right. Indeed, in many
musical contexts the making of this kind of spontaneous counterpoint was actually preferred to the performance of written composition. Morley's Gnorimus
was a strong proponent of this contrapuntal skill, and he lamented its apparent
neglect to his pupil Philomathes. "Excellent musitions have discontinued it,"
he worried, "although it be unpossible for them to compose without it, but they
rather employ their time in making of songes, which remaine for the posterity
then to sing descant which is no longer known. . . ."

For Gnorimus, counterpoint is not an object, but an action: improvisation upon a given melody. That's why he stresses the agent (the "descanter") rather than the thing produced. But Philomathes' ignorance of the topic implies a set of readers who are unsure what this old art of improvised counterpoint might be. In descanting, Gnorimus explains, the singer chooses an appropriate interval against a series of given tones, normally a plainsong melody. The specific rules for this process of improvising note against note (and, later, several notes against each given note) do not need to delay us here, for our focus is less on the technique than on how it was taught, how it was used, and why it mattered so much to Gnorimus (and Morley), despite its apparent decline.

The roots of the practice run deep in the traditions of the *maîtrises*, or cathedral choir schools, that dominated the musical landscape of northern Europe during the fifteenth and early sixteenth centuries. In these institutions, a *grammaticus* made sure that choirboys could read enough Latin to articulate and understand the texts of the prayers. Meanwhile, the master of the choirboys (*magister puerorum cantus*) helped them memorize plainsong melodies, read musical notation, and understand enough about the hexachords and modes to navigate musical space on their own as they learned to make counterpoint. Indeed, when the French theologian and University of Paris rector Jean Gerson (1363–1429) issued an important set of regulations concerning the education of choirboys at the Cathedral of Notre Dame de Paris in 1411, he identified "counterpoint" as second in importance only to the study of liturgical plainsong.

The simplest forms of these largely unwritten practices involved parallel harmonization of plainsong hymns and other tunes, a practice that had been around since at least the ninth century in the form of parallel organum. But whereas in older styles musical motion had been regulated to allow mainly parallel perfect consonance (fifths and octaves), singers of the fifteenth century allowed, or even preferred, parallel motion in imperfect consonances (thirds and sixths), punctuated by cadences at the octave and fifth. In one version of this formulaic polyphony, one group of singers sang a liturgical melody up an octave (as the highest part of the ensemble), while another group sang a contrapuntal part that moved largely in parallel sixths with the plainsong, expanding out to octaves for cadences at the ends of textual or musical phrases. This two-voice armature was then enhanced by a third unwritten part sung a fourth below the plainchant, something achieved by mentally "sighting" a clef or note where none appeared on the page. Everyone moved in close synchronization as they declaimed the liturgical text.

This practice went by different names in different places, but all of them made reference to "falseness": fauxbourdon among French-speaking musicians, who put the imaginary part below the plainsong, as explained previously; faburden in England, where the imaginary part was visualized above the plainsong but then sounded below it, so that the liturgical tune sounded in the middle of the texture; and falsobordone in Italian churches, in which four rather than three voices parts were heard in all. These practices were long a mainstay of liturgical music-making throughout the fifteenth and sixteenth centuries. They were widely taught, and were at times described in practical manuals of the day. In the fifteenth century Guillaume Du Fay arranged dozens of hymns in alternatim form in this way—one stanza as plainsong, the other in fauxbourdon style. A hundred years later copyists at the Bavarian court in Munich compiled entire volumes of Lasso's falsobordoni arrangements, some of them apparently intended as didactic models for young choristers.

Perhaps not surprisingly, each of these three traditions found its way into the compositional arsenal of techniques used in all kinds of pieces, not just elaborated plainsong. The old formula seems to have been especially useful for the clear and intelligible presentation of texts, and as such aligned nicely with humanist affinities for persuasion and oratory. In the anthology accompanying this book, we can hear it in a variety of pieces: faburden in the early-fifteenth-century carol *There is no rose* (Anthology 8) and in John Dunstable's devotional motet of about the same vintage, *Quam pulchra es* (How Lovely You Are, Anthology 7); fauxbourdon in Du Fay's elaborate motet from the 1430s, *Supremum est mortalibus* (The Supreme Good for Mortals, Anthology 9); and falsobordone in Claudio Monteverdi's madrigal *Sfogava con le stelle* (In Converse with the Stars, Anthology 26), from the very last years of the sixteenth century.

TEACHING METHODS

Traces of the methods used in teaching young choristers to improvise such music are few and far between. But we can begin to measure the sophistication of their teaching techniques through a manual by Leonel Power (ca. 1380–1445), an English gentleman, singer, and composer affiliated with the monastery of Christ Church, Canterbury, not long after Gerson issued his regulations on the education of the boys at Notre Dame de Paris. Power's modest treatise offers practical rules for those who want to be "syngers or makers or techers" on how to "sight," or mentally transpose, as many as three new "discant" parts from the written plainsong. The practice, with its emphasis on the sweet sounds of thirds and sixths, has certain affinities with faburden. In contrast to the strict parallelism between the plainsong part and its imaginary twin, however, Powers encourages singers to improvise all sorts of contrary motion relative to the plainsong, something that never happens in the simpler faburden. He also allows for the simultaneous improvisation of these discant parts by two or more singers, a practice that must have resulted in all sorts of complex intersections and even clashes. For some listeners, the results bordered on noise. When the great Christian humanist Desiderius Erasmus of Rotterdam recalled his visits to the wealthy English churches of the early sixteenth century, he disparaged the entire practice of improvised counterpoint as a corruption and confusion of sacred song:

Those who are more doltish than really learned in music are not content on feast days unless they use a certain distorted kind of music called *Faubur-dum* [*sic*]. This neither gives forth the pre-existing melody nor observes the harmonies of the art. In addition, when temperate music is used in church in this way, so that the meaning of the words may more easily come to the listener, it also seems a fine thing to some if one or other part, inter-mingled with the rest, produces a tremendous tonal clamor, so that not a single word is understood. Thus the whims of the foolish are indulged and their baser appetites are satisfied.

Erasmus's anxieties about the "baser appetites" of singers and listeners not-withstanding, plainsong was often elaborated by musicians in England and on the Continent throughout the fifteenth and sixteenth centuries. Indeed, im-provised counterpoint had a long history, if we are to believe the theorists and teachers of the period. In his *Liber de arte contrapuncti* (The Art of Counterpoint, 1477), for instance, Johannes Tinctoris (ca. 1430/35–1511) reminds his read-ers that counterpoint could have two senses: written compositions or *res facta* (literally, "something made") and spontaneous singing "over the book" (*super librum*). As Tinctoris explains, each shares the same vocabulary of allowable consonances. However, while in *res facta* all parts must agree with each other in making regulated consonances, in unwritten counterpoint the voices need only make consonances with the tenor, and not with each other:

Counterpoint that is written is usually called a "composed piece" [*res facta*]. But that which we put together in the mind we call a "counterpoint" pure and simple, and those who do this are said in common parlance to "sing over the book" [*super librum cantare*]. A composed piece differs from a counterpoint above all in that all parts of a composed piece, whether three, four, or more, are mutually bound to one another, so that the order-ing and rule of consonances of any one part must be observed with re-spect to each and all the others. . . . But when two, three, four, or more sing together over the book, one is not subject to the other. Indeed it is enough that each of them be consonant with the tenor in regard to the rule and ordering of consonances. (SR 67:401–402; 3/32:123–24)

Tinctoris does not explain how to teach this "mental" counterpoint. For him it was nevertheless a skill born of long practice and essential to musical suc-cess. "I have known not even one man," he confessed to King Ferrante, "who has achieved eminent or noble rank among musicians, if he began to compose or sing *super librum* at or above his twentieth year of age." In dedicating the *Liber de arte contrapuncti* to the king, Tinctoris may have been doing little more than offering customary tribute to his royal patron, rather than giving genuine mu-sical instruction. But he also prepared and published a number of other, more basic treatises during his time as court music tutor and advisor: studies of the Guidonian syllables, of rhythmic notation, and even the first known dictionary of musical terms, offered to Ferrante's daughter, Princess Beatrice. They could hardly have chosen a better teacher. Tinctoris was an accomplished composer, the leading theoretician of his day, and an experienced pedagogue. According to his fragmentary treatise *De inventione et usu musice* (The Origin and Practice of Music), during the 1460s he was master of choirboys at the Cathedral of Chartres. If Tinctoris warned his royal pupils of the demands of learning to "sing over the book," he probably knew only too well the patience it required of student and teacher alike.

SIXTEENTH-CENTURY TRENDS

The practice of improvisatory counterpoint legislated by Gerson and described by writers like Tinctoris was cultivated throughout the sixteenth century and beyond. When the Protestant composer and schoolmaster Adrian Petit Cocli-co (1499/1500–1562) brought out his *Compendium musices* (Musical Compendium, 1552), a compact textbook for aspiring musicians in local Latin schools (where boys pursued an increasingly humanistic curriculum over the course of the sixteenth century), his method followed the customary three-part sequence we encountered in Morley's *Plaine and Easie Introduction*: singing, making counterpoint, and composing. Coclico apparently thought the practice of counterpoint worth the trouble, despite its neglect: "A method of singing counterpoint is rare in Germany, surely for no other reason than this most beautiful art is learned thoroughly by long practice and the greatest labor. . . . A boy should apply all his forces in the learning of this most beautiful art." But how? First, Coclico explains, by learning the various harmonic intervals and their permitted sequence. In this, his list differs little from the advice offered in Tinctoris's treatise. "Having learned these types and the method," he continues,

> here is how we ought to use them: the boy provides himself with a slate on which one may write and erase; he takes a tenor from plainchant and at first writes note against note, using these types. Whenever he has gotten used to making note against note by improvisation and has become practiced in it, then he can go on to florid counterpoint. In this, when he has become trained, he will put aside the slate and learn to sing in improvising on plainchant or on figured music printed in a book or copied on a sheet of paper. But this is a task for continual exercise.

The system Coclico describes illustrates the fundamental importance of the duet at all stages of musical education, for professionals (in the old choir-school system) and amateurs (in Morley's world) alike. The graded tasks of note-against-note and florid counterpoint, too, have remained a mainstay of musical education, from Johann Joseph Fux's *Gradus ad Parnassum* (Steps to Parnassus, 1725) to textbooks of today. Coclico's *Compendium musices* is also important for what it reveals about the changing status of improvised counterpoint in the educational system. It was intended as a text for the young, or at least as a guide for those who would instruct them. But it was published in Germany at a time when, according to the preference in Lutheran schools and churches, the old obligations of choirboys to sing the sacred liturgy in elaborated plainsong were being replaced by simple congregational hymns. (We'll have more to say about Coclico and his relationship with Josquin in Chapter 8.)

Similar processes were under way in other quarters, whether in Protestant schools or in amateur households of all faiths, as musical education was increasingly distanced from the *maîtrise* system that had produced generations of choirboys and professional adult singers for Catholic religious institutions. The turn away from the plainsong liturgy was slower in Anglican England, although by the time Morley wrote his *Plaine and Easie Introduction*, polyphonic "works" rather than plainsong or its improvised elaborations were seen as the vehicles that best embodied the devotional ideals of the church and the educated gentlemen who heard them. Polyphonic music, Gnorimus and Philomathes agree, "requireth most art, and moveth and causeth most strange effects in the hearer." (Further on the "strange effects" that these works held for the "skilfull auditor" in Chapter 11.)

Sacred vocal music was only one aim of the aspiring musician, as Gnorimus attests. It was perhaps the highest form, on account of its serious subject and restrained manner, but amateurs like Philomathes had much else to keep them busy. There were secular genres like the madrigal and villanella, which Morley himself helped to promote in Elizabethan England. There was also a wealth of instrumental music: embellished versions of vocal compositions, stylized dances like the pavane and galliard in lute arrangements, ensemble canzonas for recorders or viols, and imaginative fantasias for keyboard or lute. Indeed, although instrumental skills are not taught in Morley's *Plaine and Easie Introduction*, musicians of the sixteenth century could turn to a wide range of practical tutors on almost any aspect of instrumental music-making, with advice on tunings, fingerings, reading tablature (lute notation), or instruction on the arts of improvisation. It's worth noting that these books were written in the vernacular and not, like Coclico's or Tinctoris's manuals, in Latin. They were aimed at a growing body of literate urban dwellers who looked upon music as a pastime or a measure of civility, not as religious ritual or professional training. (For more on the contexts and approaches of these manuals, see Chapter 12 and related pieces by Giovanni Bassano [Anthology 23], Diego Ortiz [Anthology 24], and Fabrizio Dentice [Anthology 25].)

At a basic level, the musical method books of the fifteenth and sixteenth centuries remind us of the inherent conservatism of musical notation, with its system of scales, solmization syllables, and mensural rhythm. There is broad agreement, too, among tutors from Tinctoris to Morley about the grammar of consonance and dissonance as it applies to polyphonic music. But as the changing status of improvised counterpoint in these texts attests, the purposes of music—and therefore the purposes of a musical education—were subject to competing forces that transformed musical learning in profound ways.

Printed tutors of the sort prepared by Coclico and Morley point to a continuing demand for musical skills among schoolboys and scholars. They also reveal the need for musical literacy among a wide range of educated amateurs for whom the ability to perform, create, and talk about music was an important social currency. (Indeed, as we will discover in Chapter 7, this civilizing role for musical skill was a central concern of the Renaissance gentleman.) With this new model of music as a means of self-formation, rather than the observance of religious ceremonies, came a new emphasis on compositions (and the language to talk about them) as the highest embodiment of musical knowledge. The path from action to object was not always straight, but it opened new possibilities for music, and for those who aspired to make it.

FOR FURTHER READING

Blackburn, Bonnie J., "On Compositional Process in the Fifteenth Century," *Journal of the American Musicological Society* 40 (1987): 210–84

Forney, Kristine, "'Nymphes gayes en abry du Laurier': Music Instruction for the Bourgeois Woman," *Musica disciplina* 49 (1995): 151–87

Murray, Russell E., Jr., Susan Forscher Weiss, and Cynthia Cyrus, eds., *Music Education in the Middle Ages and the Renaissance* (Bloomington: Indiana University Press, 2010)

Schubert, Peter N., "Counterpoint Pedagogy in the Renaissance," in *The Cambridge History of Western Music Theory*, pp. 503–33 (Cambridge: Cambridge University Press, 2002)

Sternfeld, Frederick W., "Music in the Schools of the Reformation," *Musica disciplina* 2 (1948): 99–122

Wegman, Rob C., "From Maker to Composer: Improvisation and Musical Authorship in the Low Countries, 1450–1500," *Journal of the American Musicological Society* 49 (1996): 409–79

Ⓢ Additional resources available at wwnorton.com/studyspace

PART II

Before 1500

Courtiers and clerics of the fifteenth century fashioned themselves heirs to centuries-old traditions. Courtly love, with its stylized expression of desire between men and women of different social standing, remained a favorite topic for poets and writers. Versifying nobles like Christine de Pisan and Charles d'Orléans confined themselves to literary themes and refrain forms that had been in circulation since before the 1300s. Those who moved the levers of power in the Catholic hierarchy likewise took their cue from tradition, relying on a vast bureaucracy of priests, secretaries, and other functionaries who carried out the rulings of their superiors, from local bishops to cardinals and eventually the pope himself.

Sacred and secular authorities were locked in a tight embrace. Indeed, dukes and kings often came from the same elite families whose sons were appointed to the highest positions of power in the church. Princes styled themselves defenders of the Christian faith, even when their own importance on the battlefield was more symbolic than tactical. Popes could (and often needed to) field their own armies to assert their temporal authority. Power radiated out from these big men according to protocols that bound ruler and ruled, pastor and flock, in a net of mutual obligations. Intrigue and war were a frequent means to better one's rival, but few wanted to change the system as a whole. And so the forms of fifteenth-century life in court and church were often beyond question.

Music-making was an important part of these routines. It choreographed the rituals of the church year, much as it had in previous centuries. It also marked the many aspects of life at court—in public processions that welcomed a duke to town, in the feasts that celebrated an aristocratic wedding, and in the domestic activities that filled a ruler's private moments.

Yet music was more than a symptom of these many rituals; it was also a sign of the authority and power that made them possible. Princes like the dukes of Burgundy supported music not just because it was beautiful, but because it was an appropriate means of displaying the magnificence that was the distinguishing mark of their status. Music was an aural form of display, as important to a pope as it was to a secular prince. The urge to emulate rivals and allies alike explains why music and musicians moved with surprising agility from one center of power to another. Peripatetic composers like Guillaume Du Fay were probably as self-conscious about their place in this scheme of things as were their patrons.

Among the music we will study in Part 2 of this book are works that build on old literary forms, like the rondeau, or on centuries-old contrapuntal procedures, like the cantus-firmus motet. Guillaume de Machaut, whose musical and literary works are discussed by Margot Fassler in *Music in the Medieval West*, would have been familiar with the formal outlines and poetic themes of the chansons we'll examine in Chapter 3. Johannes Ciconia, whose *Doctorum principem* we encountered in Chapter 1, would likewise have understood immediately what Du Fay was up to in the motet we will study in Chapter 4.

Yet musicians of the fifteenth century were acutely aware of their own historical position in all of this, and of the novel ideas they pioneered. As we will learn in Chapter 5, Du Fay and others extended principles of organization previously used in cantus-firmus motets to the five unchanging (or Ordinary) movements of the Christian Mass, thereby inaugurating a new kind of vast cyclic work that became a major testing ground of musical creativity. Borrowing from, emulating, and at times outdoing each other, musicians of the second half of the fifteenth century cultivated a new historical awareness as well as new ideals of sound. Their preference for counterpoint based on thirds and sixths (in contrast to the fifths and octaves preferred by musicians of the previous century), and the expanded roles for the contratenor and bassus parts in polyphonic textures, reflected a desire to accommodate new sounds with old forms.

CHAPTER THREE

Music at Court and a Songbook for Beatrice

Late in the summer of 1433 the accomplished singer-composer Guillaume Du Fay (1397–1474) took up a coveted position as leader of the musical household of Duke Amadeus VIII of Savoy. Trained in his native France at the prestigious choir school (*maîtrise*) of the Cathedral of Cambrai, Du Fay had already served in churches and elite musical establishments across the Italian peninsula, moving from the household of the powerful Malatesta family in Rimini in the early 1420s to that of the Cardinal of Bologna later in the decade, and then to the chapel of Pope Eugenius IV from 1428 until 1433, and again in 1435.

Over the ensuing decades, Du Fay frequently returned to the cathedral of his early formation, where he had family, colleagues, and important sources of income. (We'll examine some of the music that Du Fay wrote for Cambrai in Chapter 4.) But he also maintained important ties with Savoy, the duchy straddling the Alps on both sides of the modern border between France and Italy. Indeed, no less than the cathedral choir schools where musical minds like Du Fay's were shaped, the leading courts exerted a powerful influence over the movement of music and musicians throughout the fifteenth century. In an age governed by relatively intimate means of transmission, in both oral traditions and musical manuscripts, the patterns of aesthetic interchange were often highly dependent on lines of dynastic alliance, competition, and wealth. We will see all of these effects at work through Du Fay's association with Savoy, and through the operations of other musical courts of the day.

Music was an essential part of the routines of aristocratic life, with its public festivities, private entertainments, and devotional worship. The sponsorship of music and musicians reflected the aspirations of fifteenth-century princes, who took the advice of classical authorities like Aristotle very much to heart. As aristocratic patrons competed to demonstrate their magnificence, music and musicians flowed between centers of power such as Chambéry, for the Duchy of Savoy; Dijon, for the dukes of Burgundy; Milan, another ducal seat; and Naples, where a Spanish family ruled as kings.

Du Fay took part in this trade of personnel and ideas, along with many other composers, singers, and instrumentalists. Still others, like the Flemish composer, theorist, and royal tutor Johannes Tinctoris (see Chapter 2), supervised the compilation of beautiful music manuscripts in which the finest secular and sacred songs were assembled for performance in private chambers to satisfy the collecting habits of the European aristocracy. The works found in books like one Tinctoris had made for his pupil Princess Beatrice at the court of Naples can tell us much about this cultural climate and its veneration of the chivalric past. But before we turn to Beatrice's songbook, it is important to understand something of the role of music at court and the cultural priorities of the patrons who stood at the center of this remarkable world.

THE *CHAPELLE, CHAMBRE,* AND *ECURIE*

A musician working in an aristocratic household like the one Du Fay joined at the court of Savoy would by ancient convention have belonged to one of three separate administrative departments: the chapel (*chapelle*), the chamber (*chambre*), or the public court (*écurie*). Clerics like Du Fay took their place in the *chapelle*, a body of a dozen or more officials—a confessor, scribes, and skilled singers, perhaps choirboys—charged with the daily observance of the sacred liturgy for the ducal family. (The term derives from the room used to store the venerated cloak, or *capellus*, that St. Martin of Tours offered a beggar in an act of charity in the sixth century; a *chapelain*, or chaplain, is one who figuratively takes up St. Martin's work.) No doubt much of the Latin polyphony that survives from these courts had its origins in some aspect of the work of the musical chapel.

Du Fay would also have heard singers and instrumentalists specializing in the *bas*, or quiet, instruments such as the harp, lute, fiddle, recorder, and chamber organ. These musicians belonged to the *chambre*, a staff of domestic valets and advisors who took care of the ruler's personal needs. Chroniclers and paymasters tell us very little about exactly when and where these musicians played at court. They must certainly have known lots of music by heart and been expert at improvising accompaniments for each other. But from time to time they probably also performed some of the many secular polyphonic songs composed by their colleagues in the *chapelle*, as we'll see later.

Trumpeters, shawmists, and other players of *haut*, or loud, instruments took their places in the *écurie*, a collection of military guards, stable hands, heralds, and other officials responsible for public ceremony. Of their music few written traces remain, with good cause, since as improvisers of dance music and fanfares they probably had less need for notation than any of the other musicians at court. But the musical members of the *écurie*, *chambre*, and *chapelle* all had important roles to play in the elaborate routines of aristocratic life. Through their proximity and movements, many musical traditions—sacred and secular, written and unwritten—were overheard, borrowed, and adapted in the context of courtly life.

A WEDDING AT SAVOY

Perhaps the best way to recapture the sounds that Du Fay and his colleagues would have heard at Savoy is to put ourselves in the midst of the court not long after his arrival in 1433. In February 1434, Duke Amadeus welcomed a large delegation from the nearby Duchy of Burgundy that came to celebrate the wedding of Louis of Savoy, Amadeus's son and heir, to Anne de Lusignan, sister of the king of Cyprus. It's hard to imagine how officials at Savoy prepared themselves to entertain a retinue so accustomed to the best of everything: Duke Philip the Good of Burgundy wrapped himself in the finest clothing, decorated his walls with the most expensive tapestries, and outfitted his chapel and personal quarters with the best gilded objects available. He also sponsored the most highly regarded musical household of his time, then under the leadership of Du Fay's friend Gilles Binchois. When Philip's court chronicler, Jean Le Févre, copied out the official record of their days at Chambéry, he made sure to include a few fawning words about the great singers of the Burgundian *chapelle*: "Monday, the 8th day of the said month [February], the princes and princesses named above went to the great chapel of the castle in order to hear Mass, which was celebrated by the Bishop of Morienne and sung by the chaplains of the duke so melodiously that it was a beautiful thing to hear. At that moment the duke's chapel was held as the finest in all the world."

Philip's chronicler did not explain whether the Mass in question was observed wholly in plainsong, or with polyphony as well. We know that tenor masses were much prized at Philip's court during the middle years of the fifteenth century. Du Fay, like his contemporaries Binchois (1400–1460) and Antoine Busnoys (1430–1492), crafted large and immensely subtle cyclic pieces of this sort. In such works, all five movements of the Ordinary portions of the Catholic Mass—the texts that remain unchanged throughout the liturgical year—were unified via a slow-moving tenor cantus-firmus melody stretched out as a scaffold for three other voice parts. Some of these melodies were fragments of plainsong, and as such carried their own sacred meanings for those who understood their role as both structure and gloss. Other tunes were drawn from secular chansons of the day, creating a complex confluence of meanings that is best understood through of a process of analogy that elevated worldly desire in the context of a service dedicated to the divine. As we'll discover in Chapters 4 and 5, such masses were often rich in political, religious, and symbolic meanings. They were not, however, routinely used to commemorate wedding celebrations, and so we must conclude that the mass heard at Chambéry in 1434 was not distinctive enough to merit official notice.

In any event, Duke Amadeus's musicians certainly performed in the general celebrations that surrounded the wedding. Costumed singers, heralding trumpeters, and minstrels took part in outlandish displays during a week's worth of festive meals that followed the ceremony. After Mass was sung, Le Févre reports, the nobles first retreated to their private chambers, then reassembled in the castle court at Chambéry. Trumpeters from the *écurie* cleared the way as the guests entered the great room for a dinner party of almost unbelievable proportions. "The room was set out very grandly," Le Févre recalled,

> and before the tables came knights, squires, trumpeters, and minstrels, as they had the previous day. During the meal there was a sailing ship, with a man in the foremast, and the captain of the ship in the cabin at the rear. Along the side of the room were the shapes of sirens, who sang very gracefully. And from the sides of the ship were discharged plates of fish before the great table. And during the same meal trumpeters and minstrels played (as on the day before) and were given by Ymber (the bastard of Savoy [the illegitimate son of the Duke]) 50 francs, so that they cried "largesse." So passed the meal. And afterwards: the dances.

We'll return to the "largesse" of the noble patrons shortly. But first let's turn to a famous illustration of fifteenth-century courtly dances to help us imagine the scene. Figure 3.1 shows a series of couples dancing to the accompaniment of a trio of instrumentalists who play from a balcony. Perhaps these musicians were drawn in part from the ranks of the *écurie*, or perhaps they were local professionals hired for the event. They were almost certainly playing basses danses, a repertory of courtly tunes and movements for which we have ample testimony not only in chronicles, but also in some music manuscripts.

Figure 3.1: *Representation of courtly dance, from a fifteenth-century manuscript copy of* The Marriage of Renaud of Montauban and Clarisse

As the image suggests, the basses danses were accompanied by a trio of *haut* or *alta* instruments, so called on account of their "high" volume—in this case a pair of treble shawms (a double-reed instrument related to the modern oboe) plus a trombone-like sackbut or trumpet, which played the underlying basse danse tenor. Dozens of such tunes, along with basic notation of the dance steps, survive in a small corpus of manuscripts and handbooks of the late fifteenth century. We know that the tenors were played in slow triple meter, with each note given equal duration. What the shawmists did is less certain. Perhaps they improvised counterpoint in parallel thirds against the tenor notes, or perhaps they played alternating or simultaneous runs. Contemporary depictions of wind bands never show them working from a book, in contrast to representations of chapel singers, who normally have an open choirbook close at hand.

There is more than meets the eye in our image, however. The illustration is not simply a snapshot of dance at court, despite the fact that it shows the dancers in fifteenth-century dress and the musicians in an arrangement typical of fifteenth-century practice. The image appears in a lavishly illustrated manuscript of a *twelfth*-century chivalric romance, the *History of Renaud de Montauban*. The story is set at the court of Charlemagne in the *eighth* century, and the manuscript was prepared in the late 1460s at the Burgundian court for Duke Philip's son, Charles the Bold. Perhaps readers like Charles were simply incapable of or uninterested in seeing the story of Renaud in twelfth-century (or even eighth-century) costume. On the other hand, the anachronistic illustration may have been precisely the point: fifteenth-century aristocrats wanted to see themselves as heirs to a medieval chivalric tradition. Music and dance were by this measure not simply forms of mealtime entertainment; they also served as mirrors of aristocratic aspiration.

MUSICAL PATRONAGE AS ARISTOTLE'S "MAGNIFICENCE"

All of this ought to make us pause to reread Jean Le Févre's chronicle of the wedding at Chambéry in 1434. What do his reports tell us about how patrons like Philip and Amadeus wanted to be known? What was at stake for fifteenth-century princes that they displayed their wealth so lavishly and publicly? At one point Le Févre noted how members of the wedding party vied with each other to see who could prompt the greatest cry of "largesse" (in the sense of bounty, generosity, and munificence) from those who played. The generosity of Amadeus's bastard son Ymber toward the minstrels and singers was not just casual tipping; it was part of an ideology that identified generosity with magnificence. No less an authority than Aristotle had argued as much in his *Nicomachean Ethics*, a fact that was not lost on men like Philip of Burgundy and Amadeus of Savoy, whose advisors made sure that such writings were on the shelves of their personal libraries. "Magnificence," Aristotle observed, "is an attribute of expenditures of the kind which we call honourable." But it was not enough simply to spend. It was also essential that the spending be commensurate with the spender's stature. "The expenditure should be worthy of his means," Aristotle continued,

> and suit not only the result but also the producer. Hence a poor man cannot be magnificent, since he has not the means with which to spend large sums fittingly. . . . But great expenditure is becoming to those who have suitable means to start with, acquired by their own efforts or from ancestors or connexions, and to people of high birth or reputation, and so on; for all these things bring them greatness and prestige.

As Aristotle's vision of magnificence suggests, lavish patronage of the arts of the sort witnessed at Amadeus's court was not simply about aesthetic appreciation. Such practices also demonstrated in a public and self-conscious way the "high birth and reputation" of the sponsors. This explicit connection between status and display sheds light on an illustration found in a French translation of a treatise on the *Pater noster* prayer prepared by court scribe Jean Miélot for Philip the Good in about 1457 (Fig. 3.2). It depicts the duke at Mass, surrounded by members of the chapel and his courtiers. As priests officiate on the left-hand side of the image, a half-dozen singers on the right peer over a book on the choir lectern, their mouths open in song. Philip, kneeling in his own booth at the rear of the image, is revealed by an assistant who pulls back a luxurious curtain, while one of his courtiers gestures with his right hand toward the duke. No doubt the gesture was meant to call attention to Philip's Christian piety, but it also assimilates that pious devotion to the broader virtue of magnificence. The musical chapel, like the fine tapestries that cover the walls or the sumptuous garments that adorn the participants, was an expense to be witnessed, both aurally and visually. No wonder listeners at Chambéry in 1434 thought Philip's choir, in Jean Le Févre's words, "the finest in all the world."

Figure 3.2: *Philip the Good, duke of Burgundy, at Mass, from a fifteenth-century manuscript copy of Jean Miélot's* Traité sur l'oraison dominicale

TINCTORIS'S "NEW ART"

Whether Du Fay and his patron Amadeus VIII understood their relationship in such ideological terms is impossible to say. But clearly some musicians of the day were sensitive to the undercurrents of prestige encouraged by works such as the *Nicomachean Ethics*. A passage from Tinctoris's *Proportionale musices* (Proportions in Music) hints at the possibility. Written in the early 1470s, the treatise was dedicated to Tinctoris's patron, the Spanish king Ferrante of Naples, for whom he recruited singers. Music historians have often focused on Tinctoris's observations about an aesthetic transformation then under way in music, "a new art, if I may so call it," he wrote, "whose fount and origin is held to be among the English, of whom Dunstable stood forth as chief. Contemporary with him in France were Du Fay and Binchois, to whom directly succeeded the moderns Ockeghem, Busnoys, Regis, and Caron" (SR 36:292–93; 3/1:13–14).

We can trace important connections among these composers, whose careers intersected in places like Cambrai, where Tinctoris and Du Fay both served, or in the Burgundian capital, Dijon, where Binchois was the leading musician and where John Dunstable may well have visited in the retinue of John, duke of Bedford. We can also find evidence of Tinctoris's "new art," especially in the novel sense of melodic invention and a new harmonic practice founded on the euphonious sounds of parallel imperfect intervals heard in pieces like Dunstable's *Quam pulchra es* (see Chapter 4 and Anthology 7). But for Tinctoris this process of renewal was not simply a matter of aesthetic sensibilities; the real story was the piety and liberality that made the musical chapels possible in the first place. His discussion strongly echoes Aristotle's advice on the subject:

> The most Christian princes, of whom, most pious King, you are by far the foremost in the gifts of the mind, of body, and of fortune, desiring to augment the Divine Service, founded chapels after the manner of David, in which at extraordinary expense they appointed singers to sing pleasant and comely praise to our God with diverse (but not adverse) voices. And since the singers of princes, if their masters are endowed with the liberality which makes men illustrious, are rewarded with honor, glory, and wealth, many are kindled with a most fervent zeal for this study. (SR 36:292; 3/1:14)

For some princes, the urge to demonstrate the "liberality which makes men illustrious" became a compulsion that they were loath to admit publicly. Scrambling to assemble the musical markers of his own magnificence, the duke of Milan, Galeazzo Maria Sforza, sought to hide behind his surrogates as he conspired to steal away King Ferrante's best singers. Writing to his ambassador at the Neapolitan court in November 1472, the duke enlisted his help in a delicate mission of cultural piracy. "Since we have decided to make a chapel," he wrote,

> we are sending agents there to bring certain singers into our service, as you will understand more clearly from them. So that our wishes come about more easily, we want you, in a way that seems to come from you and not as if you have orders from us, to speak to those pointed out to you by the agents, urging them to enter our service. Promise them, as they have been told, that we will make them a good deal, providing them with good benefices and good salaries. We have given the money and means to the agents to bring these singers to us. Above all take care that neither his most serene majesty the king nor others might imagine that we have been the cause of removing these singers from those parts.

The "good benefices" promised by the duke were one of the most powerful recruiting tools that secular princes had for building their chapels. These sometimes lucrative church appointments supplemented the salaries singers drew from princely coffers. Some benefices required little or no work, or even physical presence in the church where they were held, provided that the holder could find a local substitute to fulfill the nominal duties of the appointment. Patrons like Galeazzo were able to exploit these appointments via their connections with the pope, who had final authority over these benefices, and who during this period was often himself a member of a ruling family like the Sforzas. If Galeazzo's furtive ambitions were in any way typical, the best singers must have been in high demand among patrons who wielded the power to confer benefices. It's not surprising that these singers were remarkably mobile. Du Fay, as we have noted, moved among a series of chapels during his lifetime, working not only for ecclesiastical institutions like Cambrai and the Papal Chapel, but also for ruling families in places like Rimini and Savoy.

Other musicians of the sort sought out by Galeazzo Maria Sforza's agents were no less peripatetic, and equally difficult to retain. The Flemish singer-composer Alexander Agricola (ca. 1445/46–1506), for instance, trained at the Cathedral of Cambrai and came to the royal court of France by 1491, whereupon he abruptly left for the Italian peninsula. Over the next decade he moved frequently among aristocratic and ecclesiastical employers in Mantua, the cathedral of Florence, the royal court of Ferrante in Naples, and the ducal court of Burgundy. All the while the French kings sought his return. Eventually he took up with the chapel of Philip the Fair in the Habsburg Netherlands, and died in Spain in 1506, probably in the company of his fellow chapel members, who had accompanied Philip on a journey there. Galeazzo Maria Sforza would have been lucky to hold onto someone like Agricola for even a few years. Similar patterns of movement can be traced for other prominent chapel singers of the

fifteenth century. The archives are rich with evidence of the efforts undertaken to entice the best singers into new and lucrative positions.

MUSIC IN MOTION

Music, too, traveled widely as a result of all of these connections, both on account of
the inevitable interchange of ideas among the professionals and through the collecting habits of their sponsors. Chroniclers of the period, as we have seen, rarely
mention particular compositions in their accounts of events. Payment registers
from court are also usually mute on the subject of musical works. But sometimes
we find hints about what must have been a brisk trade in music that moved from
court to court. In 1456, for instance, Du Fay wrote to Piero and Giovanni de' Medici,
music-loving sons of the powerful Florentine banker Cosimo, in response to a request for some of his newest music. The musician was apparently happy to oblige,
explaining that he felt "encouraged to send you some chansons which, at the request of some gentlemen of the [French] King's court, I composed recently when
I was in France with Monseigneur de Savoye" (SR 41:311–12; 3/6:33–34). The letter
suggests that Du Fay's duties in the service of patrons like Amadeus (the "Monseigneur de Savoye") extended well beyond his official role in the chapel. He apparently composed secular songs, too, at the behest of certain "gentlemen" of the
French royal court, and was free to send the pieces to the Medici in Florence.

It was not just individual pieces that changed hands in this way. Sometimes
entire manuscript volumes were imported, both as practical resources for local singers and as lavish presentation copies for their patrons. The duke of
Burgundy once sent the king of Naples a manuscript that contained six different
polyphonic tenor masses, all anonymous and all based on the famous *L'homme
armé* tune. (We'll return to the many meanings of the "armed man" tradition
and other aspects of the tenor mass in Chapter 5.) The works and the book that
contained them have been interpreted as symbolic expressions of membership
in the aristocratic Order of the Golden Fleece, an organization to which both the
giver and the recipient belonged.

A SONGBOOK FOR A PRINCESS

There must once have been many such presentation books, but only a few survive
in libraries around the world. (The duke of Burgundy's manuscript can still be
seen in a Neapolitan library.) One of the most beautiful is a parchment songbook
made as a musical gift for King Ferrante's daughter Beatrice in the early 1470s
and now preserved at Yale University (Fig. 3.3). Like other deluxe books of the
fifteenth century, the Mellon Chansonnier—so called after its modern donor,

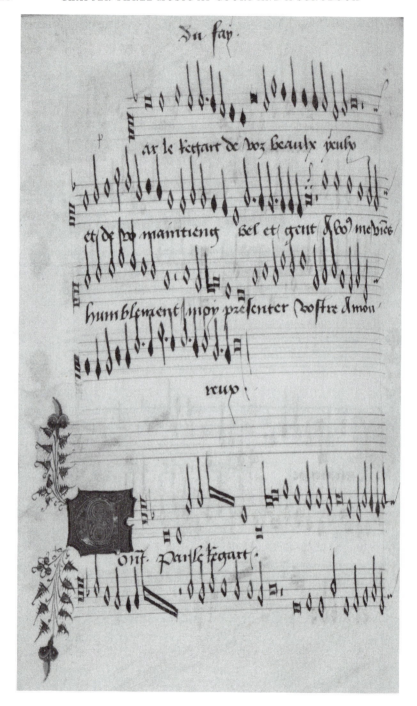

Figure 3.3: (a) *Guillaume Du Fay's* Par le regard, *from the Mellon Chansonnier, showing the cantus voice part above and a section of the contratenor part below*

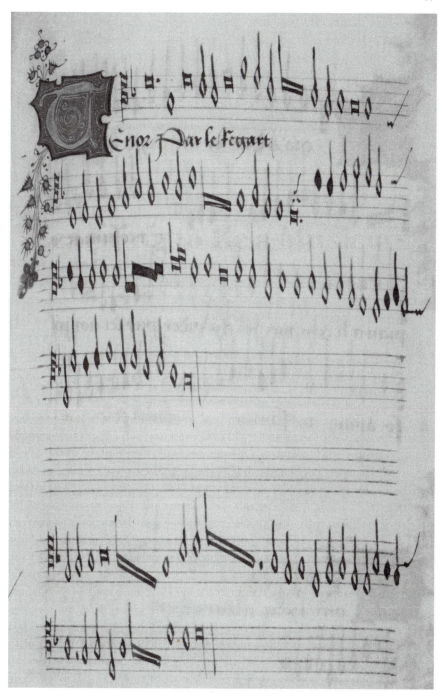

(b) *The tenor voice part is shown above and the continuation of the contratenor part below.*

Paul Mellon—was carefully copied by expert scribes. (Further on the work of these master craftsmen in Chapter 9.) The editor was almost certainly Beatrice's musical tutor, whose writings we have encountered so frequently in our survey of fifteenth-century music. Tinctoris evidently thought enough of his royal pupil (and of his own standing at court) to compose a devotional Latin song, *O virgo miserere mei* (Lady, have mercy on me), in her honor. The piece survives uniquely in the Mellon Chansonnier, with the dedication "Beatissime virgini domine beatrici de Aragonia" ([To the] most beatific virgin Lady Beatrice of Aragon).

Beatrice's songbook preserves a rich cross-section of sacred and secular music to Latin, French, Italian, English, and Spanish texts. It concludes with another Latin song by Tinctoris, *Virgo Dei throno digna* (O virgin worthy of God's throne). As with *O virgo miserere mei*, it is not entirely clear whether the virgin in question is divine or human, and perhaps this was the point. In any case, there is no doubt about who the supplicants are. "O virgin worthy of God's throne," the prayer intones, "only hope of musicians, to the devoted throng of singers be merciful and kind." Tinctoris seems to be hinting, not so gently, that no less than the heavenly Virgin, Beatrice ought not to forget the needs of her own musicians. In transposing the language of devotional prayer to the world of courtly patronage, Tinctoris's piece shows how the sacred and secular realms were brought surprisingly close through music.

A MUSICAL ALLEGORY

The opening work in Beatrice's chansonnier seems no less significant or suggestive: "Bel acueil" (Fair welcome), it begins, appropriately enough. The music is by Antoine Busnoys, a leading French composer of the fifteenth century from whom we will hear more shortly. But the turn of phrase is not merely formulaic; it invites the reader to enter the world of courtly love. Bel Acueil is an allegorical figure from the *Romance of the Rose*, a chivalric romance by the early thirteenth-century poet Guillaume de Lorris. Like Pity, Courtesy, and Courage, Fair Welcome represents the moods and faculties of those who subject themselves to the moral universe of the god of love, Amours, and his court. The chanson's refrain sets the scene:

Bel Acueil, le sergant d'Amours,
En bien soit faire ses esploys
M'a ja cité par pluseurs foys
D'aller a l'une de ses cours.

Fair Welcome, the servant of Love,
Knows how to turn his deeds to good account;
He has already summoned me, and many times
To go to one of his courts.

In the world of Fair Welcome, love was above all a service, often compared to the kind one might render to the Divine or to one's sovereign. The relationship of lover to beloved was thus imagined as that of vassal to lord or, in Christian terms, devotee to God or saint. Love was also a kind of physical suffering to be endured, wherein the beloved alone held the cure for the lover's ailment. The physical consummation of love, although often hoped for, was only obliquely described, and rarely realized, in texts from this tradition. Descriptions of physical love were instead displaced outside the courtly register to the world of the pastoral.

Whether the mental and moral universe imagined in such poetry was ever a social reality is beside the point. In the fifteenth century such literary conventions could be serious, ironic, or even parodic. But they were an important source of inspiration for aristocratic poets like Charles d'Orléans and Christine de Pizan, who used them as vehicles for the exploration of love in all its varied forms. That fifteenth-century readers and musicians would still be interested in this old-fashioned literature reminds us that courtly audiences of the period saw themselves as heirs to codes of conduct set out in the lyrics of the medieval troubadours and trouvères. Like the painted image of court dancers from the *History of Renaud de Montauban* explored above, *Bel acueil* shows how fifteenth-century courtiers actively cultivated old chivalric ideals through new poetry and music.

SONGS BY DU FAY AND BUSNOYS

Most of the pieces in Beatrice's songbook are in three-part textures: a lyrical cantus, which weaves a flowing duet with the tenor, plus a contratenor that makes lively rhythmic and melodic counterpoint with them. Consider, for instance, Du Fay's setting of *Par le regart* (By the Look), a poem that shares the lovelorn rhetoric of many of the songs in the collection (for a facsimile of this piece as it appears in the Mellon Chansonnier, see Fig. 3.3; a modern edition appears as Anthology 4). It is an entreaty to a lady of "fair and noble demeanor" by a suitor who presents himself "humbly" and is already held captive "by the glance of [her] beautiful eyes." The poem is cast as a rondeau, one of the old *formes fixes* (fixed forms) that trace their origin to the conventions of repetition and return first explored by the trouvères in the thirteenth century and codified by poets like Guillaume de Machaut in the fourteenth century. Like other rondeaux, *Par le regart* begins and ends with a refrain—in this case, four lines of rhymed text. The middle stanzas present a routine of successive departure and reprise: first a half stanza with half refrain (just the first two lines), then a full stanza and full refrain. Du Fay's music traces this progress with two contrasting musical sections, so that the overall plan might be represented as **ABaAabAB** (with capital letters indicating the two-part refrain). Du Fay's chanson does not so much express its text, as in an art song of the nineteenth century, as present it.

Another song from the Mellon Chansonnier reveals different aspects of the literary, musical, and social worlds that intersected in Beatrice's album. In Antoine Busnoys's *Ja que li ne s'i attende* (Although He Does Not Expect It), it is not the man who petitions, but the woman who professes fidelity (Anthology 5). There is an added wrinkle here, for the opening line of the song can also be heard—if we assemble the first few syllables as a single word—as "Let Jacqueline wait." This in turn is precisely what the speaker proposes to do in the body of the poem, allowing her love to be perceived by all who look upon her heraldic colors, blue and white, which her lover wears upon his armbands. Encryptions of the name "Jacqueline" or "Jacqueline d'Acqueville" circulate in a number of other songs from the orbit of the French royal court (as an acrostic in *Je ne puis vivre ainsi*, for example, also set by Busnoys, which likewise appears in the Mellon Chansonnier). The "Jacqueline" in question could have been any of several women with that name from Busnoys's world, including a Parisian noblewoman or a lady-in-waiting to a Scottish princess resident at the French court.

Despite professions of fidelity, courtly love was often framed as adulterous or involving incompatible social stations, something that helps to explain why the suitor in Busnoys's song would not expect more than a public rebuke of his affections. The deliberate ambiguity of the opening poetic line is pointedly resolved by the music, which links the first four syllables that together sound out the woman's name in a single melodic phrase in the cantus part. This poem is a virelai, another of the classic refrain schemes inherited from the fourteenth century (**AbbaA**). Its design repeats the sonic play on Jacqueline's name at the end of the poem.

In addition to the contrasting literary registers and forms, *Par le regard* and *Ja que li ne s'i attende* reflect changing approaches to musical counterpoint and harmony, especially with respect to the role of the contratenor part in the overall texture. Through them, composers discovered new expressive possibilities for the representation of form, rhyme, syntax, and meaning. These developments were in turn joined by still other innovations in the years after 1500 as composers explored new kinds of texts and newly expanded musical spaces (see Chapter 10).

A DOUBLE-TEXTED CHANSON

Like Busnoys, Johannes Ockeghem (ca. 1410–1497) was for a time associated with the church of St. Martin of Tours in the Loire Valley. He was also chapel master to the French royal court, where he served starting in about 1454. Given his long tenure at court, he is certain to have been familiar with poetry of the sort we have just encountered. But Ockeghem's double-texted *S'elle m'amera—Petite Camusette* (If She Will Love Me—Little Snubnose) appends a new literary dimension to the tradition of courtly expression. It seems to be a composite of two different poems, one drawn from the courtly register, the other from the pastoral. Such combinative chansons, as modern scholars call them, constitute a special genre in which literary as well as musical counterpoint adds many layers of possible meaning. The first text, which appears in the cantus part, is probably the refrain from a five-line rondeau (three lines for the A section and two for the B; the version below comes from the Mellon Chansonnier, which differs slightly in wording and spelling from that found in other sources that begin "S'elle m'amera"). The speaker of this poem wonders how he will find "grace" in his lover's eyes:

Cantus Text	
Petitte Camusette, j'ay	*Little Snubnose, I have*
Proposé me mettre en essay	*Proposed at least to try*
D'acquerir quelque peu vo grace:	*To obtain, however little, your grace;*
Force m'est que par la je passe	*Needs be that I pass that way*
Ceste foys j'en feray l'essay.	*This time I'll make the try.*

Meanwhile, the lower voices tell a disjointed tale of a more humble sort, shifting quickly from direct address ("Little Snubnose, you've put me to death") to a fragmentary tale that seems to come from a different world. "Robin and Marion are going to the wood to play" transports us into a landscape of shepherds, shepherdesses, and errant knights. The *pastourelle*, or pastoral lyric, was part of a long literary tradition with origins in the lyrics of the troubadours and trouvères. This second text probably derives from an old dance-game, the *rondet*, in which a leader would sing out a refrain, which would then be repeated by a chorus.

Text for the Lower Voices
Petitte Camusette, la mort m'avés mis.
Robin et Marïon s'en vont au boys jouer.
Ilz s'en vont bras a bras; ilz se sont endormis.
Petitte Camusette, la mort m'avés mis.

Little Snubnose, you've put me to death.
Robin and Marion are going to the wood to play.
They're going off, arm in arm; they've gone to sleep.
Little Snubnose, you've put me to death.

Although the verbal counterpoint of two texts sung simultaneously makes them virtually impossible to comprehend, chanson composers often combined more than one poem in the same song. Indeed, as we saw with Johannes Ciconia's *Doctorum principem* in Chapter 1, some motets had as many as three texts, even in different languages. In Ockeghem's chanson, the juxtaposition of courtly and pastoral registers produces some interesting conjunctions of word and tone (Ex. 3.1). As the speaker of the rondeau wonders whether he will "pass that way," the two lovers in the pastoral text have already gone off, arm in arm, to "sleep." In musical works like

Example 3.1: *Johannes Ockeghem,* S'elle m'amera–Petite Camusette, *mm. 16–36.*
Ockeghem, *Collected Works,* 3 vols., ed. Richard Wexler and Dragan Plamenac
(Philadelphia: American Musicological Society, 1992), 3:88–89.

this one, we can begin to measure the compatibility of those two ways of thinking
about love, in all its forms. As we'll discover in Chapter 10, singers and composers
of later years, too, were subtle readers of poetic texts of all kinds.

PERFORMING CHANSONS AT COURT

Documents from the courts of Naples, Savoy, and Burgundy are surprisingly silent on who performed these songs and in what contexts. As we've witnessed in

Du Fay's letter to the Medici brothers, the composition and copying of chansons seems to have taken place on the margins, so we should perhaps not be surprised that accountants had little to say about it. Du Fay's letter also suggests that these activities were largely private matters—exchanges and perhaps even performances undertaken out of earshot of official chroniclers. The evidence of the pieces themselves, no less than of books like the Mellon Chansonnier, is equivocal for the fifteenth century. Purely vocal performance was certainly the norm, despite the fact that the contratenor parts, with their frequent leaps and silences, seem less well suited to the voice than the cantus and tenor, with their smooth, flowing lines. Sources like the Mellon Chansonnier similarly seem to favor the cantus and tenor parts as the vocal ones, since only these voices carry poetic texts. On the other hand, these songbooks often leave to singers the job of fitting extra stanzas beneath the notes. Presumably a skilled chapel singer could do this for the contratenor part no less than for the other voices.

Beatrice's tutor Tinctoris suggested a still wider range of roles for the musicians of the *chambre* in the adaptation and performance of written repertories. In a treatise compiled in about 1480, *De inventione et usu musicae* (The Origin and Practice of Music), he paused to consider the accomplishments of important instrumentalists. Writing of the lute players heard at private entertainments, Tinctoris observed that "some teams will take the treble part of any piece you care to give them and improvise marvellously upon it with such taste that the performance cannot be rivalled. Among such, Pietrobono, lutenist to Ercole, Duke of Ferrara, is in my opinion pre-eminent." Tinctoris may have been preaching to the converted, for his readers at the court of Naples were probably well aware of the exceptional abilities of Pietrobono de Burzellis (ca. 1417–1497).

Not long after Beatrice, sister-in-law to Pietrobono's employer in Ferrara, moved to Buda as the new queen of Hungary (she married King Matthias Corvinus in 1476), she persuaded the lutenist to come to her court. But what, exactly, did he play for her? If Pietrobono was anything like the lutenists that Tinctoris so admired, he was entirely familiar with mensural notation (the system of rhythmic notation that preceded the use of time signatures; see Chapter 2). How else could they "improvise marvellously" upon the "treble part of any piece you care to give them"? What is more, Pietrobono's name in Ferrarese and other archival documents normally turns up in association with a player identified simply as his *tenorista*. Such arrangements are clearly implied by Tinctoris's reference to "teams" of players in his comment noted above. The role of the *tenorista* must have been to cover the tenor part. But in what sort of polyphony? One possibility is that they played music from the basse danse repertory, with Pietrobono spinning out improvised counterpoint against a slow-moving tenor. Another possibility is that Pietrobono and his *tenorista* were playing arrangements of polyphonic chansons or Italian songs of the sort we have seen in the Mellon Chansonnier, a scenario made even more likely by the fact that

Pietrobono was a singer as well as a player. If, as his functional title suggests, the *tenorista* took that line, then players of Pietrobono's quality would, according to Tinctoris's testimony, have had no trouble playing the remaining cantus and contratenor at once, or even all three parts: "Others will do what is much more difficult; namely to play a composition alone, and most skillfully, not only in two parts, but even in three or four."

Tinctoris does not say whether singer-instrumentalists like Pietrobono also collaborated with the chapel singers like Du Fay who composed secular songs of the sort we have just encountered. But it's hard to imagine that they would have avoided each other. Such music existed at the narrow perch between oral and written traditions. Clearly, the court lutenists and other members of the *bas* consort were comfortable with the complexities of written counterpoint composed by Tinctoris, Du Fay, and Busnoys. All of this suggests a rich interplay between different types of music—vocal and instrumental, written and oral, sacred and secular—in the private spaces of aristocratic households in places like Tinctoris's Naples. As we will see in subsequent chapters, these forms of musical expression often intersected, with beautiful results, during the fifteenth and sixteenth centuries.

Aristocratic households of the fifteenth century were places of luxury and display. Rulers like Duke Philip the Good of Burgundy and the men who sought to emulate him fashioned themselves in the image of ancient models. They saw themselves as heirs to Aristotle's teaching no less than to the fanciful codes of behavior set out in traditional chivalric poetry or in the ideals of Christian militancy. Music was put to work in the service of these ideas in many ways. Heraldic trumpeters announced their sovereign's every public move. Court chapels saw to the observance of the divine liturgy. Skillful instrumentalists provided entertainment for the important guests who assembled at weddings and other feasts where elites invited. And men like Tinctoris compiled treatises and supervised the production of manuscripts for sophisticated princes and princesses.

Guillaume Du Fay did not remain long at the court of Savoy during the 1430s, for Duke Amadeus soon abdicated his throne in favor of a role as hermit-knight, and eventually as Antipope Felix V. After an informal association with the court over the next 20 years, Du Fay eventually returned to his native Cambrai for a long and successful career as a church musician. He seems not to have composed much new secular music after the 1450s, when his connection with Savoy finally waned. From the works we have considered in this chapter, and the many testimonies about musical life we have encountered, it is clear that music, for all its ephemeral and contingent qualities, provided noble patrons with a persuasive means to manifest their piety, chivalry, and magnificence for all to hear. Meanwhile, thanks to the collecting, recruiting, and other exchanges put in motion by their patrons, the composers, singers, and players of the early

Renaissance were exploring new ways of interacting and new combinations of texts and tones.

Now that we understand the place of secular music in the aesthetics and ideals of courtly households of the mid-fifteenth century, we turn to consider the great variety of sacred music composed by men like Du Fay, and the many ritual, devotional, and symbolic meanings these works could carry.

FOR FURTHER READING

Alden, Jane, *Songs, Scribes, and Society: The History and Reception of the Loire Valley Chansonniers* (New York: Oxford University Press, 2010)

Atlas, Allan W., "Alexander Agricola and Ferrante I of Naples," *Journal of the American Musicological Society* 30 (1977): 313–19

Fallows, David, *Du Fay* (London: Dent, 1982)

Higgins, Paula, "Parisian Nobles, a Scottish Princess, and the Woman's Voice in Late Medieval Song," *Early Music History* 10 (1991): 145–200

Planchart, Alejandro Enrique, "Guillaume Du Fay's Benefices and his Relationship to the Court of Burgundy," *Early Music History* 8 (1988): 117–71

Prizer, William F., "Music at the Court of the Sforza: The Birth and Death of a Musical Center," *Musica disciplina* 43 (1989): 141–93

Reynolds, Christopher, "Musical Careers, Ecclesiastical Benefices, and the Example of Johannes Brunet," *Journal of the American Musicological Society* 37 (1984): 49–97

Wegman, Rob C., "Johannes Tinctoris and the 'New Art,'" *Music & Letters* 84 (2003): 171–188

Ⓢ Additional resources available at wwnorton.com/studyspace

CHAPTER FOUR

Piety, Devotion, and Ceremony

W hat roles did music play in Christian worship of the fifteenth century? What claims were made on its behalf? In this chapter we will explore these questions through the plainsong melodies, polyphonic hymns, and ceremonial motets and tenor masses of composers like John Dunstable, Guillaume Du Fay, and Jacob Obrecht. Religious life was changing, and nowhere so plainly as when wealthy private donors instituted special "votive" services in honor of the Virgin Mary and local saints. Music had especially important work to do in these contexts, mediating between heavenly audiences and earthly believers in ways that religious painting or sculpture could not. Music was an important way for individual donors, religious confraternities, and musicians to demonstrate their piety. It also allowed popes and kings to enshrine their authority with sacred sounds. Thanks to its central role in the presentation of these aspirations, music took on a new measure of autonomy and portability that had a profound impact on later generations.

In exploring these themes, we will highlight some important developments in sacred musical styles and forms that emerged during the fifteenth century. As the works of English composers circulated throughout Europe, Continental musicians were captivated by the fresh sounds of an idiom founded on flowing, declamatory melodies and harmonic combinations that emphasized successions of thirds and sixths. These same preferences also shaped the development of new sounds in Continental chansons of the period. Indeed, English compositions are to be found in the book Johannes Tinctoris compiled for Beatrice of Aragon (see Chapter 3). The English sounds also made their mark in the world of sacred music. In emulating these ideals, and through musical innovations of their own, composers like Du Fay and Obrecht found the means to invest religious observances with new and persuasive force that could be heard, felt, and shared.

The story of these developments continues in Chapter 5, where we will take up some of the most elaborate and deeply symbolic religious compositions of the fifteenth century, such as the large-scale cantus-firmus motets and cyclic tenor masses of Du Fay, Obrecht, Johannes Ockeghem, and Josquin des Prez. Before turning to these grand works, however, we will take time here to put the ceremonial and expressive functions of fifteenth-century sacred music in their broad cultural context, from English towns to the Italian peninsula, and to explore the means and meanings they put in play.

MUSIC IN CHURCH

According an entry in a Latin dictionary compiled by the Genoese scholar and priest Johannes de Balbis (d. ca. 1298), images were brought into churches for three fundamental reasons: "*First*, for the instruction of simple people, because they are instructed by them as if by books. *Second*, so that the mystery of the incarnation and the examples of the Saints may be the more active in our memory through being presented daily to our eyes. *Third*, to excite feelings of devotion, these being aroused more effectively by things seen than by things heard." Balbis's closing remark would appear to put music at a distinct disadvantage, for by his reasoning "things heard" were by their very nature less persistent and thus less effective than visual forms when it came to his three priorities of instruction, exemplification, and devotion. Music nevertheless had an important place in spiritual practice, often in ways that offer interesting analogies with the functions proposed by Balbis. Indeed, music could sometimes be combined with images, as shown in a famous music manuscript compiled between 1516 and 1523 for Marguerite of Austria (Fig. 4.1). Music also offers some contrasts with visual representation, for it could move among contexts in ways that durable forms like paintings and sculpture could not.

Plainsong had been the foundation of Catholic worship in monasteries and cathedrals for hundreds of years. Among the first requirements of any young cleric was literacy in both Latin grammar and musical practice. It was essential that those taking part in worship understood how and when to sing the various prayers. Sacred melodies were differentiated according to their place in individual services (such as the Mass or the Hours of the Divine Office) and the place of those services in the broader cycle of the church year (from major feasts like Christmas or Easter to minor ones for saints of local importance). There were literally hundreds of musical prayers to learn, and many combinations in which they might be heard. Only

Figure 4.1: (a) *Miniature of the Virgin, from a manuscript of chansons and motets copied for Marguerite of Austria between about 1516 and 1523*

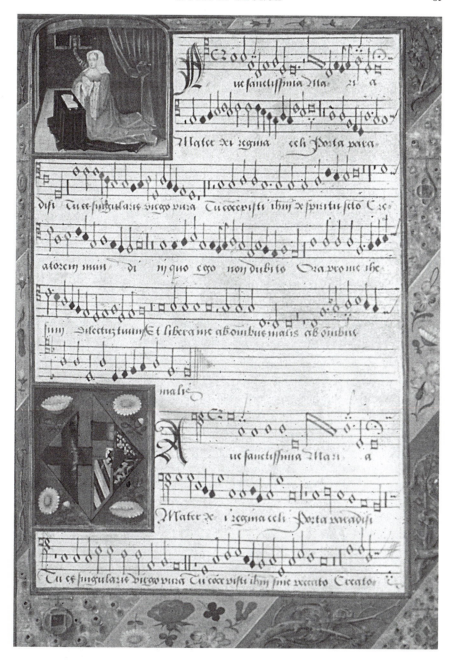

Figure 4.1: (b) *Miniature painting showing Marguerite of Austria in a devotional pose facing a miniature of the Virgin*

skilled theologians were qualified to debate the finer points of Christian doctrine, but even novice clerics were expected to have a practical understanding of liturgical melodies and their proper place in sacred rituals, without which services would simply grind to a halt.

Christian services in important ecclesiastical centers like Canterbury, Paris, and Rome had much in common, in part because of institutional inertia that resisted change. In other respects, however, the liturgy was a local affair, as Margot Fassler shows in *Music in the Medieval West*. Each town—and in larger towns each church or monastery—had its own sacred calendar, with observances to mark an important saint's day, to commemorate an early Christian martyr associated with the town, or perhaps to remember the arrival of an important sacred relic. Such observances were sustained through the interests of private donors—influential individuals, members of a religious confraternity or trade guild, and others who sought to demonstrate their piety, exchanging material wealth for spiritual merit. When new services were instituted, there was often need for new music to accompany them.

DU FAY AND A NEW MARIAN SERVICE FOR CAMBRAI

In 1457 a dying priest of the cathedral of Cambrai, Michel de Beringhen, endowed a new service in honor of the Virgin Mary, to be observed on the fourth Sunday of each August in perpetuity following his death. The *Recollectio omnium festorum Beate Mariae Virginis* (Recollection of All the Feasts of the Blessed Virgin Mary), as its title suggests, recalled in a single day each of the important feasts associated with Mary's life that had been observed throughout the liturgical calendar for centuries. Some of the prayers for this new service were borrowed from existing feasts, such as the Assumption and Annunciation, but many others had to be specially created. For this work de Beringhen turned to friends and colleagues from the cathedral of Cambrai.

The record of the new Marian service, preserved among the archives of the cathedral, tells us much about the kinds of labor that went into memorial endowments like these. The new prayers were written by the dean of the cathedral chapter and professor of theology at the University of Paris, Gilles Carlier. A messenger was sent hundreds of miles away to the court of Savoy, where Du Fay—who, as we saw in Chapter 3, had a long-standing association with Cambrai—set about composing plainsong melodies for Carlier's texts. Local scribes then copied the words and music of the service into over two dozen different books used around the cathedral, while other officials saw to it that de Beringhen's donated property would provide for the perpetual observance of the feast. For all of this his name would be included among the annual memorial prayers recited in church. Ecclesiastical officials were as good as their word: Du Fay's and Carlier's chants are still to be seen in the old service books of the cathedral, where the *Recollectio* was observed, with some modifications, for over two centuries.

The original record of the foundation tells us nothing about what de Beringhen might have hoped to achieve through his endowment. Acts of charity, and especially donations to support the work of religious institutions, were understood to accrue merit that could win the soul rapid movement through Purgatory and the other trials that followed death. According to some authorities, the support of musical worship seems to have been regarded as especially effective in this regard. Carlier himself once wrote a long and eloquent eulogy of music and its power to invoke heavenly favor. Sacred song, in his words, "earns the companionship of the angels." (Figure 4.2 shows a fifteenth-century sculptural representation of a chorus of angels.) Music could play a powerful mediating role between heaven and earth, drawing down sympathetic effects of the former upon the latter. "If at the death of certain saints," Carlier reasoned, "sweet-sounding hymns were heard, to their comfort, is it any wonder if hosts of angels support God's servants in their devout jubilation when, in the presence of Christ's beloved bride, the Church, they make musical offerings—not just rooting out malicious lies but also encouraging the hearer's feelings to devout grief?"

Perhaps the singing clerics at Cambrai did not need such lofty language to justify their participation in new services such as the one endowed by de Beringhen. Certainly, some of the more humble members of that chapter could have used the extra income they stood to earn as a result of their colleague's

Figure 4.2: *Luca della Robbia, Singing Angels (from series of sculptural friezes for the cathedral of Florence, scenes illustrating Psalm 150)*

deathbed generosity. The singer-priests of Cambrai, like members of most cathedral chapters (as the groups of clerics were called), were not monks but secular clergy, which is to say they lived in the world at large, in ordinary homes in the neighborhoods around the church. They needed money to pay for rent, furniture, food, and books, among other things. Depending on their seniority, they might hold a prebend, through which income from church property like farms and forests would provide a steady salary. But absenteeism was high, and so a system of extra payments was often implemented as an encouragement for those who sang services like the one endowed by de Beringhen.

Carlier's remarks on the affinities of heavenly and earthly singing, however, are part of an ambitious defense of polyphonic music and its rightful place in sacred ceremony. In it, he responded to the queries of a "devout man" who wondered why in so many religious institutions of the day "Gregorian or plain chant is neglected, while the sweet jubilation of harmoniously blended voices sounds forth in divine worship." What sorts of polyphonic music might Carlier have had in mind? What do we know about how it was used? And how might that knowledge help us understand surviving compositions from Cambrai and other religious institutions of the fifteenth century?

POLYPHONY AT THE MARGINS OF THE LITURGY

Much of this polyphony was tied in one way or another to plainsong. As we noted in our exploration of musical education in the fifteenth century (Chapter 2), cathedral choir schools like the one at Cambrai routinely taught young singers how to harmonize plainsong melodies with techniques like fauxbourdon, sometimes in stanza-by-stanza alternation with unadorned plainsong. Du Fay himself composed many hymns and other plainsong settings in this style. The demands they placed on singers were not burdensome, and in their simplest forms they would not disrupt the flow or order of the service.

Carlier, however, may also have been thinking of more ambitious works, such as polyphonic motets. In these compositions, plainsong prayers and sometimes newly crafted pious Latin texts were set for three, four, or even more voice parts in elaborate contrapuntal combinations. Not long before his death in 1474, for instance, Du Fay stipulated that during his own dying moments his colleagues at Cambrai should sing one of his elaborate settings of an antiphon in honor of the Virgin Mary, *Ave regina celorum* (Hail, Queen of Heaven). As cleric, composer, and the benefactor who endowed the extra sacred service during which the piece was to be sung, Du Fay was in a special position to inscribe himself in the performance. Around an ornamented version of the *Ave regina celorum* plainsong, the composer added petitions on his own behalf: "Have mercy on your dying Du Fay, or as a sinner he will be cast down into the fires of hell," and "Have mercy on your supplicant Du Fay, and may you see beauty in his death" (Ex. 4.1).

Example 4.1: *Guillaume Du Fay,* Ave regina celorum, *mm. 86–96. From Guillaume Dufay,* Opera Omnia, *ed. Heinrich Besseler, 6 vols., Corpus Mensurabilis Musicae, 1 (Rome: American Institute of Musicology, 1947–66), 5:127.*

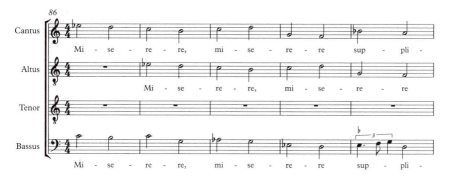

As it happened, there was no time to organize a performance of *Ave regina celorum* before the composer drew his last breath. But when the motet was sung at his funeral, Du Fay's colleagues were at last able to sing on his behalf what he himself could no longer ask. A half-century later, proceeds from the sale of Josquin des Prez's estate (he died in 1521) similarly endowed services in his memory, including the stipulation that during sacred processions his six-voice motet *Pater noster/ Ave Maria,* which combined the two prayers "Our Father" and "Hail Mary," be sung before an image of the Virgin Mary that hung outside his former home. The singer's prayer, it seems, had a long life as a special genre of composition in the fifteenth and early sixteenth centuries.

For clerics like Josquin, Du Fay, and de Beringhen, musical appeals to or praises of the Virgin Mary reflected widely held views of her power as an intercessor in the court of heavenly judgment. Linked with the virtues of virginal purity and maternal compassion, Mary emerged in theologies of the fourteenth and fifteenth centuries as a crucial mediator between the penitent and the divine. It's thus no surprise that during this period many churches were out-fitted with special Lady Chapels and other spaces given over to the veneration of the Virgin. In these alcoves spiritual confraternities, guild members, and wealthy private donors could demonstrate their devotion through charitable acts. Music—especially polyphonic music—became an important part of these "votive" or voluntary offerings, for reasons that Carlier's logic and Du Fay's or Josquin's pleading music make abundantly clear.

A MEMORIAL MASS BY OBRECHT

Given the expense of ensuring that the best singers would be provided with the best musical materials in order to undertake this work of pious persuasion, it's also not surprising that particularly rich traditions of devotional music emerged in cities where economic power was concentrated. The prosperous Flemish town of Bruges was one such place. It was there, in 1487, that the wealthy widow Adriane de Vos set aside funds to cover payment for Masses to be said in a private chapel that she and her late husband, Donaes de Moor, had founded behind the main altar of the church of St. James; the chapel was dedicated to the couple's patron saints, St. Donatian and St. Adrian.

Some of these new services were surely observed in plainsong, but others required polyphony. Jacob Obrecht (1457/58–1505) was the logical man to fulfill the commission. He held an appointment at St. Donatian and soon emerged as a leading composer of his generation. He responded to the request with a work of astounding richness and complexity, the *Missa de Sancto Donatiano* (Mass for St. Donatian). In such tenor masses, as we have noted, all five movements of the Ordinary (or unchanging) texts of the Mass were unified via a slow-moving cantus-firmus melody that served as structural foundation and spiritual commentary at the same time, since those who knew in advance about the tunes used in this way could understand what casual listeners might miss. Some tenor melodies were fragments of plainsong; others were drawn from secular songs of the day.

Obrecht's mass contains both kinds of cantus firmi (Anthology 6). It uses a sacred melody in the tenor, *O beate pater Donatiane* (O Blessed Father Donatian), beseeching St. Donatian (for whom both Donaes de Moor and the cathedral were named) to plead with Jesus for forgiveness on behalf of his human petitioner. We know from liturgical books of early sixteenth-century Bruges that this particular Latin antiphon (a chant originally sung as a refrain to the verses of a psalm) was suitable for any kind of private votive ceremony. As such it fit the needs of Adriane de Vos's endowment perfectly. Obrecht also used a second cantus-firmus melody: a Dutch secular song, *Gefft den armen gefangen* (Give to the Poor Prisoners), that calls on listeners to give alms and in doing so earn pious merit. Adriane and Donaes are known to have done precisely this, creating an almshouse and endowing funds to support the inmates of the local debtor's prison.

Music became a medium through which wealthy laymen and women, no less than the princes who controlled chapels or the priests and other officials who staffed them, could present their piety for all to hear, once they knew what to listen for. Humble music like plainsong could do the job, as Michel de Beringhen hoped when he endowed the *Recollectio*. For Adriane de Vos and her departed husband, the most elaborate polyphonic genre of the day was the choice.

DUNSTABLE, THE SONG OF SONGS, AND MUSICAL DEVOTION

From Du Fay's humble plainsong service of 1457 and Obrecht's elaborate mass of 1487, we now turn to consider yet another kind of sacred music, in this case from early-fifteenth-century England. *Quam pulchra es* (How Lovely You Are) by John Dunstable (ca. 1390–1453) might at first glance seem an unlikely vehicle for religious expression. It is a setting of verses drawn from the biblical Song of Songs, a love poem of frank eroticism, here offered as the lyrical exchange between a man and a woman. By later religious standards that presume a sharp distinction between physical and spiritual affinities, this poetic sensuality might appear utterly at odds with the needs of pious worship. As allegorized by generations of Jewish and Christian commentators, however, these texts had long been viewed through a decidedly spiritual lens. Bernard of Clairvaux, a French theologian of the twelfth century, identified the Song of Songs as suited to those who were fully prepared for spiritual marriage with Jesus. Believers were routinely taught to think in this analogical way, a frame of mind no less crucial to the historical understanding of the many tenor masses based on secular love songs than to the interpretation of the Song of Songs. Thus it should not be surprising that in Dunstable's England, as in other Christian contexts of the fifteenth century, passages from the Song of Songs had become thoroughly integrated into the liturgy. *Quam pulchra es*, used as a processional antiphon for feasts of the Blessed Virgin Mary, was among them (Anthology 7).

Quam pulchra es et quam decora, carissima in deliciis.
Statura tua assimilata est palme, et ubera tua botris.
Caput tuum ut Carmelus, collum tuum sicut turris eburnea.
Veni, delecta mi, egrediamur in agrum,
Et videamus si flores fructus parturierunt, si floruerunt mala Punica.
Ibi dabo tibi ubera mea.
Alleluia.

How lovely and wonderful you are, most beloved, most sweet in your delights.
Your stature is like a palm tree, and your breasts like a cluster of grapes.
Your head is like Mount Carmel, your neck like an ivory tower.
Come, my love, let us go into the fields,

And see if the flowers bear fruit and the pomegranates are in flower.
There will I give you my breasts.
Alleluia.

On the surface, there is nothing to rule out the possibility that polyphonic settings like Dunstable's were used in sacred services, particularly in light of the ample number and variety of similar antiphons in veneration of the Virgin that survive in English sources. The treble part, however, is apparently unrelated to any known plainsong melody. In this respect it stands apart from some of Dunstable's other settings of Marian hymns and antiphons, such as *Ave maris stella* and *Ave regina celorum*, in which a borrowed plainsong melody figures prominently in one of the three vocal parts. In short, while this setting of *Quam pulchra es* pays homage to the liturgical uses of the Song of Songs, it also marks out a space in which the specifically processional function of that antiphon has given way to a reflective stance. Singers and listeners alike are able to attend to the text as it is sung in the sweet-sounding harmonies (based on successions of thirds and sixths) and declamatory phrases (like the solemn chords on "Veni" at the center of piece) that were so typical of the new English style of the early decades of the fifteenth century.

Perhaps compositions such as this served to commemorate the Divine Service rather than merely to accompany it. The source tradition for Dunstable's piece suggests just this: *Quam pulchra es* is preserved in mixed manuscripts of sacred and secular songs compiled for aristocratic patrons on the Continent rather than in any liturgical books from English cathedrals or churches. The call of musical devotion, it seems, was heard in private households no less than in the church. In short, whatever we might guess about the origins of Dunstable's antiphon, its circulation was hardly limited to English religious establishments, or to those parts of the Divine Service associated with its text. As such it stands as a reminder that music could circulate quite independently of the divine liturgy. Even Balbis would be forced to admit that "things heard" could incite inner, private devotional fervor no less than the outer, public forms of things seen.

THE SOUND OF SACRED PROCESSIONS

Every church and monastery guarded its own sacred relic—a fragment of the True Cross, a vial of Holy Blood, parts of a saint's body—that was venerated for its historical, healing, or intercessory powers. Stored in an ornate silver-and-crystal reliquary, the relic was on special occasions paraded through town, spreading its protective power or reenacting its original "translation" from afar. Carried under an elaborate canopy and surrounded by clerics bearing huge candles and singing plainsong melodies, relics were often taken on a path that traced out the boundaries of the local parish. These processions could be moments of profound religious experience. A painting by the Venetian artist Gentile Bellini, *Processione in San Marco* (Procession in St. Mark's Square, 1496), commemorates one such moment on St. Mark's Day in April 1444, when the son of a Brescian merchant was miraculously healed just as his father kneeled to pray before the passing fragments of the True Cross. (The merchant can be seen in Fig. 4.3 just to the right of the canopy under which the relic is held.)

To judge from Bellini's painting and the many official chronicles of this annual procession, the assembly for St. Mark's Day brought together representatives of the most important religious and political institutions of the Venetian Republic. There were members of the great charitable confraternity of San Giovanni, local friars, priests from various congregations around the city, government officials, and their elected leader, the doge (who was important enough to merit a canopy of his own). Bellini's painting offers only mute testimony to the miraculous events of 1444, but music clearly had an important role to play: singers, lutenists, and harpists prepared the way for the True Cross, while bands of trumpets, sackbuts, and shawms cleared

Figure 4.3: *Detail of sacred relics and kneeling patron at the right from a commemorative painting of a sacred procession before the Basilica of San Marco in Venice held in on St. Mark's Day in April 1444, from Gentile Bellini's* Processione in San Marco *(1496)*

Figure 4.4: *Detail of musicians, from Gentile Bellini's* Processione in San Marco *(1496)*

the way for the doge (Fig. 4.4). There is little reason to doubt the acoustical splendor of the scene; we know from fiscal records of the day that the confraternity of San Giovanni spared no expense in hiring specialist singers and instrumentalists for the annual procession.

The citizens of Venice were hardly unique in using music as a way to participate in sacred public commemorations. In the Tuscan town of Siena, what began as a collective offering of thanks to the Virgin Mary blossomed into an annual contest that pitted the various political wards (each with its own banner, or palio) against one another in a public celebration that was part religious festival and part athletic forum, with multisided boxing matches, horse races, and jousting tournaments. By the fourteenth century the Palio was a focal point of communal life in which confraternities and merchants' associations vied with each other to sponsor the most flamboyant banners and processions. Trumpets, shawms, and drums accompanied each banner in its progress through the town, while singers, blind lutenists, and others took part in floats and other costumed assemblies organized by the wards. The Sienese Palio is still an annual event involving the entire town and thousands of tourists (Fig. 4.5).

Figure 4.5: *Modern-day observance of the Palio in Siena (1997)*

MUSIC FOR CORPUS CHRISTI PROCESSIONS

Of all the public processions that took place in European towns of the fifteenth and sixteenth centuries, however, none was as universally observed as the great Feast of Corpus Christi. Celebrated each year in early summer (the Thursday after Trinity Sunday), the holiday was first promoted in the thirteenth century as a way to encourage the veneration of the mystery of the Eucharist. Transformed during the Mass into what was believed to be Jesus's body, the Eucharist was held aloft during the Corpus Christi ritual in an ornate portable display stand and carried in solemn procession out of the church and through the town for all to see. The stand, or monstrance, was covered by a canopy, flanked by clerics carrying huge candles, and accompanied by solemn plainsong melodies that celebrated its healing powers. This public display was also an important opportunity for local interests to assert their own status as they jostled with each other to draw close to the Eucharist and express their collective piety.

Many communities compiled an official guide to the Corpus Christi ritual that spelled out in great detail which magistrates, religious orders, and craft guilds could take part in the procession, and above all in what order they could walk. In the prosperous English market towns of the fifteenth and early sixteenth centuries, these groups vied to see who could supply the best costumes, carpentry, and music for cycles of religious dramas staged along the parade route. These street dramas played out moralizing stories of prophecy, redemption, sin, and salvation in English for all to understand. Scripts for plays in places like Chester, York, and Coventry survive in considerable number, for they were part of annual traditions repeated well into the sixteenth century around the time of Corpus Christi, Easter, and Christmas, much as they had been for centuries (as we learn in Margot Fassler's *Music in the Medieval West*).

Unfortunately, the music for these English sacred dramas does not survive along with the scripts in any great abundance. It was in all likelihood performed from memory without notation by instrumentalists or singers according to who was at hand, or which guild had the funds to hire the musicians. Trumpets and other loud instruments might announce the plays, as would have been necessary in a noisy urban environment. Musical cues also served structural functions within the dramas, indicating the passage of time or scene changes. On a deeper symbolic level, contrasting combinations of voices and instruments were used to suggest a kind of moral order, from the harmonious singing of angels to the rough dance music or bawdy songs of the lower world. Apparently, the audience felt free to join in with the liturgical melodies, either to accompany a "procession" in the imaginary world of the drama or in a final Te Deum of thanksgiving. Breaking down any semblance of theatrical illusion, music afforded an opportunity for ordinary citizens to be participants as well as observers. Ceremony and expression could through such sonic forms be one and the same.

A CEREMONIAL CAROL

There is no rose, an English carol of the early fifteenth century, invites consideration in this context. To judge from its subject matter, the song was ideally suited to a Nativity play of the sort enacted in churches or town squares around Christmastime, but it could just as easily have been a part of a Corpus Christi pageant. In five brief couplets (rendered below in modern English), the song recalls the mysteries of Mary's life and reminds listeners of their profound import for Christian believers. The miraculous birth, the Holy Trinity, the joyful songs of heavenly and earthly witnesses are set out in rhymes that even simple folk could understand:

There is no rose of such virtue
As is the rose that bore Jesus,
Alleluia.

For in this rose was contained
Both heaven and earth in a little space,
A thing to wonder at.

By that rose we may well see
That he is God in persons three,
But of equal form.

The angels sing to the shepherds,
"Glory in the highest to God."
Let us rejoice!

We leave behind this worldly mirth
And follow this joyful birth.
Let us go.

Carols like *There is no rose* had their origins among the monophonic songs that were common musical property in English towns of the fourteenth and fifteenth centuries. Analogous traditions of popular religious song existed elsewhere in Europe, from the processional laude in the Italian peninsula to the monophonic noëls heard in France and the *Leise* melodies of German-speaking lands. Such songs stood outside the Mass and other official rituals of the church, which could be observed only by priests, and were probably a convenient way for preachers to translate theological concepts into memorable texts and tunes for those who could not read.

Over the course of the fifteenth century, church composers frequently used some of these monophonic tunes in polyphonic settings. An anonymous version of *There is no rose* (Anthology 8) joins this tradition of borrowing and adapting from popular sources. It reveals the handicraft of a skilled musician, with its flowing contrapuntal motion and harmonic vocabulary built around successions of thirds and sixths. Whether it was meant for private singing, for after-dinner entertainment in a household wealthy enough to hire local singers to perform it, or for mealtime music in a church school, *There is no rose* shows how popular tunes and the craft of polyphonic composition could be joined in the expression of pious virtues shared by all.

MUSIC FOR CEREMONIES OF STATE

Fifteenth-century kings and popes also surrounded themselves with the sights and sounds of liturgical ceremony. Princes used a musical vocabulary borrowed from sacred processions to remind everyone of their divine right to rule. According to the French chronicler Jean Froissart, when Isabella of Bavaria, queen consort to the French monarch Charles VI, made her official entrance into Paris in 1389, heralding trumpets and plainsong melodies punctuated the route. Similarly, when Philip the Good, duke of Burgundy, made his "pleasant entry" into Bruges in December 1440, sounds and images were arrayed in ways that put princely authority, civic pride, and religious doctrine in close alignment. A chronicle of Philip's day sets the scene: as the duke and his entourage waited outside Holy Cross Gate, officers of the city approached as barefoot penitents. The procession was soon joined by members of religious orders, representatives of craft guilds, foreign merchants, and others. The occasion marked Philip's magnanimity in pardoning the town for a violent revolt in which one of his field marshals and an entire battalion of soldiers had been killed. Now that order had been restored, the duke was ready to forgive the citizens of Bruges, who joined in singing the customary Te Deum. In short, music embodied worldly political order, while rendering appropriate thanks to the divine.

The entire assembly turned through the gate in a solemn procession through the town and up to the market square. Eighty trumpeters marked important stations along the route. Church bells rang from every quarter. What Froissart found most remarkable about the procession, however, were the platforms of "living pictures." The ones prepared for Philip's return to Bruges were reportedly the most elaborate that the local citizens had ever witnessed. The costumed actors in these tableaux didn't actually speak, but instead held static poses, while painted banners linked the visual displays with moralizing or sacred texts. Music frequently animated the tableaux. In some, singing children took the parts of angels. In others, various combinations of *bas* instruments (lutes, harps, organs, and soft winds) evoked the harmony of a heavenly realm that otherwise remained beyond human experience. The tableaux were arranged in a didactic sequence aimed to align Philip's reign with prototypes from Christian theology. The wealthy citizens of Bruges apparently wanted to remind themselves of Philip's clemency, and the procession soon became an annual observance.

Other honorific compositions must have been heard along these triumphal routes. Many are now lost; others are hidden among the laudatory works that appear without special designation in the music books of fifteenth- and sixteenth-century Europe. But sometimes a printer or scribe will give us a hint, as when in the 1530s Pierre Attaingnant designated a motet by Mathieu Gascongne as having been written "for our king." The king in question was Francis I, but the text of *Christus vincit, Christus regnat, Christus imperat* (Christ Conquers, Christ Reigns, Christ Commands), with its repeated refrain and long list of patron saints, was equally suitable for any French monarch. Indeed, it had been sung at coronations, festal crown-wearings, and other royal ceremonies since the time of Charlemagne. French kings were not just political figureheads; they were the physical embodiment of a divine presence. Their regimes melded statecraft and religion in ways that are often hard for us to fathom from the perspective of republican democracy. So we should not be too surprised that the sounds of their secular public ceremonies echoed those heard in the public rituals of the Christian church with which they were so closely allied.

DU FAY'S MOTET FOR POPE AND EMPEROR

As we observed in Chapter 3, Guillaume Du Fay's long musical career took him the length and breadth of Europe as a relatively young man. His powerful Italian patrons seem to have been especially fond of commemorating important occasions like marriages and political accords with elaborate motets. These works were a far cry from the lyrical, often intimate devotional pieces we have just encountered. With their repeating, carefully organized tenors and complicated interplay of upper voice parts, they were also relatively old-fashioned. (Recall Egidius of Murino's exposition of the basic premise of the motet, which we discussed in Chapter 1.) Nevertheless, they reveal how musical techniques that began in the elaboration of the liturgy were used to frame some very worldly concerns with musical markers of the sacred.

Du Fay's *Supremum est mortalibus* (The Supreme Good for Mortals), a four-voice motet composed in April 1433 to mark a peace treaty concluded between his employer, Pope Eugenius IV, and Sigismund, king of Hungary and emperor-elect, embodies many of these qualities. The concord between the two is manifest in sound as their names are declaimed in slow-moving chords at the climax of the piece: "May our eternal pontiff be EUGENIUS AND OUR KING SIGISMUND" (Ex. 4.2; for the complete text, see Anthology 9).

Unusually among Du Fay's large-scale motets, the tenor is not a borrowed plain-song melody, but it briefly quotes a fragment of chant, *Isti sunt duae olivae* ("Here are two olives," originally from a feast in honor of Saints John and Paul), immediately before the choir sounds out the names of his dedicatees. Replacing the two apostolic figures with pope and king was an audacious, if private, move, since only those already in the know would have been aware of the reference in the tenor part. But there is still more to the story, for sacred sounds are heard even when the tenor is silent. Here Du Fay calls for something quite unexpected: fauxbourdon. Perhaps the idea was prompted by a reference to the "psalm-like" sound of streams, one of four phrases in the motet where Du Fay calls for the special fauxbourdon texture. Perhaps, too, the harmonious sounds of fauxbourdon (see Chapter 2) seemed to fit the passage in the third section of the text that recalls the "sweetness" of a holy peace. Fauxbourdon is also heard at the very outset of the motet and right after the slow declamation of the names of the honorees, for the concluding "Amen" (shown in Ex. 4.2). Perhaps Du Fay meant to frame the accord between Eugenius and Sigismund with sounds his listeners would have associated with the divine liturgy, anointing a political event with a persuasive musical force that would have been hard to resist.

Our encounter with de Beringhen's endowment for the *Recollectio*, Dunstable's *Quam pulchra es*, and Du Fay's *Supremum est mortalibus* demonstrates, first and foremost, that despite Johannes de Balbis's concerns about the efficacy of "things heard," music could and did play a vital role in the service of the sacred. It served the same functions that Balbis allowed for the presence of images in church: to instruct the simple, to model pious behavior, and to inspire personal devotion. But music also accomplished what images could not. It mediated, in Gilles Carlier's view, between heaven and earth, providing listeners with the sense that musical prayers had implications far beyond the confines in which they were made.

We have seen how private patrons—guild members, clerics, and musicians themselves—sought salvation in the musical work of local churches, sponsoring all kinds of new services and music. Music marked the public sphere with sacred sounds in ways that could be heard by all, as during processions of holy relics and the Eucharist. Music could also imprint the political ambitions of earthly rulers with the stamp of the sacred, as we've observed in the chronicles of princely official entrances and in Du Fay's elaborate motet for Pope Eugenius and King Sigismund. Mediating between the divine order and human aspirations, music was a powerful

Example 4.2: *Guillaume Du Fay,* Supremum est mortalibus, *mm. 107–20. From*
Guillaume Dufay, Opera Omnia, *ed. Heinrich Besseler, 6 vols., Corpus Mensurabilis*
Musicae, 1 (Rome: American Institute of Musicology, 1947–66), 1:63.

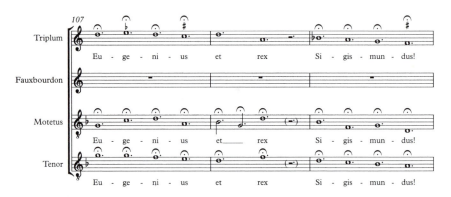

expression of ritual action and pious devotion alike. Having seen how even modest musical forms, no less than Du Fay's motet, could serve these twin purposes, we turn in Chapter 5 to explore the structure and significance of some of the most challenging works that he and his colleagues crafted during the fifteenth century.

FOR FURTHER READING

Blackburn, Bonnie J., "For Whom Do the Singers Sing?" *Early Music* 25 (1997): 593–609

Bloxam, M. Jennifer, *Saint Donatian Mass: Jacob Obrecht,* http://obrechtmass.com

Borgerding, Todd M., "Imagining the Sacred Body: Choirboys, their Voices, and Corpus Christi in Early Modern Seville," in *Musical Childhoods and the Cultures of Youth*, ed. Susan Boynton and Roe-Min Kok, pp. 25–48 (Middletown, CT: Wesleyan University Press, 2006)

Brown, Howard Mayer, "The Mirror of Man's Salvation: Music in Devotional Life about 1500," *Renaissance Quarterly* 43 (1990): 744–73

Haggh, Barbara, "The Celebration of the 'Recollectio Festorum Beatae Mariae Virginis,' 1457–1987," *Studia musicologica Academiae Scientiarum Hungaricae* 30 (1988): 361–73

Kreitner, Kenneth, "Music in the Corpus Christi Procession of Fifteenth-Century Barcelona," *Early Music History* 14 (1995): 153–204

Maurey, Yossi, "Heresy, Devotion and Memory: The Meaning of Corpus Christi in Saint-Martin of Tours," *Acta musicologica* 79 (2006): 159–96

Wright, Craig, "Dufay at Cambrai: Discoveries and Revisions," *Journal of the American Musicological Society* 28 (1975): 175–229

Ⓢ **Additional resources available at wwnorton.com/studyspace**

CHAPTER FIVE

Structures and Symbols in Cantus Firmus and Canon

In Chapters 3 and 4, we saw how music was used in sacred ceremony to express different forms of piety and devotion. Among the musical compositions deployed in these contexts were the relatively intimate genre of plainsong and small-scale pieces like *There is no rose* and Dunstable's *Quam pulchra es*. Large-scale motets and cantus-firmus masses could join in this work of ritual performance and pious expression. The crafting of such long and cleverly organized pieces represented the culmination of a lineage of musical thought that stretched back to the very roots of polyphonic practice in Europe. Through them, we can begin to measure the weight of tradition, and in particular the legacy of a Scholastic mentality that delighted in glossing and layering even the humblest source materials to create works of astounding intellectual richness.

The need to organize sound around borrowed melodies and abstract, even inaudible, structures is among the most basic of musical impulses. Musicians of the fifteenth and sixteenth centuries were virtuosos in this respect. Our investigation will begin with ceremonial motets and cyclic tenor masses by composers like Guillaume Du Fay and Josquin des Prez, in which borrowed melodies provide a structural scaffolding for large spans of musical time. Johannes Ockeghem and other composers liked to include witty, even obscure, directions in their works that challenged singers to make audible order from cryptic clues in the written score. Each of these kinds of pieces involves more than mere musical abstraction; for musicians of the fifteenth century, they were no less important for their philosophical and spiritual meanings. Poised between the ritual, devotional, and political uses of music on one hand, and speculative claims about the character, origins, and purposes of music on the other, works like these can tell us much about the musical past and how fifteenth-century musicians saw themselves as part of a great intellectual tradition.

CANTUS FIRMUS AND THE CEREMONIAL MOTET

For musicians of the early fifteenth century, composing was quite literally the craft of putting things in order. When Egidius of Murino offered guidance to aspiring composers in his *Tractatus cantus mensurabilis* (see Chapter 1), he suggested that the first thing to do when creating a motet was to select a tenor melody with a text suited to the occasion and "arrange it and put it in rhythm." To this secure foundation the composer could then add one, two, or three more voice parts. Organizing music around a borrowed cantus firmus (literally, fixed melody) in the tenor part had been the basis of European polyphony as far back as the ninth century. Around 1200, Leonin, Perotin, and other masters of organum at Notre Dame de Paris first applied cantus-firmus technique in systematic fashion to the elaboration and notation of liturgical polyphony. By Egidius's day, around 1350, this compositional habit had become more or less obligatory in crafting music for important occasions. Indeed, Italian statesmen, aristocrats, and church officials seemed to expect this sort of musical commemoration of their achievements. The early-fifteenth-century motet *Doctorum principem* by Johannes Ciconia (ca. 1370–1412), which we examined in Chapter 1 (also see Anthology 2), is built on three statements of a tenor melody, around which the various voices move in coordinated rhythm as they sing the praises of Ciconia's patron, Archpriest Francesco Zabarella. The invocations of Zabarella's name herald each repetition of the underlying tenor. Thus the work's political message and its hidden structure reinforce each other nicely.

Among the many motets that Guillaume Du Fay (1397–1474) composed for his Italian patrons over the course of his long career are several that illustrate this tradition of musical order-making. In his *Supremum est mortalibus* of 1433 (see Chapter 4 and Anthology 9), a freely composed tenor melody is stated twice, with each statement rhythmically organized around three presentations of the same basic series of durations. In Ciconia's piece, Zabarella's name is sounded out for each of the tenor repetitions. In Du Fay's, the names of the dedicatees, Pope Eugenius and King Sigismund, are heard only after the regular pattern of the tenor breaks off and all four voices move in slow, coordinated harmonies.

Du Fay's *Nuper rosarum flores* (Recently Blossoms of Roses), probably written to mark the consecration of the cathedral of Florence in 1436, takes a more systematic approach. In keeping with the compositional method proposed by Egidius, Du Fay chose as his tenor an excerpt from the plainsong liturgy used to mark the inauguration of sacred spaces: "Terribilis est locus iste" (Awesome is this place) it begins. The ceremonial nature of its tenor tune assured that Du Fay's motet was appropriate for the event it marked. The slow-moving tenor and contratenor are stated in successive metrical transformations that follow a series of proportions, 6:4:2:3. Indeed, the tenor is notated only once, with a verbal canon (or "rule") explaining how to sing it in each of the four different mensurations. Meanwhile, the upper voices repeat their own melodic patterns in new rhythmic guises. But there is evidence that the mensural relationships held symbolic as well as procedural importance. The proportions inscribed in Du Fay's motet underscore analogies between the structure of the newly completed Florentine cathedral and that of King Solomon's Temple in Jerusalem, which was described in biblical sources in the same mathematical proportions of 6:4:2:3. The musical impulse to create order, it seems, could be used to connect past and present through the medium of sound.

THE *CAPUT* MASSES

The chief innovation of what we now call the cyclic tenor mass is the idea that the several, independent movements of the Ordinary (that is, the unchanging texts of the Kyrie, Gloria, Credo, Sanctus, and Agnus Dei) of the Mass would be joined together by a single recurring theme, in this case concentrated in the tenor part as a cantus firmus. In addition to the symbolic or associative functions the tenor melody might bring, it presented composers with a way of extending to mass movements the possibilities of rational planning often heard in elaborate political motets of the sort just described. First invented by English musicians of the early fifteenth century, the tenor mass rapidly spread to the Continent, where composers like Du Fay, Antoine Busnoys, Johannes Ockeghem, Jacob Obrecht, and Josquin des Prez created vast cyclic compositions by borrowing from both liturgical and secular sources.

The *Missa Caput*, or "Head" Mass, dating from the 1440s, was among the earliest of these new tenor-based settings of the Ordinary. In it, an anonymous composer (once thought to be Du Fay, but probably an unknown Englishman) joined the five unchanging sections of the Mass through the use of a common tenor: a fragment from a liturgical melody used in England during Holy Week, which culminates in Easter.

The *Missa Caput* was also important for the way in which it added a fourth voice *below* the tenor cantus firmus. This "contratenor bassus" (later, simply bassus) opened up all sorts of new musical possibilities for composers, particularly around cadences, since the borrowed tenor part need no longer determine the final tone of those articulations, as it normally did in pieces like Du Fay's *Supremum est mortalibus*. The tenor could now just as easily form a fifth with the surrounding parts, or engender more-flexible movement among them (see the discussion of Du Fay's *Missa L'homme armé* below and Anthology 10).

Finally, in linking the generic text of the Ordinary with the extramusical associations of a given tenor cantus firmus, such works could be inscribed with all sorts of meanings, as we noted in our explorations of music at court and musical devotion. Obrecht's *Missa de Sancto Donatiano* (Mass for St. Donatian; see Chapter 4) combined two cantus-firmus melodies in ways that invoked the intercessory powers of that saint to plead on behalf of wealthy, pious donors. Local, even personal meanings could be put into play through the organizing principle of the cantus firmus. But tenor masses could also trace out meanings that were symbolic, or even hidden, all depending on the sacred or secular source of the borrowed tune. Some of the meanings these tunes brought to the mass might seem obvious; others must have been apparent only to those in the know, or even to the composer alone.

Relying on a fragment from the Maundy Thursday service, the *Missa Caput* was long understood in the liturgical context of its slow-moving tenor melody. The "head" (*caput*) in question was that of the Apostle Peter, who, as the Gospel relates, asked Jesus to ceremonially wash his head and hands as well as his feet. Viewed from the standpoint of the Easter liturgy, the reference seemed to point both toward Jesus's power to cleanse others of sin and toward Peter's eventual role as head of the new Christian church. But recently other likely meanings have been suggested: in some sources the mass is identified as *Missa Caput draconis* (Head of the Dragon) and accompanied by illuminated borders or initials depicting the mythical beast as it was defeated, pierced, or crushed underfoot by an armed man or woman. The dragon, in keeping with a long tradition of Christian images and teachings, might in this case symbolize Satan or sin, while the armed figure stands for either Jesus or the Virgin Mary.

This reading helps us to understand how other composers treated the tune in their own tenor masses on the *Caput* melody. Ockeghem, for example, "pushed the head down" by radically transposing it from its notated register to the lowest-sounding voice of the texture (Ex. 5.1). In the Agnus Dei movement of Obrecht's *Missa Caput*, the tune gradually descends through the four voice parts until it reaches the bottom of the ensemble. Musical actions embedded in these compositions thus mimetically enact a moral victory over sin, echoing a tradition of dragon-bashing that was well known in fifteenth-century England and France, from paintings to popular processions. Carefully inscribing one sacred text (the *Caput* melody) in another (the Mass), the anonymous composer of the original *Missa Caput* built a work of astonishing richness that is still yielding new interpretations and meanings.

Example 5.1: *Johannes Ockeghem,* Missa Caput, Kyrie, *mm. 16–24. From Johannes Ockeghem,* Collected Works, *ed. Dragan Plamenac, 2nd ed., 3 vols. (Philadelphia: American Musicological Society, 1959), 2:37.*

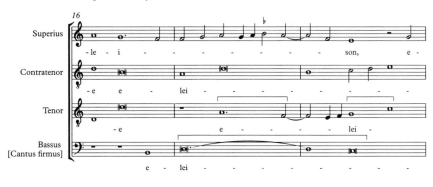

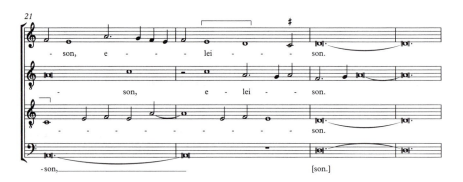

Lord, have mercy

THE *L'HOMME ARMÉ* TRADITION

Masses built on the humble folk melody *L'homme armé* (The Armed Man) also join this tradition of symbolic order-making. This secular monophonic tune first entered the repertory of polyphonic music in the mid-fifteenth century, notably in the works of composers active at the courts of Burgundy and France. There survive over two dozen different treatments of it from the fifteenth and sixteenth centuries, many of them written in response to each other, suggesting a culture of competition, emulation, and historical self-consciousness. As in the case of the *Caput* masses, these works are significant both musically and culturally. The *L'homme armé* masses stand at some distance from other tenor masses, which turned either to sacred plainsong (Du Fay's *Missa Ave regina celorum*) or to lines drawn from polyphonic chansons (Ockeghem's *Missa De plus en plus*). One explanation holds that the "armed man" of the song was an emblem of the resurgent Christian knight prepared to do battle with the "Turk" also mentioned in the words of the folk tune. This reading seems to align with the political priorities of the Burgundian court, where several of the earliest treatments of the tune circulated (see below).

DU FAY'S CANONIC AGNUS DEI

The closing Agnus Dei from Du Fay's *Missa L'homme armé* follows the conventional division of the sacred text into three symmetrically arranged sections that mirror the threefold repetitions of the phrase "Lamb of God." (For a detailed analysis of this piece, see Anthology 10.) The *L'homme armé* melody can be heard in each—if we are careful to listen for it. (See Example 5.2 for a transcription of the melody as it appears in a mass by Antoine Busnoys—one of the first composers to use it as a cyclic cantus firmus in this way.)

Example 5.2: *Anonymous tune,* L'homme armé, *as given in the* Tu solus *section of the Gloria of Antoine Busnoys's* Missa L'homme armé, *quoted from Antoine Busnoys,* Collected Works: The Latin-Texted Works, *ed. Richard Taruskin, Monuments and Masters of the Renaissance, 5 (New York: Broude Brothers Trust, 1990), pp. 16–17. Text added to show alignment of musical and poetic phrases.*

L'homme armé doibt on doubter.	*The armed man is to be feared.*
On a fait partout crier	*Everywhere the cry has been raised*
Que chascun se viegne armer	*That each must arm himself*
D'un haubregon de fer.	*With an iron hauberk.*

In Agnus I the melody appears in the tenor part in long notes, serving much the same structural role that the tenor part served in Du Fay's and Ciconia's motets. With its frequent leaps and repeated motives, the tune is relatively easy to recognize, even at this slow pace, particularly since we have already heard it in each of the preceding movements. In Agnus III the tenor continues this structural function, although now the sequence of rhythms and pitches seems anything but familiar (it is in fact going backward!). About two-thirds of the way through the Agnus Dei III, things suddenly become clearer: the tenor moves at the same pace as the other voices, allowing us to plainly hear the *L'homme armé* melody in its entirety.

The plan behind the obscure beginning and sudden reversal in Agnus III would have seemed less murky to Du Fay's singers than to his listeners. A witty Latin canon, or rule, hinted at their task: "Cancer eat plenus sed redeat medius" (Let the crab go forward whole, but return half). To sing the piece correctly they needed to decode the two reversals implied by the canon as they read the melody on the page. "Whole" and "half" in this case suggest rhythmic diminution, namely: sing the melody first in its notated values, then twice as fast. Going "forward" and "returning" suggest retrograde motion. This seems simple enough, until we remember that crabs always scuttle in *reverse*. So the slow backward version comes first, then the tune in its original sequence, now at twice the pace.

Canonic instructions like these were fairly common in fifteenth-century sources. Indeed, when the theorist and composer Johannes Tinctoris compiled a dictionary of musical terms for his pupil Princess Beatrice in Naples, he described a canon as "a rule showing the purpose of the composer behind a certain obscurity." Of course, Du Fay could have achieved the same result by simply writing out the tenor in its entirety, without worrying whether his singers, much less his listeners, noticed the scheme behind the notes. Tinctoris's definition nevertheless suggests that "a certain obscurity" was part of the game, and that singers would have expected this sort of challenge from time to time.

Thinking in terms of hidden allegories and symbols was very much part of an educated person's way of reading and interpreting all kinds of texts, not simply musical ones. Princess Beatrice, who was certainly capable of participating in the intellectual game, was once given a manuscript devoted exclusively to *L'homme armé* masses, many peppered with cryptic canonic inscriptions that take the "armed man" (and the singers) back and forth through musical space and time. It is a mega-cycle in which the tune has been divided into six segments, each forming the basis of an entire mass. Now not just the musical work but also its performers (and informed listeners like Beatrice) joined in the act of representation. Clearly, these works were not simply meant to be heard or enjoyed; they were intellectual projects that demonstrated and demanded specialist skills and ways of understanding sounds.

JOSQUIN DES PREZ AND THE "ARMED MAN"

Josquin des Prez (ca. 1450–1521) took two turns with the melody in tenor masses of his own. In the *Missa L'homme armé super voces musicales* (Armed Man Mass upon Musical Syllables), he used solmization syllables—the six *voces* of the hexachordal system that every singer knew by heart—as the backdrop for the progressive transformation of the tune (Anthology 11; for a facsimile of a manuscript containing the first pages of this composition, see Fig. 9.1). Each movement of this mass presents the tune starting on a new syllable and pitch level—C (*ut*) for the Kyrie, D (*re*) for the Gloria, and so on—until the final Agnus Dei, where it appears starting on A (*la*). The ceremonial text of the Mass is played out against the abstract space of music itself, and as a result it is not the text that gives order to the music but musical space that gives order to the text. Josquin has one more trick up his sleeve. As in Du Fay's *Missa L'homme armé*, the tenor part is silent during the Agnus II movement. The systematic exploration of musical *space* enacted by the successive transpositions of the cantus-firmus tune is temporarily set aside for an equally remarkable exploration of musical *time*, for Agnus II is a three-voice mensuration canon.

We've already seen the mensural system used as a template for thematic transformation in Du Fay's *Nuper rosarum flores*, where the same notation is read in a series of different mensural contexts, both slow and fast, as well as duple and triple. Josquin, however, characteristically took things to another level altogether, deriving three-part polyphony from a single notated part as it is read in three different meters *at the same time*. The voices begin together in different transpositions, but as the singers interpret the same note-shapes under different mensural signs and at different pitch levels, they gradually diverge (Fig. 5.1). The fact that the movement makes musical sense to our ears at all is testament both to Josquin's ability to imagine how the same line might combine with itself at different paces, and to the singers' ability to interpret the puzzle correctly. But such pieces were not always viewed with approval by sixteenth-century musicians. When the Swiss humanist and music theorist Heinrich Glarean considered elaborate canons in his *Dodecachordon* (the 12-String Lyre; 1547), he worried that some of these pieces might have been composed more as a "display" of their creators' abilities than to provide "enjoyment which truly refreshes the hearing."

(a)

(b)

Figure 5.1: *Josquin des Prez, mensuration canon from* Missa L'homme armé super voces musicales, *as presented in a theoretical treatise of the sixteenth century:* **(a)** *Heinrich Glarean,* Dodecachordon (*Basel, 1547*), *Book III, p. 442, with* **(b)** *resolution of canon in modern notation, with arrows showing relationships among the voice parts in canon*

Glarean's doubts notwithstanding, Agnus II from Josquin's *Missa L'homme armé super voces musicales* could well have hinted at hidden meanings of the sort that Tinctoris suggested might stand behind the "obscurity" of canonic instructions. In a number of sources from the years around 1500, Josquin's mensuration canon is labeled with language that suggests a theological premise underlying the musical plan. Whereas Glarean marked his example "Ex una voces tres" (From one voice three; see Fig. 5.1a), these earlier sources variously call it "Tria in unum" (Three in one), "Trinitas" (Trinity), and "Sancta Trinitas, salva me" (Holy Trinity, save me). Perhaps Josquin's triple canon stands as a "symbol" of the Trinity, the Catholic dogma that taught of one God in three persons, as explained as a matter of faith in the Credo of the Mass.

SYMBOLIC MEANINGS

Why should a Trinitarian canon appear in the context of a mass based on the decidedly secular, even militaristic, *L'homme armé* tune? Scholars have long associated the *L'homme armé* mass tradition with chivalric cultures of the fifteenth century, and above all with the Order of the Golden Fleece, an elite club of European rulers organized by Duke Philip the Good of Burgundy in 1430. The figure of the "armed man" mentioned in the borrowed tune aligned neatly with this ideology. Its inscription as the foundation of settings of the Catholic Mass, according to this view, must have resonated with the self-image of this elite band as protectors of Christian as well as chivalric values, particularly in the decades following the rapid expansion of the Turkish (Ottoman) Empire in the East, culminating in the capture of Constantinople (Istanbul) in 1453. Indeed, some music historians have noted that the tenor cantus firmus of Busnoys's *Missa L'homme armé* (one of the earliest, probably written in the 1460s; see Ex. 5.2) contains 31 semibreves—exactly the number of knights in the Order of the Golden Fleece!

Recently it has been suggested that the canonic wanderings of the *L'homme armé* tune in these works represent archetypes of moral (and therefore internal) rather than real combat. In classical mythology, heroic figures like Orpheus undertook harrowing journeys to hell and back. In Christian theology of the fifteenth century, too, Jesus's death and resurrection offered a model for believers anxious to triumph over sin and death. Linking these journeys of salvation with the spiritual pilgrimages undertaken in mazes, labyrinths, and moral writings of the time, the image of the armed man offered a visual token of the sort of spiritual armor one might need along the way. By this measure we can read not only the *L'homme armé* melody but, more important, the various twists and turns it takes in pieces like Du Fay's Agnus III or across the movements of Josquin's *Missa L'homme armé super voces musicales* as symbolic enactments of spiritual journeys. Heard in this context, the theological reading of Josquin's mensuration canon takes on special force as an example of a symbolic as well as a musical process.

OCKEGHEM'S MUSICAL PUZZLES

Josquin was by no means the only composer fond of crafting works in which many voices could be produced from one. Corresponding more closely to the modern meaning of "canon" as a work founded on some kind of exact imitation of one part by another, these works often required as much skill on the part of singers as of the composer. Johannes Ockeghem (ca. 1410–1497) was especial-ly famous for designing clever musical riddles, building his *Missa prolationem* (Prolation Mass) entirely around such premises. As in the case of the canonic Agnus II by Josquin, each movement of this mass derives more than one voice part from a single notated line. One pair of parts is written down, but with two different mensuration signs (which determine the meters, or "prolations," of the title, as we learned in Chapter 2), so that each sounding voice moves accord-ing to its own independent meter. As if that were not enough, in each successive movement or section Ockeghem has each new canon begin at a different melodic interval, so that as the singers move from "Kyrie" to "Christe" to "Kyrie," and so on, they intone a canon at the unison, second, third, and so on, until all melodic and temporal combinations are presented.

Looking back on works like these from the vantage point of the middle of the sixteenth century, Glarean thought them sometimes a little too skillful for their own (or the listener's) good. He called them *catholica*, a Greek term suggest-ing encyclopedic versatility that had never before been used with reference to musical compositions. Such pieces could be sung, Glarean explained, "in many modes, almost according to the will of the singers." Ockeghem's *Missa cuiusvis toni* (Mass in Any Mode) falls clearly in this category. There are no clefs in any of the voice parts; singers are meant to choose a set of clefs so that the tenor follows a standard mode while the other three parts follow suit.

For modern historians, works like these reinforce an image of Ockeghem as a practitioner of intellectual sophistry played out in esoteric musi-cal riddles, hidden designs, and obscure symbols that carry us back to the mystical origins of music itself. His immediate contemporaries appear to have encouraged us in this regard. Indeed, his colleague Busnoys com-posed a motet, *In hydraulis* (Of Water Organs), that compared Ockeghem to Pythagoras and Orpheus, the mythological founders of musical thought and art. Josquin's musical epitaph for Ockeghem, *Nymphes des bois/Requiem* (Nymphs of the Woods/Requiem), alludes to his love of puzzles, symbols, and artful combinations. It uses a liturgical tenor from the Introit of the Requiem Mass, perhaps in reference to Ockeghem's own famous Requiem, which may have been the earliest polyphonic setting of that Mass. Josquin's piece combines a French text in the other voices with the Latin tenor, also perhaps an allusion to Ockeghem's similarly bilingual lament for Busnoys, *Mort, tu as navré/Miserere* (Death, You Have Wounded/Have Pity).

Josquin's notation, moreover, recalls Ockeghem's preference for signs and ciphers. Instead of open, white note-shapes, Josquin's piece is notated all in black (a sign of mourning, presumably). For the tenor, instead of a clef we have French instructions that tell the singers to sing the melody a semitone lower than written. *Nymphes des bois/Requiem* is a rich and moving tribute to a composer whose command of canonic structures is as impressive today as it must have seemed in his own time. Through Ockeghem, we are reminded of the ways in which abstract order and symbolic meaning were at play in motets and masses of the fifteenth century, much as they had been for generations of musicians who turned borrowed melodies into works of great complexity.

OLD STRUCTURES, NEW LISTENERS

It is plain from writings like Glarean's that musicians of the sixteenth century were acutely aware of the tenor mass as it was crafted by the best composers of the fifteenth century. Yet by the mid-1500s composers had largely abandoned this layered and Scholastic approach to unifying the various movements of the mass in favor of a technique centered on adaptations of models that were themselves polyphonic. Scholars have called these polyphonic adaptations of other polyphonic works "parody masses." Contrary to contemporary connotations, the term does not imply an attempt to poke fun at the source materials. Indeed, the more usual term used in sixteenth-century music publications was "imitation mass" (*Missa ad imitationem . . .*). The process can be revealing, for composers frequently adapted polyphonic ideas from their models in new imitative combinations, or stretched and compressed whole passages from the source in inventive ways.

Orlando di Lasso, Giovanni Pierluigi da Palestrina, Tomás Luis de Victoria, and other composers wrote many pieces in this way, using as their source material not only motets but also chansons and madrigals. Inasmuch as many of these polyphonic models were crafted as persuasive vehicles for the delivery of their verbal texts, the resulting masses took on new rhetorical stances that echo contemporary controversies about religious faith and doctrine. Indeed, as we will discover in Chapter 9, the source materials and their adaptations are as interesting culturally as they are in terms of compositional technique, for they can be understood in the context of humanist debates about music and its proper relationship to language. Thus, while sixteenth-century musicians appreciated the old cantus-firmus tradition, they were less concerned with abstract intellectual schemes than with new possibilities for organizing sound around verbal meaning.

Modern musicians have long been fascinated by the sorts of cycles, symbols, and structures we have considered in this chapter. Perhaps they matter to us because they mirror some of our own changing values and concerns. In recent decades, cantus-firmus sets like the various treatments of *L'homme armé* have been evaluated from the standpoint of their cultural or theological contexts. But for a long time before that they were discussed in terms that highlighted their aesthetic unity, or their place in a great chain of specifically musical homage and borrowing. Such values sound conspicuously like those used to explain what matters about the abstract symphonic tradition in the nineteenth century. The recent interest in Renaissance cycles of pieces organized by literary text or narrative theme has its legacy in discussions of nineteenth-century art songs and the *Liederkreis*, or song cycle, tradition.

Preoccupation with hidden musical numbers, abstract canons, and other precompositional devices likewise invites comparison with modernist concerns for the inaudible and symbolic. The serial composer Anton von Webern (1883–1945) was a serious student of Renaissance music and completed a doctoral thesis on the liturgical music of one of Josquin's most famous contemporaries, Heinrich Isaac. Certainly, Webern did not need the Renaissance to teach him how to organize melodies in rigorously contrapuntal ways. Knowing the connection, however, helps us hear more-recent music as part of a long tradition that sought order and proportion in sound. It is to this tradition, with its deep roots in ancient and Scholastic modes of speculative thought, that we now turn.

FOR FURTHER READING

Bloxam, Jennifer, "A Cultural Context for the Chanson Mass," in *Early Musical Borrowing*, ed. Honey Meconi, pp. 7–36 (New York: Routledge, 2004)

Haggh, Barbara, "The Archives of the Order of the Golden Fleece and Music," *Journal of the Royal Musical Association* 120 (1995): 1–43

Kirkman, Andrew, *The Cultural Life of the Early Polyphonic Mass: Medieval Context to Modern Revival* (Cambridge and New York: Cambridge University Press, 2010)

———, "The Invention of the Cyclic Mass," *Journal of the American Musicological Society* 54 (2001): 1–47

Lockwood, Lewis, "Aspects of the 'L'homme armé' Tradition," *Proceedings of the Royal Musical Association* 100 (1973–74): 97–122

Long, Michael P., "Symbol and Ritual in Josquin's *Missa Di Dadi*," *Journal of the American Musicological Society* 42 (1989):1–22

Prizer, William F., "Brussels and the Ceremonies of the Order of the Golden Fleece," *Revue belge de musicologie / Belgisch Tijdschrift voor Muziekwetenschap* 55 (2001): 69–90

———, "Music and Ceremonial in the Low Countries: Philip the Fair and the Order of the Golden Fleece," *Early Music History* 5 (1985): 113–53

Robertson, Anne Walters, "The Man with the Pale Face, the Shroud, and Du Fay's *Missa Se la face ay pale*," *Journal of Musicology* 27 (2010): 377–434

Trachtenberg, Marvin, "Architecture and Music Reunited: A New Reading of Dufay's *Nuper Rosarum Flores* and the Cathedral of Florence," *Renaissance Quarterly* 54 (2001): 741–75

Wright, Craig, "Dufay's *Nuper rosarum flores*, King Solomon's Temple, and the Veneration of the Virgin," *Journal of the American Musicological Society* 47 (1994), 395–441

🄯 Additional resources available at wwnorton.com/studyspace

PART III

Around 1500

Part 3 of our study revolves around a series of cultural and political upheavals that erupted on various fronts during the last decades of the fifteenth century and the first ones of the sixteenth century. These upheavals did not begin all at once, nor were they suddenly complete early in the new century. But inasmuch as they embodied new ways of thinking or behaving, they encouraged the reexamination of old patterns of life, and thus served to spur still other currents of change that took hold of European culture during the sixteenth century.

The political landscape of the Italian peninsula was radically transformed in the years around 1500. The region had long been the scene of both cooperation and rivalry among different city-states like Milan (where members of the Sforza family reigned), Florence (where the Medici banking family held sway), and Rome (seat of papal authority and many important aristocratic families). Some citizens were ruled by strongmen, others by oligarchies; still others experimented with self-organizing republics of the sort that thrived in Siena and Venice. Starting in the 1490s, however, a series of invasions led by French kings disrupted the relative stability that prevailed among this patchwork of competing centers of power.

The cynical pragmatism that Niccolò Machiavelli expressed in *The Prince* (1513) and *On the Art of War* (1519–1520) was one response to this social and political turmoil. A very different attitude is reflected in Baldassare Castiglione's *Book of the Courtier* (1528), which offers a portrait of the ideal courtier whose grace and modesty, expressed above all in the studied cool of *sprezzatura*, served as a guide for generations of Renaissance gentlemen. As we will discover in Chapter 7, Castiglione's book has much to teach us about the place of music in this social world.

Meanwhile, thinkers both north and south of the Alps were coming to terms with a new intellectual movement, humanism, that pitted itself against the old Scholastic order. For generations, scholars had relied on rigorous logic as their main method of inquiry. Their basic mode of argumentation was the Aristotelian syllogism—the deduction of a conclusion from two or more premises—which helped them to resolve differences and contradictions in authoritative texts. In contrast, advocates of the *studia humanitatis* (studies of humanity) employed the new methods of philology, which helped them to correct ancient texts that had been corrupted in transmission over the centuries, and of rhetoric, which allowed them to persuade their readers about the moral lessons gleaned from ancient philosophy and historical writing. Humanists hunted in monastic libraries for long-forgotten classical sources. Certain ancient pagan texts presented challenges for scholars raised in the Christian tradition. But many humanists (like the Dutch scholar Desiderius Erasmus or the English statesman Sir Thomas More) were convinced Christians; their unquestioned position as defenders of religious thought freed them to apply new scholarly methods to biblical and other ancient texts.

Where music is concerned, however, by far the most important of the humanist projects under way in the decades before 1500 was what scholars now call Neo-Platonism, especially as it was promoted by Marsilio Ficino, a priest, philosopher, and magician active in Florence during the last decades of the fifteenth century. Encouraged by his patron Cosimo de' Medici, Ficino translated the complete works of Plato from the original Greek into Latin. He did the same for other classical authors, as well as producing an ambitious set of commentaries that sought to explain the esoteric and often mystical connections among medicine, magic, and astrology for Renaissance readers.

As we will learn in Chapter 6, music figures importantly in Ficino's writings, above all the idea of solo song as the medium best suited to mediate between heavenly bodies and the human soul. Castiglione likewise gives pride of place to solo singing, often to the accompaniment of lute or lyre. The old forms of polyphonic counterpoint, traditionally the domain of professional singer-composers trained in the ecclesiastical choir schools, were by no means eclipsed around 1500. But a new generation of amateur gentlemen, some of whom we'll meet in Chapter 7, seized upon the ideal of solo singing as the best way to demonstrate their civility. This in turn stimulated a demand for settings of vernacular poetry arranged for solo performance, above all in the popular Italian frottole that proliferated during the early sixteenth century. Meanwhile, new career possibilities were opening up for professional musicians. Men like Heinrich Isaac operated as freelancers, without obligation to a particular court or ecclesiastical chapel. As we will see in Chapter 8, Josquin des Prez, who enjoyed an outsized reputation during his lifetime, is a paradigmatic example of the enhanced image and status of the composer.

Last but not least, the comparatively new technology of music printing (which emerged around 1500, decades after it had been pioneered for verbal texts) brought about profound changes for composers and performers alike. In ways that we will explore in Chapter 9, it gave music new mobility across boundaries of geography and class; it also gave composers and editors new authority over the works they offered the public, securing the connection between words and music in ways that had important implications for the remainder of the century.

CHAPTER SIX

Number, Medicine, and Magic

R enaissance medical writings, occult philosophy, and mathematical thought can teach us much about how music was understood during the fifteenth and sixteenth centuries. How do we know music: through sense or reason? And how can we put its powerful effects to good use? Will it regulate us? Should we regulate it? The answers to these questions are as varied as the sources we might consult, from mathematicians and astronomers to physicians and philosophers.

In this chapter, we will trace the competition between old and new agendas. Scholastic modes of thought on proportion and order in music persisted throughout the Renaissance. But in the late fifteenth century there emerged new humanist ideas about music, language, and the power of solo song that soon captivated the musical imaginations of generations of thinkers (see Chapter 14). Renaissance scholars, like those today, did not hesitate to let each other know who was right and who was wrong. They understood music as a source of healing, as a means of spiritual, even magical enlightenment, and above all as a marker of universal order.

MUSIC, NUMBER, PROPORTION

Musica, according to ancient authorities, was subject to the same rules of proportion and perfection that governed other parts of the cosmos. Nowhere was the rational basis of music more evident than in its affinities with mathematics and number. In the Scholastic curriculum of European universities and church schools, music took its place alongside the other mathematical arts of the quadrivium: arithmetic, geometry, music, and astronomy (revisit Fig. 1.1). When the French theologian and mathematician Jacques Lefèvre d'Etaples (Jacobus Faber Stapulensis) brought out his *Musica libris demonstrata quattuor* (Music Explained in Four Books) in 1496, it was paired with his guide to a treatise on arithmetic by the sixth-century Roman statesman Severinus Boethius, himself the author of the most influential musical treatise of the Latin Middle Ages. Lefèvre proposed new approaches to tuning and intervals, but he did so through the lens of classical authority, using Euclid's geometry to inform his own approach to certain problems.

Even Gioseffo Zarlino (1517–1590), the Venetian priest, choirmaster, and music theorist whose work on modes we discussed in Chapter 2, led a double intellectual life as a scholar of astronomy and the calendar. His writings on the latter subject were gathered in a book that has been all but ignored by musicologists: *De vera anni forma, siue, De recta eius emendatione* (On the True Form of the Year, or, On Its Proper Correction, 1580), written not long before Pope Gregory XIII declared the great calendrical reform of 1582, the basis of our modern calendar. In his music-theoretical writings such as *Le istitutioni harmoniche* (The Harmonic Foundations, 1558), Zarlino aligned himself with the traditional viewpoint that music was an amalgam of nature and number. Citing no less an authority than Avicenna, the influential Persian physician and philosopher active in the tenth and eleventh centuries, Zarlino insisted that "music has as its principles those of natural philosophy and those of number." But music, he continued, "cannot be said to be simply mathematics, nor simply natural, but is instead partly natural and partly mathematical and is consequently a mixture of one and the other. And on account of this from natural science music has the reason of its consonance (which consists of sounds and syllables); and from mathematics it has the reason of its form, namely proportion."

Zarlino's observations contributed to an intense debate about musical practice, especially the treatment of contrapuntal dissonance and the status of the melodic modes in polyphonic composition. Yet the ancient concepts of rationality and proportion in music were largely unquestioned in the fifteenth and sixteenth centuries. The mathematical basis of harmony was among the lessons taught to schoolboys. When the Lutheran pedagogue Martin Agricola (ca. 1486–1556) turned to the subject of musical proportion in his *Musica instrumentalis deudsch* (Instrumental Music in German, 1529, revised 1545), for instance, he began with a famous story told of the fifth-century B.C.E. Greek philosopher and mathematician Pythagoras and popularized by Boethius: pausing one day to listen to the sound of blacksmiths as they hammered away at their work, Pythagoras wondered why they made so harmonious a blend. The explanation,

Figure 6.1: *Pythagoras at the forge, from Martin Agricola's* Musica instrumentalis deudsch *(1545)*

he discovered, was to be found in the relative weight of the hammers—or, more accurately, in the rational proportions of their respective weights (Fig. 6.1).

Pythagorean doctrine taught that weights in the basic proportions of 12:9:8:6 yield musical intervals of foundational importance. As Agricola explains: "An octave was heard between the first and the fourth hammers in dupla [1:2] proportion. The first and third, called sesquialtera [2:3], clearly sounded a fifth. The first and the second, sesquitertia [3:4], gave a fourth without any jest. The second and the third, sesquioctava [8:9], provided a whole tone." From these proportional relationships, Agricola continues, it is possible to derive an entire musical system by applying basic rules for adding and subtracting ratios in ways that his pupils knew well from their studies of mathematics. This "speculative method," as Agricola aptly calls it, informs much musical thought and even practice, an approach to discovering correct intervallic proportions "useful for all organ makers and other elegant, clever and speculating minds."

The story of Pythagoras and the weights was a revered topos of musical thought in the Renaissance. The fifteenth-century composer Antoine Busnoys wrote a motet, *In hydraulis* (Of Water Organs), in honor of his colleague Johannes Ockeghem that compared his works to Pythagoras's with reference to the elemental ratios explained by Agricola. While the text of the motet recalls the Pythagorean relationships, an abstract tenor cantus firmus sounds them out in various melodic and rhythmic combinations.

THEORY VERSUS PRACTICE

Agricola's more empirically minded students would soon have discovered that Pythagorean proportions looked better on paper than they worked in practice. The story of the hammers, for instance, does not correspond to acoustical reality, and Pythagorean tuning is not really practical in performance for any but a limited set of tones. As Pythagorean theorists quickly recognized, a series of 12 acoustically perfect fifths (each with a proportion of 3:2 between frequencies) would arrive at a tone slightly *higher* than a corresponding series of seven acoustically perfect octaves (with a proportion of 2:1), rather than winding up in exactly the same spot. This discrepancy is known as the Pythagorean comma, brought about by the simple mathematical fact that the factors of two (the basis of the octave) and the factors of three (the basis of the fifth) diverge to infinity.

How and whether to accommodate this slippage between theoretical proportion and sounding practice was a source of continuing tension for writers of the fifteenth and sixteenth centuries, as it had been since antiquity. The problem became particularly acute when dealing with fixed pitches such as those on keyboard instruments or harps. (Voices, brass, and unfretted stringed instruments can adapt by "tempering" the pitch to its correct position.) The modern solution spreads the error across all 12 chromatic steps in a system known as "equal" temperament, where each half tone increases in frequency relative to the previous one by the twelfth root of two. In the years around 1500 there were other systems, including "mean tone" temperament, in which acoustically pure major thirds were produced by tempering the fourths and fifths.

Renaissance theorists also struggled to explain the basis of imperfect consonances, which they sensed from musical practice to be pleasant sounds, but which they also knew from Pythagorean doctrine to stand outside the bounds of the most basic numerical proportions. The tension between practical experience and received wisdom is striking. Composer-theorists like Franchinus Gaffurius (1451–1522) and Johannes Tinctoris (ca. 1430/35–1511) had no trouble writing polyphony in which successions of thirds and sixths were a foundation of contrapuntal style. (See Chapter 3 for a discussion of Tinctoris's "new art.") Yet in their theoretical writings these same intervals, viewed from the standpoint of speculative thought handed down since the time of Boethius, had no rational basis as harmony per se. The question was not so much whether thirds and sixths could be explained by arithmetic proportions; they could, of course, as Agricola and others were ready to point out. The problem was that these proportions could not be derived from the Pythagorean *tetraktys* (Fig. 6.2), an elemental triangle formed by ten points arranged in four rows that held mysterious, sacred meaning according to ancient teachings: the whole-number ratios of one row to the next correspond to the equally elemental musical intervals

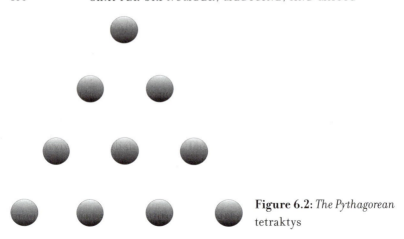

Figure 6.2: *The Pythagorean* tetraktys

of the octave (2:1), fifth (3:2), and fourth (4:3). No wonder music theorists felt obliged to tailor their conceptual schemes for consonance to this model, even if in practice they knew otherwise.

Zarlino's approach to this problem reflects the profoundly contradictory tendencies of these traditions. He wanted to find a space for *sense* to operate alongside *reason*. "In order to have perfect knowledge concerning music, it does not suffice to appeal to the sense of hearing, even if it is most keen, but rather one should seek to investigate and know the whole, so that reason is not discordant with sense, nor sense with reason; and then everything will be well." The accommodation of experience with axiom in turn allowed Zarlino to expand the Pythagorean universe of mystical sounding number without questioning the need for some rational basis for consonance in the first place. His innovation—which was more progressive than revolutionary— was a set he called the *senario*: with six basic numbers instead of Pythagoras's four, Zarlino had at his disposal all of the arithmetic proportions he needed to account for the major third, the minor third, and the major sixth. (How to justify the minor sixth with respect to this system was another problem, which need not detain us here.) For Zarlino the priest, the scriptural significance of six, with its resonance in the cycle of divine creation in six days of work, was enough to seal the case.

Even after this "extension" of the old explanatory model to new intervals, however, another fundamental stumbling block remained: no instrument or ensemble could use Pythagorean proportions without encountering all sorts of problems. As the Venetian mathematician Giovanni Benedetti pointed out in response to a query from the composer Cipriano de Rore, the use of the "correct" proportional intervals dictated by Pythagorean mathematics would result in musical mayhem. In choral performance, ensembles would be likely to fall in pitch (as they in fact often do), while keyboard players would find it impossible to tune their instruments in ways that would allow the use of enharmonically equivalent notes (such as D♯ and E♭) in a single composition.

Zarlino's pupil Vincenzo Galilei (late 1520s–1591) argued that the Pythagorean ratios had little validity in the first place. Testing old maxims about the lengths of strings and the notes they produced, Vincenzo discovered that the tension and thickness of the strings determined the sounding result no less than their length. With numerical ratios of lengths no longer a reliable guide to what he heard, he was forced to use experience rather than reason to judge the result. Pointing the way to a new, experimental approach to consonance and dissonance, and new expressive purposes for these sounds, thinkers like Vincenzo put into play a revolutionary idea: art need not conform to the laws of nature. As we'll see in Chapter 14, this development would have important resonance with stylistic and aesthetic controversies of the following decades, above all in the momentous debate between the music theorist Giovanni Maria Artusi and the composer Claudio Monteverdi.

MUSIC AND MEDICINE

While Zarlino and his fellow music theorists debated the problems of proportion and consonance, other thinkers considered music from the standpoint of medical teaching. Indeed, the musical and medical arts had much to learn from each other. According to some, the human pulse was a kind of music that could be read by a physician and in turn regulated by the application of the correct sounds. Tinctoris had this tradition in mind when he listed such therapeutic powers among the virtues of music in a treatise titled *Complexus effectuum musices* (A Compendium of the Effects of Music), prepared for his pupil Princess Beatrice of Aragon about 1473. He was hardly the first to make the claim, citing as his authorities Isidore of Seville, a sixth-century theologian, the Persian scholar Avicenna, and Galen, a Greek physician of the second century. To Galen's way of thinking, the musical distinction between upbeat and downbeat was analogous to the pattern of diastolic and systolic in the movement of our blood.

For centuries the idea that body and soul were bound together in a kind of musical harmony was a commonplace of medical science. For Gaffurius in the late 1400s, the connection went back to the moment of birth, and even before. "Music itself," he wrote, "comes together in our birth, particularly since the number of days and months which correspond to the pregnancy of women is controlled by musical ratio." This corporeal music (*musica humana*), in turn, took its place in a universe bound together by harmony, as Boethius famously envisaged it, poised between the unheard celestial music of the spheres (*musica mundana*) and the sounds we know through earthly instruments and voices (*musica instrumentalis*) (SR 14:140–41; 2/6:30–31).

Nowhere were the mutual affinities of sound and body more acutely connected than in the case of melancholia, a complex set of physical and psychic ailments that puzzled philosophers, doctors, poets, and theologians of the fifteenth and sixteenth centuries. In the conservative world of the great medical faculties like Montpellier and Padua, melancholia took its place in the scheme of four bodily humors inherited from ancient authorities like Galen via medieval and Arabic sources: blood, phlegm, yellow bile, and black bile. (The latter was quite literally the substance of melancholy, which derives from the Greek words *melaina* [black] and *khole* [bile].) Passed down through generations of Scholastic physicians, this tradition allowed that one's temperament depended in part upon the relative balance or temporary imbalance of these humors and their corresponding qualities, such as hot and cold or wet and dry. (For a mosaic-like representation of the four basic human temperaments and their physical qualities, see Fig. 6.3.) Well into the sixteenth century doctors explained both disease and feeling according to this "humoral" model, advising patients on the appropriate substances that might rebalance the equation of essences. The French satirist François Rabelais mocked the humoralist doctors he encountered while studying medicine at Montpellier during the middle years of the sixteenth century.

Melancholia occupied an anomalous position within this system of complementary qualities, for it could also emerge without apparent physical cause. The notion of groundless anxiety is central to an important distinction made in many writings about the difference between melancholy, the humoral substance, and *melancholia*, the affective condition supposedly formed in a middle

Figure 6.3: *The four humors, from Leonhart Thurneisser's* Quinta essentia *(1574), showing the four temperaments and their various elemental, physical, and astrological attributes arrayed in four quadrants*

region of the brain variously called the imagination or fantasy. It was here, our authorities agree, that sensory impressions were projected, inscribed, and sometimes erroneously interpreted by the understanding in ways that could in turn be read as bodily signs as well as mistaken judgments. When things went wrong, the imagination could be a fearsome organ, as ancient physicians like Galen emphasized. "The true melancholic," according to the French royal physician André Du Laurens, "wishes to flee and yet cannot move." If he closes his eyes for rest, "he is assailed by a million phantoms and hideous specters, by fantastic chimeras, and by appalling dreams. If he tries to call someone to his aid his voice stops short, and can speak only in stammering."

The symptoms of this imaginary melancholia, to judge from descriptions like Du Laurens's, were no less varied than its causes. But there are a number of common themes in these accounts: the blank, downward gaze, the interrupted speech, the returning visions, and the incessant deferral of rest. It's easy to imagine how one might represent some of these visually or dramatically, as in Albrecht Dürer's classic engraving (Fig. 6.4) or Shakespeare's *Hamlet*, whose

Figure 6.4: *Albrecht Dürer*, Melancholia *(1513)*

title character is perhaps the most famous theatrical melancholic. But can we identify musical counterparts for the signs of melancholy? The problem is particularly tricky, since we must also constantly gauge the forms and processes of a medium that is itself largely beyond the power of language to represent. And yet by virtue of this peculiar condition perhaps music is uniquely disposed to articulate stances, attitudes, and conditions of subjective experience in ways we find so difficult to communicate through other means.

DOWLAND, DU FAY, AND THE SOUNDS OF MELANCHOLIA

Perhaps no composer of the Renaissance was more closely attuned to melancholia than the Elizabethan lutenist John Dowland (1563–1626), author of works such as the *Melancholy Galliard* and *Flow my tears*. (See the anthology to Wendy Heller's *Music in the Baroque* for an extended discussion of *Flow my tears*.) Dowland's great cycle *Lachrimae, or Seaven Teares Figured in Seaven Passionate Pavans* (published 1604) features a persistent melodic marker: a descending linear fourth ending with a plangent half step that scholars have dubbed the "tear motive." It is also sometimes called the "Phrygian tetrachord," since it corresponds to the first four notes of the mode starting on E (see the first four notes of the cantus part in Ex. 6.1). Heard in countless instrumental romanescas (a popular variation form) of the period, and familiar to students of seventeenth-century opera as the *lamento* bass line, this tetrachord also appears in vocal music from the middle years of the sixteenth century. For instance, *Mille regrets* (A Thousand Regrets), a chanson long credited to Josquin des Prez, is saturated with the obsessive repetition of this motive (see Chapters 8 and 10).

The widespread use of the tear motive hints at a long and deep musical tradition of melancholic reflection. Indeed, many composers took an interest in the musical depiction of the passions, and especially in the signs and sounds of melancholia, long before the Elizabethan fascination with the condition overshadowed their efforts. These pieces represent the physical and mental symptoms of melancholia as it was described by Renaissance doctors. The stalled descent of the tetrachord, like the static gaze of Dürer's melancholic, seems "stuck" without focus or resolution.

Music could certainly be enlisted in the study of humoral medicine, according to the learned physicians. But we can hardly imagine from their suggestions that a musical representation of melancholy would ever have been used to treat the condition. Judging from medical advice on visual remedies for the sadness of old age—a parade of delightful feminine forms, beautiful colors, and precious jewels—doctors would instead have been disposed to prescribe some kind

Example 6.1: *John Dowland,* Lachrimae antiquae, *mm. 1–8. From* Lachrimæ or seaven teares figured in seaven passionate pavans *(London, 1604), fols. 3ᵛ–4ʳ.*

of musical *opposite* to counteract the melancholic distortion. One influential medical text, Bernard of Gordon's *Lily of Medicine* (ca. 1300), repeated the conventional wisdom that in the treatment of melancholia "there must be musical instruments and, in short, everything that cheers the soul."

The scene of one such cure may be played out in Guillaume Du Fay's rondeau *Ce moys de may* (This Month of May, from the 1440s; Ex. 6.2). With its lively, syncopated rhythms and sharp melodic profiles, the music seems to illustrate the release from melancholy proposed in the refrain:

Ce moys de may lies et joyeux	*This month of May, be happy and joyful,*
Et de nos ceurs ostons merancolye;	*And banish melancholy from our hearts.*
Chantons, dansons et menons chiere lye,	*Sing, dance, and be of good cheer,*
Por despiter ces felons envieux.	*To spite these foul, envious ones.*

At the crucial word "merancolye," the voices suddenly change course to trace a linear descent, not unlike the tear motive later used by Dowland and Wilbye, ending with a tentative Phrygian cadence to A. To judge from this work, some of

Example 6.2: *Guillaume Du Fay, Ce moys de may, mm. 10–15. From Guillaume Dufay, Opera Omnia, ed. Heinrich Besseler, 6 vols., Corpus Mensurabilis Musicae, 1 (Rome: American Institute of Musicology, 1947–66), 6:59.*

the musical iconography of melancholia seems already to have been in place by the middle years of the fifteenth century.

Robert Burton's great compendium of writings on the subject, *Anatomy of Melancholy* (1621), suggests that melancholy music might serve to relieve rather than provoke the condition. He allowed that while "many men are melancholy by hearing musicke, but it is a pleasant melancholy that it causeth . . . it expells cares, alters their grieved mindes, and easeth in an instant." Perhaps this is how we ought to understand songs like *Draw on, sweet Night* by Dowland's contemporary John Wilbye (1574–1638). This madrigal imagines a time and space free of the cares of "painful melancholy," but which in rehearsing them "expells" (to use Burton's word) the cares it seems to represent. The piece begins with a gentle ebb and flow that seems already to imagine this quiet space. But soon an undercurrent of obsessive memory and interrupted speech all but overwhelm the speaker, thanks to Wilbye's artful counterpoint (Anthology 12). This may be what Burton had in mind in suggesting his homeopathic cure: a temporary, shared melancholy that would allow musical readers to sing (and hear) it from the safe distance of their drawing room, and thereby regulate or relieve themselves of the very humoral illness they imagined through sound.

MUSIC AND NEOPLATONIC MAGIC

Even as Scholastic medical teachings on the humors persisted, they were challenged by competing perspectives on the nature and origin of melancholia, particularly as it was associated with artistic genius. This debate was played out vividly in *Solitaire premier* (First Solitaire), a treatise on the merits of poetry and artistic creativity published in 1552 by Pontus de Tyard (1521–1605), a French poet, philosopher, and priest who frequented elite literary circles of the day. The work unfolds as a series of conversations between Solitaire and his beloved pupil Pasithée as they discuss the merits of poetry and the artistic visions that make it possible. As the title suggests, it was the first of what eventually became the five books of his *Discours philosophiques* (Philosophical Discourses, 1587), each of which focuses on a different theme: poetry, music, time, astrology, and the cosmos itself. Tyard's outlook on these subjects, voiced through the persona of his alter ego Solitaire, is steeped in the esoteric world of the Neoplatonic writings that circulated in the intellectual circles of the sixteenth century. Music and listening were especially important in this literature, as we'll soon discover. But Tyard did not simply present this ideology, he staged it in order to put it in dynamic counterpoint with other ways of understanding poetry, song, and artistic genius.

One day, Tyard begins, Solitaire overheard Pasithée as she sat alone, tuning her lute, then singing an ode to its accompaniment. Solitaire stood transfixed by the sweetness of the music. "I felt ravished by a celestial harmony," he recalls. Pasithée, too, is struck by Solitaire's suddenly changed expression and wonders whether he ought to consult a doctor. No, Solitaire insists, this is no medical ailment but instead a kind of artistic alienation he calls "furor." Then follows a long explanation of each rival position. For Pasithée, Solitaire's condition begins in the body and its four humors. This furor, she concludes, is nothing more than an affliction of the brain, a "folly" that arises from a profound defect in these substances, which in certain conditions can cloud the imagination and disturb us in remarkable ways. André Du Laurens and the Montpellier doctors would have agreed with this explanation, which corresponded precisely to ancient humoral doctrines.

Solitaire does not deny the basis of this first type of bodily alienation. But to this he annexes distancing of a sort that stems from other, secret forces "characterized by a hidden divine power, by which the reasoning soul is inscribed." This is the real source of "divine furor, or what the Greeks term Enthusiasm." Solitaire's explanation of the place of music and sound in this process of occult revelation is especially interesting. The soul, we learn, seeks to return to the perfection of its divine origins. But while in the body it is fragmented, "its superior part is asleep, stunned (as we might say) by so heavy a fall, and its inferior part is agitated and full of perturbations, from which arise a horrible discord, disorder and unharmonious proportion." Song is the only remedy,

> awakening the sleeping part of the soul by the tones of music; comforting the perturbed part by the suavity of sweet harmony, then chasing away the dissonant discord by the well tuned diversity of musical accord; and finally reducing the disorder to a certain well and proportionately measured

equality ordered by the graceful and grave facility of verses regulated by the careful observance of number and measure. (SR 66:396–97; 3/31:118–19)

FICINO AND THE COSMIC DIMENSION

Solitaire's grand claims for this prophetic music remind us in some ways of the outlandish creeds of artistic genius served up in the nineteenth century by Romantic visionaries like E. T. A. Hoffmann and Richard Wagner. But for Tyard's readers this language had obvious affinities with a long tradition of Neoplatonic writings on the soul, the cosmos, and the magical forces that bind them together. Indeed, the passage just quoted from Tyard's *Solitaire premier* comes directly from the work of the most famous of these musical humanists, Marsilio Ficino (1433–1499; Fig. 6.5). As priest, philosopher, physician, and astrologer to the powerful Medici household in Florence, and as guiding authority of the city's Accademia Platonica, Ficino tirelessly advocated solo song as the most powerful form of musical, and indeed human, expression.

Ficino's experience owes much to the largely unwritten traditions of musical delivery practiced in Italy throughout the fifteenth century. Through the singing of contemporary virtuosos, often to the accompaniment of a bowed instrument called the lira da braccio, Ficino claimed to have rediscovered the secret of ancient Orphic singing. (For an early-sixteenth-century depiction of a lira da braccio in the context of a scene from classical mythology, refer to Fig. 7.2.) Rehearing the vocal practice of the new Golden Age in light of Neoplatonic philosophy, he put music at the center of the universe. Ficino's influential *De vita*

Figure 6.5: *Anonymous,* Portrait of Marsilio Ficino, *philosopher, priest, magician*

libri tres (Three Books on Life, 1489), a commentary on Plotinus's writings from the perspective of magic, medicine, and astrology, affords music a crucial mediating role between body, soul, and the cosmos, synchronizing distant realms through harmony and movement:

> Song is a most powerful imitator of all things. It imitates the intentions and passions of the soul as well as words; it represents also people's physical gestures, motions, and actions as well as their characters and imitates all these and acts them out so forcibly that it immediately provokes both the singer and the audience to imitate and act out the same things. By the same power, when it imitates the celestials, it also wonderfully arouses our spirit upwards to the celestial influence and the celestial influence downwards to our spirit. (SR 64:387; 3/29:109)

In Ficino's scheme of things, the sun, stars, and planets, each equipped with their own musical affinities, had corresponding affinities with our souls. Even the conservative music theorist Gaffurius (cited above in connection with the defense of Pythagorean notions of proportion and "human" music) was no less convinced of the operation of this kind of celestial harmony, as revealed in a woodcut appended to his *Practica musicae* (The Practice of Music, 1496; Fig. 6.6). In it we can see an entire celestial tone system arrayed in an imaginary hierarchy of planets, tones, and elements in a great chain of harmonic being that stretches from Apollo and the Muses in the heavens to the lowly earth and its four elemental substances.

The idea of a universe bound together by a kind of cosmic harmony can itself be traced back through a long line of Scholastic commentators to Boethius in the sixth century and beyond. Christian theologians imagined it as a kind of divine mystery. The sixteenth-century Protestant reformer Jean Calvin, echoing St. Augustine, allowed that music "has a secret and almost incredible power to move our hearts in one way or another" (SR 57:366; 3/22:88). But Ficino's notions take things to a new level, for when properly aligned through astrological prognostications, the human soul could temporarily retrace its divine origins to "catch an influence that resembles them" (SR 64:387; 3/29:109). Harmony was the key to this process, and poetic furor (or artistic genius, as we might call it) was its means. Thus in Ficino's philosophy music served a magical mediating role, not only between performer and listener, but also between the soul and its celestial source. Sound could have a healing power that was more than physical. "Now the very matter of song," he observed, "is altogether purer and more similar to the heavens than is the matter of medicine" (SR 64:387; 3/29:109). No wonder the Neoplatonist Solitaire sought to rebuff Pasithée's humoral approach to hearing and artistic alienation.

Tyard's dialogue, in short, shows how musical melancholia played out the tensions between rival intellectual systems—one humoral and Scholastic, the

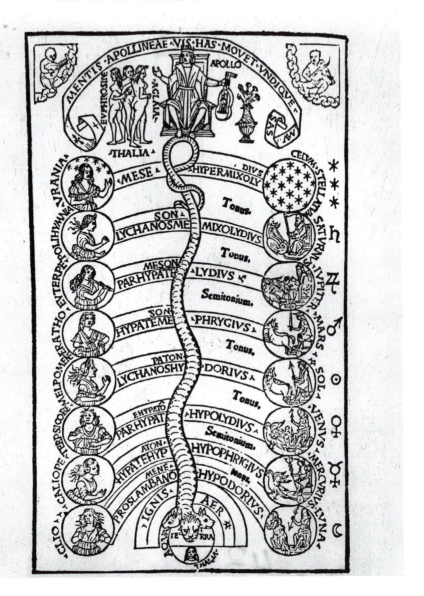

Figure 6.6: *Apollo presiding over the music of the spheres, planets, and earth, from Franchinus Gaffurius's* Practica musicae *(1496)*

other reflecting the values of Neoplatonism—during the sixteenth century. His preferred musical medium, and that of the salon of his aristocratic dedicatee, Catherine de Clérmont, the countess de Retz, was the air de cour, a genre of solo song that enjoyed renewed cultivation during the third quarter of the sixteenth century. The same was true for the generations of cultivated men and women who were guided by Baldassare Castiglione's *Book of the Courtier* (1528), to which we will turn in Chapter 7. Yet whether solo song or elaborate polyphonic counterpoint, in all these systems music had some important cultural work to do.

In addition to its communicative or curative role, music was a means by which performers and listeners could join an elite club, at least temporarily. Melancholia, after all, was for Renaissance thinkers above all an affliction of social distinction, understood as the defining ailment of prominent men. Such assumptions trace their lineage through an equally prominent tradition of philosophizing on the subject that owes its origins to a question posed in the treatise *Problems* by an anonymous author known as Pseudo-Aristotle: "Why is it that all those who have become eminent in philosophy or politics or poetry or the arts are clearly of an atrabilious [black-biled] temperament, and some of them to such an extent as to be affected by diseases caused by black bile [melancholy], as is said to have happened to Heracles among the heroes?" By the fifteenth and sixteenth centuries, the display of melancholia was seen as a sign of noble, masculine virtue. It is not difficult to imagine why Renaissance poets and philosophers cultivated the symptoms and reflective processes of melancholia as a way of drawing close to this presumed aura. Music extended the circle of exclusivity still wider, broadcasting the sounds of social distinction through a series of concentric circles—from poet to composer, and from performers to listeners—in ways that would be hard to control.

The idea of music as a means of regulation of society no less than ourselves is another important theme in Renaissance thought. Some writers extended the idea of harmony to the social body, with its hierarchy of ruler and ruled and competing communities of faith. Thomas Vautrollier, a French Protestant printer exiled to London during the late sixteenth century, addressed one of his new books to the Catholic count of Arundel, praising "the admirable beauty of the harmony with which wisely administered republics temper the diversity of their various parts." (For more on Vautrollier and the political implications of sacred music, see Chapter 11.) Concepts of "harmonical governance" were also circulating elsewhere in Europe, notably through the writings of the French political philosopher Jean Bodin, whose *Six Books of the Republic* (1576) was widely read. Wracked by spasms of sectarian violence between Protestant and Catholic, many societies were in sore need of "tempered" diversity.

Exactly how the progressive choirmaster Zarlino or the practically minded teacher Agricola would have understood the esoteric visions of Ficino, Tyard, or Vautrollier is difficult to say. Their readerships—aspiring composers and young music students—were focused on the challenges of learning to perform and compose well enough to sustain themselves musically in the world of priests and pastors. Debates about the rival claims of sense and reason upon music, or discussions about music, the humors, and the soul, in their view were probably best left to philosophers. For a new generation of amateurs who needed to find their way in the cultural landscape of the humanistic academies and courts that emerged starting especially in the years around 1500, the balance of practical and philosophical knowledge about music tipped in the opposite direction. For Renaissance courtiers and the hopeful readers who wanted to imitate them, it was not enough to be able to make music; it was equally important to know how to talk about it from a philosophical standpoint. As we will discover in Chapter 7, persuasive talk about music was an important skill for the Renaissance gentleman. Viewed from a still broader perspective, we can observe in these debates the intersection of the larger intellectual forces of Scholasticism and humanism as they sought to make sense of music in all its complexity.

FOR FURTHER READING

Austern, Linda Phyllis, "Musical Treatments for Lovesickness: The Early Modern Heritage," in *Music as Medicine: The History of Music Therapy since Antiquity*, ed. Peregine Horden, pp. 213–48 (Aldershot: Ashgate, 2000)

Blackburn, Bonnie J., "Leonardo and Gaffurio on Harmony and the Pulse of Music," in *Essays on Music and Culture in Honor of Herbert Kellman*, ed. Barbara Haggh, pp. 12–49 (CESR Collection Épitome Musical. Paris and Tours: Minerva, 2001)

Brooks, Jeanice, *Courtly Song in Late Sixteenth-Century France* (Chicago: University of Chicago Press, 2000)

Cohen, David. E., "'The Imperfect Seeks its Perfection': Harmonic Progression, Directed Motion, and Aristotelian Physics," *Music Theory Spectrum* 23 (2001): 139–69

Drake, Stillman, "Renaissance Music and Experimental Science," *Journal of the History of Ideas* 31 (1970): 483–500

Haar, James, "The Frontispiece of Gafori's *Practica Musicae* (1496)," *Renaissance Quarterly* 27 (1974): 7–22

Tomlinson, Gary, *Music in Renaissance Magic: Toward a Historiography of Others* (Chicago: University of Chicago Press, 1993)

Van Orden, Kate, *Music, Discipline, and Arms in Early Modern France* (Chicago: University of Chicago Press, 2005)

Wienpahl, Robert W., "Zarlino, the Senario, and Tonality," *Journal of the American Musicological Society* 12 (1959): 27–41

ⓒ Additional resources available at wwnorton.com/studyspace

CHAPTER SEVEN

Music and the Ideal Courtier

The courtly ideal of the Renaissance gentleman—civilized, educated, urbane—is deeply ingrained in our popular understanding of the period. The role of the courtier had been a fixture of aristocratic life as long as princes needed advice. And as long as there were rivals for a prince's favors, courtiers found ways to compete for influence. At court, what mattered increasingly in the years around 1500 were not accomplishments in battle, but skills with language and words. In this respect the courtier's interests aligned with those of the humanist, for whom persuasive speaking and writing were the highest virtues. Music, too, was drawn into this world, particularly in alliance with poetry and language. But it was not enough for a gentleman simply to know about music; he had to display the proper attitude toward its performance as well. The stakes of the game were high and missteps could bring a social fall. But what were the rules of this game? And who set them?

CASTIGLIONE'S *BOOK OF THE COURTIER*

For historians interested in the changing character of courtly culture in the fifteenth and sixteenth centuries, the answers to these questions are complex. They nevertheless often begin in the same place: *Il libro del cortegiano* (The Book of the Courtier) by Baldassare Castiglione (1478–1529). By far the most influential "courtesy" book of the period, it was avidly read, imitated, and critiqued by generations of men and women across Europe. First published in Venice in 1528, *The Book of the Courtier* rapidly became a best-seller, both in its original Italian and in French, English, German, and Latin translations, often with commentaries, notes, and marginalia to guide aspiring courtiers. As we'll soon discover, Castiglione has important things to say about music and musical performance in relation to vernacular language, a central concern of the book.

The Book of the Courtier presents itself as a series of imaginary conversations that took place over the course of four evenings at the court of Urbino, a small hill town near the Adriatic coast, not long after the death in 1508 of the reigning duke, Guidobaldo da Montefeltro. (Castiglione was himself a diplomat in the service of this duke, although he is only briefly mentioned in the dialogue.) The speakers all have the names of real people, including Count Lodovico da Canossa from Verona and Federico Fregoso from Genoa, a relative of Guidobaldo. The fourth and final book of conversations gives pride of place to Castiglione's close friend Pietro Bembo, a Venetian nobleman who later served as secretary to Pope Leo X and became a cardinal of the Catholic Church in 1539. Bembo was also an extremely influential authority on matters of language and style. In his *Prose della volgar lingua* (Prose in the Vernacular) of 1525, he advocated the emulation of the Italian verse of Petrarch and Boccaccio, celebrated poets of the fourteenth century, much as Latin humanists sought to imitate ancient writers like Cicero and Virgil. As we will see in Chapter 10, Bembo's writings shaped tastes for generations of poets and musicians. His appearance in *The Book of the Courtier* was no accident: he took an active hand in preparing it for publication, reading printer's proofs in Venice while Castiglione was an ambassador to the Spanish court.

Each of the four "books" of *The Book of the Courtier* takes as its focal point some aspect of the perfect courtier (see the excerpts from Books 1 and 2 in SR 45:325–29; 3/10:48–51). What manner or "air" should the courtier take on in relation to his peers, toward women, and above all toward his prince? How should the court lady carry herself? How should the ideal prince behave? Castiglione does not simply tell us the answers to these sorts of ethical questions. Instead, his speakers offer opinions, tell stories, debate rival positions, and generally force the reader to consider the possibilities without knowing how to resolve the differences. On a few central points our informants nevertheless agree. The ideal courtier, Count Lodovico reminds his friends, should "be born of a noble and genteel family." On account of this accident of birth the courtier must be prepared to defend family honor through virtuous action. Failure to do so would be a terrible mistake. "Should he stray from the path of his forebears," the count continues, he "stains the family name, and not only fails to achieve anything but loses what has been achieved already." For men like Lodovico, the best place to keep family honor clean had always been the battlefield. The profession of arms was the chief occupation of his ideal nobleman.

Count Lodovico nevertheless also recognized that in his own day members of the nobility had to cope with changing circumstances. In the Italian peninsula in particular, the emergence of strongmen such as the Sforza princes in Milan or the Medici family in Florence pulled warriors and members of the minor nobility to court. It was here that titles were meted out, legal disputes settled, and alliances forged. Increasingly dependent on the favor of a powerful local authority figure rather than a king, as was the case in France, old warriors needed to civilize themselves in order to compete for their prince's attentions. The pursuit of virtue on the battlefield was increasingly balanced by the need to control one's self at court—in conversation, movement, demeanor, and even the performance of music. *The Book of the Courtier* is about finding this virtue in behavioral "grace" no less than in the profession of arms.

FEDERICO DA MONTEFELTRO: THE IDEAL PRINCE

The court of Urbino was itself in many ways the model of this transformation in behavior. Duke Guidobaldo da Montefeltro loomed large in Urbino, thanks to a dynastic legacy that would have been impossible to ignore. The Montefeltro mark was to be seen everywhere—in the palace itself, in its famous collection of sculpture and books, and above all in the magnificent official double portrait of the young Guidobaldo and his father, Federico, that was made for them ca. 1480 (Fig. 7.1). It is one of the most famous images of the Italian Renaissance.

The panel shows Federico in full armor, covered in his ducal robe, and surrounded by symbols of power and authority. The ducal sword strapped to his side points down toward his commander's baton, and up toward a dazzling hat that represents his position as chief of the pope's army. Meanwhile, the young Guidobaldo, poised strategically beneath the hat as if to receive it, toys with his father's scepter. Perhaps the viewer is meant to understand that Guidobaldo will one day inherit them both. Federico, however, is concerned with neither sword nor crown. His gaze is focused instead on a massive open book, which he reads while leaning it against a shelf containing more books. The courtiers of Urbino could hardly have missed the point: the ideal alignment of arms and letters was plainly represented by the straight line between sword, book, and hat.

Federico enjoyed a long and successful career as a condottiere, or mercenary captain, in the bloody rivalries among the various city-states of fifteenth-century Italy. He was nevertheless remembered by successive generations no less for his learning. Sent to study the classics at a humanist academy near Mantua, Federico immersed himself in the study of scripture, theology, philosophy, and history, as well as mathematics, architecture, music, sculpture, and literature. The ducal palace of Urbino (which survives today as a UNESCO World Heritage site) housed an unrivaled store of treasures, both newly commissioned and

Figure 7.1: *Pedro Berruguete,* Double Portrait of the Duke of Urbino, Federico da Montefeltro, and his Son Guidobaldo, *ca. 1480*

plundered from the towns he subdued over the course of his military career. As Castiglione recalls in *The Book of the Courtier*, the elder duke also "collected many very excellent and rare books in Greek, Latin, and Hebrew, all of which he adorned with gold and silver, deeming these to be the supreme excellence of his great palace." He assembled his remarkable collection of books in an equally remarkable library (*studiolo*) that was plastered with images of the world's greatest thinkers, and with trick images of books, scientific objects, and musical instruments that seemed to spill forth from hidden cabinets.

THE COURTIER AND THE THEATER OF APPEARANCES

Poised at the threshold of this studious treasure trove, the viewers of Federico's portrait probably wondered what he was reading and how they, too, might prepare themselves to establish credibility in the eyes of so accomplished a ruler. Skill in battle was certainly the most important way, as Count Lodovico explains. But simply fighting was evidently not enough; it was no less important to make sure that your accomplishments in battle were noticed by the right people and at the right time. "Whenever the Courtier chances to be engaged in a skirmish or an action or a battle in the field, or the like," Federico Fregoso observes, "he should discreetly withdraw from the crowd, and do the outstanding and daring things that he has to do in as small a company as possible and in the sight of all of the noblest and most respected men in the army, and especially in the presence of and, if possible, before the very eyes of his king or the prince he is serving." Like Shakespeare's Falstaff, who insists that "the better part of valor is discretion," Fregoso imagines a world in which military virtue is an elaborate piece of theater performed before a particular audience. Indeed, this same principle of managed appearances recurs as a refrain throughout the civil conversations of *The Book of the Courtier*. "Whether in word or deed," Count Lodovico advises, the courtier ought "to avoid affectation in every way possible as though it were some very rough and dangerous reef; and (to pronounce a new word perhaps) to practice in all things a certain *sprezzatura*, so as to conceal all art and make whatever is done or said appear to be without effort and almost without any thought about it."

Sprezzatura—literally, neglect—has remained an elusive condition precisely on account of its strongly performative aspect. For Castiglione's little circle of courtiers, it was not something one possessed in any permanent sense, but instead was a way of doing something according to a particular set of codes. Count Lodovico characterized it as a "cool ease" of physical movement. For another of the courtiers it was to be found "in showing no concern, and in seeming to have one's thoughts elsewhere rather than in what one is doing." Sixteenth-century translators puzzled over the term, rendering it as "*nonchallance*" in French or "recklessness" in English. Castiglione's notion of feigned indifference was universally understood as the mark of a civilized man. The ideal courtier was the original master of "the cool."

With regard to musical performance, the idea of "showing no concern" emerges as a way of making things seem easier than they actually are, and thereby accruing social prestige in the eyes of one's peers. As Federico Fregoso explains: "And although he may know and understand what he does, in this also I would have him dissimulate the care and effort that is required in doing anything well; and let him appear to esteem but little this accomplishment of his, yet by performing it excellently well, make others esteem it highly."

Given the overwhelming concern to maintain clear lines of demarcation between the noble courtier and the world at large, musical performance was tightly circumscribed according to its social context. Performing music in private for one's peers was laudable, for it accorded well with what humanists had discovered about the place of performance in the ancient *convivium* (banquet) staged in Plato's dialogues and other newly discovered writings. On the other hand, to be heard singing or playing in public (other than in a masquerade) risked a social fall. In *The Book of the Courtier* Fregoso complains of those who perform too readily, and before an unknown audience, "so that it seems that they have put in an appearance for that alone, and that that is their principal profession." Musical performance, he continues, ought to be "a pastime" and "not in the presence of persons of low birth or where there is a crowd." Of course, sound could and did pierce the circle of exclusivity in ways that other forms of behavior might not. But Fregoso (and through him Castiglione) uses music as a marker of social differences that inscribe the distinguishing "grace" of nobility through a performance that is no less carefully managed than the strategic withdrawal from a crowded battlefield in order to be "seen."

SONGS FIT FOR A COURTIER

The preferred medium for this nonchalant musical performance was solo song, often to the accompaniment of a supporting instrument. The ability to read, to understand, and to take part in the performance of polyphony in mensural notation was a valued skill among Castiglione's courtiers. But in the solo voice "we note and follow the fine style and the melody with greater attention in that our ears are not occupied with more than a single voice, and every little fault is the more clearly noticed—which does not happen when a group is singing, because then one sustains the other." (As we saw in Chapter 6, humanists like Marsilio Ficino prized solo singing as the acme of musical expression.)

The presentational quality of solo vocal performance reminds us of the importance placed in Castiglione's world on the careful staging of one's self for one's peers. But there is an intimacy established here, too, for the courtier ought to "adapt himself to the occasion and will know when the minds of his listeners are disposed to listen and when not." Echoing an important humanist commonplace that held the soul itself as a kind of harmony, Castiglione also allowed that familiar (and in particular feminine) company made music an apt medium for shared experience: "It is especially appropriate when ladies are present, because their aspect touches the souls of the listeners with sweetness, makes them more receptive to the suavity of the music, and arouses the spirits of the musicians as well."

French and English translations of Castiglione's text often suggest that the solo singing mentioned by Federico Fregoso was done to the accompaniment of the lute (see, for instance, Thomas Hoby's text of 1561: SR 45:325–29; 3/10:47–51). It's an understandable transformation. For northern European gentlemen and ladies of the second half of the sixteenth century, accomplishment on the lute was among the foremost signs of civility; the French parliamentarian and literary scholar Jacques Gohory described it as "the moste noble and melodious instrument of Musicke." The lute was also a practical choice for amateurs. Frets solved tricky problems of intonation, and tablature—which tells the player which strings to

Figure 7.2: *Apollo playing the lira da braccio among the nine Muses, from Raphael's* Parnassus *in the Stanza della Segnatura, Vatican Palace, Rome*

pluck and where to place the fingers—saved laborious study of mensural notation. It was not hard for a would-be gentleman to acquire enough basic skill on the instrument to impress listeners with his feigned "recklessness." Publishers rushed in to fill the need with instruction manuals, books of dance music for the lute, arrangements of polyphonic vocal music (either for lute alone or to accompany a solo singer on the treble part), and solo songs written expressly for lute and voice.

Castiglione's Italian original, however, described the preferred vehicle somewhat differently: "cantare alla viola" (singing to the accompaniment of the viol) or "cantare alla viola per recitare" (sung recitation to the viol). Castiglione's readers would have understood these as allusions to the viola da braccio or lira da braccio, bowed string instruments that were often associated with music-making in the comparatively private confines of elite households (for a representation of a lira da braccio, see Fig. 7.2).

SERAFINO AQUILANO, SINGER AND POET

Federico Fregoso's emphasis on recitation probably was meant to evoke traditions of improvised singing (see Chapter 12), as practiced by professional poet-performers like Serafino Aquilano (1466–1500) and evoked in Italian epic verse of the day. Reciters had long been a part of the Italian musical landscape in the fifteenth century, as we noted in our discussion of Pietrobono, whose improvisatory singing and lute playing were praised by Tinctoris (see Chapter 3). Yet this unwritten tradition is only obliquely acknowledged in the story of polyphonic practice as it was told by contemporary music theorists like Tinctoris and Gaffurius, and as it is studied by musicologists today. Men like Serafino perpetuated these improvisatory and oral traditions, which had been the musical means for the delivery of many different types of poetry, including sonnets, canzoni, *strambotti*, and other conventional rhyme schemes, often delivered as the singer accompanied himself on the lute or lira da braccio.

Among Serafino's listeners in the private chambers of cardinals like the music-loving Ascanio Sforza, these traditions took on profound meaning. For Paolo Cortesi, host and founder of a private academy of aristocratic literati who gathered in his Roman villa during the 1490s, Serafino's performances were far more than entertainment; they were a means of moral edification and even magical healing (see SR 43:316–21; 3/8:38–43). Vincenzo Calmeta, a poet and literary commentator who also took part in Cortesi's little academy, vividly recalled Serafino's remarkable art, which inspired many imitators. Filtering his perception of modern song through humanistic readings on the power of its ancient counterpart, Calmeta calls Serafino and his colleagues not just poets or singers but *citaredi*, a term that evokes the ancient Greek *kithara*, or lyre (see SR 44:323; 3/9:45). This same fusion of ancient and modern is reflected in a famous mural of the Greek god Apollo that the painter Raphael made for the Vatican palace in Rome (Fig. 7.2). Here we see the fashionable lira da braccio in the hands of the ancient god identified with the power of music and affective song.

Men like Calmeta helped to shape the cultural preferences of Castiglione's courtiers. Indeed, among the speakers in *The Book of the Courtier* is Bernardo Accolti, one of the most famous singers of his day, and by all accounts a gifted practitioner of *sprezzatura* improvisation. He represents the physical manifestation of the ideal articulated by Fregoso. In sharp contrast to the ideals of rational proportion embodied in the figure of Pythagoras and the polyphonic art associated with his teachings, solo singing was aligned with Orpheus, who represents the affective, rhetorical dimension of music. Here was a musical idiom perfectly suited to the humanist program embraced by *The Book of the Courtier*.

MARCHETTO CARA AND THE FROTTOLA

We know relatively little about the improvisatory traditions practiced by singers like Serafino or Bernardo, for while the poetry survives, the music does not. Yet among the patrons assembled in places like Urbino during Castiglione's day were men and women who were thoroughly familiar with such solo song. The

"Duchess" of *The Book of the Courtier*, Elisabetta Gonzaga, a member of the family that ruled the duchy of Mantua, was sister-in-law to Isabella d'Este, who moved to Mantua from her native Ferrara after her marriage in 1490 (she was 16 at the time). Although it was unusual for the women of aristocratic families like the Este and Gonzaga dynasties to maintain their own chapels or musical households, Isabella is known to have supported various players, singers, and composers, including Marchetto Cara (1465–1525), a composer, singer, and lutenist whose performances were highly regarded by courtly listeners. In *The Book of the Courtier* Cara is mentioned as an example of all that is moving about Italian song, which rivals Latin oratory for its effects upon listeners. "In a manner serene and full of plaintive sweetness," Castiglione's Lodovico explains, "he touches and penetrates our souls, gently impressing a delightful sentiment upon them."

Like other composers active at the music-loving courts of northern Italy in the years around 1500, Cara wrote frottole that took a variety of poetic forms, chiefly stanzaic designs with witty refrains. The subject matter of these songs ranged freely among the perennial themes of lyric poetry: the sufferings of love, the beauties of nature, and the uncertainties of fortune. The music followed rhyme and refrain in close coordination, with formulaic tunes that offer a glimpse of the procedures one might use in declaiming poetry to musical accompaniment, although with little sense of the flexible, nonchalant improvisation so prized by Castiglione's courtiers. Indeed, among the 11 books of frottole published by the Venetian music printer Ottaviano Petrucci during the early years of the sixteenth century are pieces designed as "models" for the declamation of particular poetic forms. The titles of these formulas suggest that they were understood to dwell at the intersection of speech and song, much as they did at the intersection of written and unwritten musical traditions. The *First Book of Frottole*, for instance, offers a model piece described as "modus dicendi capitula" ("a way of reciting capitoli," an Italian poetic form equivalent to the *terza rima* that Dante had invented around 1300 for his *Divine Comedy*). In the *Fourth Book of Frottole*, an anonymous piece is marked "modo de cantar sonetti" ("way of singing sonnets"; Fig. 7.3). Still others are called "aer" (literally, aria), in this case meaning both melody and breath.

These designations highlight the humanist fascination with the eloquence of ancient Latin authors and more recent Italian masters such as Dante, Petrarch, and Boccaccio. The humanists also grappled with the problem of finding modern-day counterparts for the profound ethical effects identified in ancient writings on the union of music and poetry. Castiglione's courtiers were certainly familiar with these tropes: Count Lodovico, reacting to a critique of music as unsuitable to "real men," launches into a long litany drawn from classical history on the power of music to "induce a good new habit of mind and an inclination of virtue." Identifying music with ancient teachings on the harmony of the universe, he recalls the principle that "the world is made up of music, that the heavens in their motion make

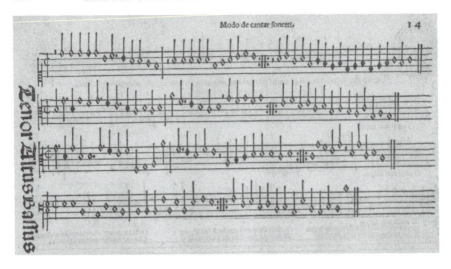

Figure 7.3: *Polyphonic model for the musical performance of any sonnet, from Ottaviano Petrucci,* Libro quarto de frottole *(1507)*

harmony, and that even the human soul was formed on the same principle, and is therefore awakened and has its virtues brought to life, as it were, through music."

In the world of Castiglione's courtiers, these ethical effects were most evident in the inspired declamatory songs of men like Serafino, who visited Urbino and other courts of northern Italy during the late 1490s. Cara's singing probably inspired some of these same associations. Indeed, these modes of largely unwritten solo delivery, by professionals and the amateurs who imitated them, were widespread in the Italian peninsula during the fifteenth and early sixteenth centuries, at least until they were supplanted by a new vogue for polyphonic genres like the chanson and madrigal in the middle of the sixteenth century. Yet even here, as we will learn in Chapter 10, the old priorities of persuasion and expression through vernacular song retained their force.

A FROTTOLA IN DETAIL: TROMBONCINO'S
OSTINATO VO' SEGUIRE

Professional poet-improvisers like Serafino and trained musicians like Cara probably needed no instructions on how to join text and tone in the ways set out by Petrucci. But Petrucci's model pieces could have been useful for courtiers and others interested in carrying off a carefully rehearsed "performance" with detached *sprezzatura*. Alongside such schematic approaches, Petrucci also issued dozens of frottole with music specifically tailored to the shape and meaning of the poetry. *Ostinato vo' seguire* (I Shall Resolutely Follow), a song by Isabella d'Este's wind-playing singer Bartolomeo Tromboncino (1470–1534), can serve as an example of the genre. The poem takes as its theme the cruel decrees of fortune and the fortitude of one magnanimous enough to withstand them. As the various stanzas explain, neither "pleasure nor pain" will change his resolve. Fortune has its reasons, but what matters to the persona imagined by this poem is that regardless of the outcome he will have found "honor," "great desire," and above all magnanimity. The melodic flourishes at the end of each line underscore these ideas, just in case we were not listening (Anthology 13).

Castiglione's courtiers would probably have endorsed the musical expression of these sentiments without hesitation, for the values called out so boldly in Tromboncino's modest song align neatly with the qualities they sought in an ideal ruler. The model prince, they agreed, would display the fundamental virtues identified since antiquity with important men: justice, temperance, liberality, gentleness, honor, and greatness of spirit. As we saw in our encounter with courtly patrons of the fifteenth century in Savoy and Burgundy (Chapter 3), aspiring rulers needed to look no further than Aristotle's *Nicomachean Ethics* or *On Virtues and Vices* for confirmation of these qualities. Indeed, the words that Castiglione puts into the mouths of his courtiers sound like loose paraphrases of Aristotle's formulations. But how might his ideal courtier help to instill these attributes in his prince, particularly when so many despotic rulers suffered from "ignorance and self-conceit" that made them unreceptive to advice, easy to anger, or capricious in distributing favors? The solution, it seems, was to teach through carefully chosen examples. And so the courtier was advised "to incite his prince" to ethical virtues by considering "famous captains and other excellent men to whom the ancients were wont to make statues . . . in public places, both to honor these men and to encourage others, so that through worthy emulation they may be led to strive to attain glory too."

Examples worthy of emulation came in other forms, too, such as music and poetry, that might keep the courtier's "mind continually occupied with worthy pleasures, yet always impressing upon him also some virtuous habit along in these enticements, as I have said, beguiling him with salutary deception." Considered from this utilitarian perspective, a piece like Tromboncino's *Ostinato vo' seguire* seems rather more than a fashionable courtly pastime or a vehicle for the facile display of *sprezzatura*. The catchy tune and vocal flourishes are pleasant, to be sure, but they are also "worthy pleasures." For any prince who took the trouble to listen, *Ostinato vo' seguire* conveyed a message of "virtuous habit." Cultivate temperance in the face of uncertain fortune, it advises. Devote yourself to the highest form of love. And above all, find the greatness of heart that is the essence of magnanimity. The courtier's musical ploy, it seems, could sometimes be the persuasive vehicle of an important political message.

MUSIC, THE COURT LADY, AND THE COURTESAN

We can only guess what Tromboncino's patron Isabella d'Este (Fig. 7.4) thought of this musical parade of male virtue. Judging from the ideas put forth in Castiglione's *Book of the Courtier*, she would certainly have understood much about the values expressed in this and similar frottole. The courtiers say only enough about Isabella to indicate their profound respect. They prefer to remain silent rather than publicly praise a lady "of whose admirable virtues it would be offensive to speak as restrainedly as anyone must do here who would speak of her at all." Perhaps, given the participation of Isabella's sister-in-law, Duchess Elisabetta, in the imagined conversations, it would have been a grave error to have her compared (even implicitly) to a relative and generational peer. In any case, Isabella would have been held in especially high regard by the courtiers

Figure 7.4: *Titian*, Portrait of Isabella d'Este *(created 1534–36)*

of Urbino, for when Cesare Borgia toppled Duke Guidobaldo from his throne in 1502, she brokered a deal that brought the duke and duchess to her own court in Mantua as refugees.

Behind the courtier's guarded comment rests the conviction that the ideal court lady (the central theme of Book 3 of Castiglione's treatise) shares the same "virtues of mind" identified with the male courtier who would serve a patron like Isabella. The court lady would at the very least need to be as well informed about painting, literature, and music as Isabella, whose clients included not only Tromboncino but also artists such as Andrea Mantegna and Leonardo da Vinci, and the poet Ludovico Ariosto. Castiglione himself enjoyed her protection for a time. So we should not be surprised to learn that, according to *The Book of the Courtier*, the court lady should "have knowledge of letters, of music, of painting, and know how to dance." But to what end? Not, it seems, chiefly to engage in performing herself, but instead "in order that she may know how to value and praise cavaliers more or less according to their merits." Thus, although the lady courtier ought to be a ready audience, sponsor, or judge for the activities of male peers, her own role as a participant in these activities was narrowly circumscribed. Like Princess Beatrice of Aragon in Naples a quarter-century before, the lady serves as patron of an elite chamber or salon. Noble women were certainly well informed on matters of music, but where and when they were free to express their knowledge or demonstrate their skill was quite another matter.

The profession of arms (a "robust and strenuous manly" exercise) was by definition out of bounds to a woman. Her participation in music and dance, too, was confined to modes of performance that would constrain the body rather than reveal too much of it. "And so when she dances," as Giulio de' Medici (nephew of Lorenzo the Magnificent and later Pope Clement VII) explains, "I should not wish to see her make movements that are too energetic and violent; nor, when she sings or plays, use those loud and oft-repeated diminutions [ornaments] that show more art than sweetness; likewise the musical instruments that she plays ought in my opinion to be appropriate to this intent."

Giulio's comments help us to understand the frequently repeated claims of Isabella's preference for the sweet sounds of strings. They tell us something, too, of the anxiety already attached to virtuosic display by women singers, who were certainly capable of executing "oft-repeated diminutions" on the order of the vocal flourishes we heard in Tromboncino's frottola. (For more on these ornaments and female virtuosity, see Chapter 12.) For a nobleman, performing in public risked a social fall to the level of the professional artisan. For a noble woman, however, singing or playing in almost any context risked a confusion with the role of the courtesan-prostitute, whose voice was often heard as a marker of sexual power and transgression. A famous French painting of the early sixteenth century puts the intersection of gender, music, and moral codes plainly (Fig. 7.5). The outdoor scene stages music-making by women among public pleasures of

Figure 7.5: *Anonymous,* Prodigal Son with Courtesans, *early 16th century*

food, drink, and erotic desire. Courtesans play lute and flute as a young gentleman gestures toward a music book on the table before them. It was certainly
possible for women to make music privately (see, for instance, the pious domestic scene depicted in an Italian painting of the late sixteenth century shown in
Fig. 9.5). But anything that resembled public performance by women was to be
avoided at all costs.

We can read something of this anxiety in the frank warning that the
aforementioned Pietro Bembo offered to his daughter Elena in 1541 (see
SR 47:332–33; 3/12:54–55). Musical performance, he advised, was a vanity
incompatible with feminine chastity: "Playing music is for a woman a vain
and frivolous thing. And I would wish you to be the most serious and chaste
woman alive." Such worries must have exerted terrible negative pressures on
aspiring women composers, too. Writing music was accepted in convents and
private households, but venturing into the public sphere required the protection of someone with unassailable social credentials. Thus when Maddalena
Casulana (active 1566–1583) took the unusual step of publishing some of her
madrigals for four voices in 1568—it was the first publication ever devoted exclusively to music by a woman—she enlisted the help of "the Most Illustrious
and Excellent Lady Donna Isabella de' Medici Orsina, Duchess of Bracciano"
(SR 50:337; 3/15:59).

Seeking out a prestigious patron was not unusual even for male composers. But Casulana sought to turn the tables on men, who marked music as a

feminine vanity but a male virtue. For her, men were committing "a vain error" in "esteem[ing] themselves such masters of high intellectual gifts that they think women cannot share them too." To judge from the very capably written music in this and her other books of madrigals, Casulana's argument had much merit. The social stigma associated with performance and composition by women was nevertheless a persistent facet of Renaissance courtly culture. In the 1590s, when the reigning members of the Este family in Ferrara brought skilled female singers into the ducal chamber, they were promptly married off to noble courtiers and inscribed on the rolls of Duchess Margherita's private household. Women, it seems, were gradually being heard as performers and composers, even as they were constrained by contradictory impulses of aesthetic value and social stigma.

By the end of the sixteenth century, the example of Ferrara shows us that women could do more than merely listen or offer criticism of male music-making. On the other hand, the old social codes (so clearly expressed in *The Book of the Courtier*) that identified the display of feminine skill with the courtesan's taint kept these talented women far from the general public. Paradoxically, the better the members of Duchess Margherita's *concerto delle donne* (consort of ladies) could sing, the more urgent it was to coop them up and to sustain the image of them as court ladies performing among their peers. (For more on the "singing ladies of Ferrara," see Chapter 12.)

FORTUNES OF THE COURTIER AESTHETIC

The concerns expressed in *The Book of the Courtier* had still other important implications for music-making in sixteenth-century Europe, both within and beyond the confines of courtly society. Gentlemen with real skills had to work hard to make sure their musical display did not compromise their elite status. When the nobleman and soldier Giulio Cesare Brancaccio (1515–1586) came to the ducal court of Ferrara in the 1580s, he was drawn into the *musica secreta* (private music), as the private ensembles there were known. Brancaccio possessed a magnificent bass voice, made even more impressive by its wide range and his skill with the same sorts of virtuosic ornaments and effects for which the three newly ennobled singing ladies were so adored. Yet Brancaccio began to worry about what his performances at court and his lavish stipend might mean for his aristocratic standing. Was he an accomplished amateur, or a mere professional? By 1583 Duke Alfonso d'Este's demands for rehearsed performances with the *concerto delle donne* had become too much. "Signor Guilio Cesare," in the words of an ambassador who was there, "said very angrily that he did not want to join in and that he was not one of His Highness's musicians and [also said] other not very nice things to his master." Brancaccio left Ferrara with his gentlemanly honor barely intact.

Other musical noblemen were more successful in maintaining the aversion to performance that Castiglione's courtier code prescribed. The skilled Neapolitan lutenist and singer Fabrizio Dentice (? 1539–1581) moved in some of the same aristocratic circles as Brancaccio. But as a descendent of an ancient noble family, Dentice was apparently very careful about when and where he played, and only did so after demonstrating a reluctance appropriate to his rank. A chronicler at the Farnese court in Parma recalled that Dentice was an excellent lutenist, but that as a gentleman he "disdained the pursuit of this profession and the title of lute player. Duke Ottavio was barely able with his supplications to have him take the lute in hand, since as a Cavalier of very noble affiliations, he believed such a profession would compromise his noble status." Dentice's attitude may help explain why his works survive only in private manuscripts, far from the public eye and ear. (For an analysis of one of Dentice's elegant lute fantasias, see Anthology 25; for more on the arts of improvisation he practiced, see Chapter 12.)

What did Castiglione's *Book of the Courtier* mean for the growing numbers of literate townsfolk—students, officials, and would-be gentlemen—who read, imitated, and critiqued it? Few true amateurs had the skills to justify Brancaccio's ire or Dentice's careful detachment among their peers and superiors. Some might have worried, however, about other kinds of social gaffes made through and on account of music. Remember Philomathes, the young gentleman from Thomas Morley's *Plaine and Easie Introduction to Practicall Musicke* (1597), whom we met in Chapter 2. When two other gentlemen at a banquet asked him to help resolve an argument over music, he felt obliged to demur, even at the risk of being considered discourteous. Philomathes's problem was not just that he knew little of music, but rather that his protest of ignorance was taken simply as the obligatory reluctance that was expected of all refined gentlemen. When his ignorance was revealed as genuine, the game was up and he lost much stature in the eyes of his peers.

Worse still, Philomathes was equally incapable of making music when the mistress of the house brought out the partbooks and requested him to sing. "But when after manie excuses, I protested unfainedly that I could not, everie one began to wonder. Yea, some whispered to others demaunding how I was brought up." By then Philomathes did not even want to appear to be pretending. And yet by the conclusion of the *Plaine and Easie Introduction*, the tutor Gnorimus brings Philomathes gently back to the idea of music as an opportunity for composers as well as courtly amateurs to display themselves favorably. It is tempting to read this advice as a mirror of our own ideas about individual expression through music. But in light of what we have learned of the world of the courtier, Gnorimus's remarks probably have some important analogies with the temporary self constructed in Castiglione's elaborate social ballet of appearances and illusion. By the late sixteenth century, the act of composing polyphony, no less than a solo turn with voice and lute, had become a marker of the courtier ideal.

From this brief exploration of music and manners in Castiglione's *Book of the Courtier* we have learned that music was in many ways an ideal testing ground for the elaborate strategies of appearance imagined by Renaissance gentlemen like Fabrizio Dentice as they navigated the tricky landscape of life at court. When the game of make-believe was well played, courtiers could hope to parlay their feigned "neglect" of professional standards into prestige in the eyes (and ears) of their fellow courtiers. The game was not without risks, as Giulio Cesare Brancaccio and Morley's Philomathes discovered. Genuine accomplishment and ignorance alike could result in a social fall. For women of the Renaissance court, too, music provided an opportunity to demonstrate their knowledge even as it risked transgressing into behaviors deemed unacceptable. This was the anxiety against which Maddalena Casulana and members of the *concerto delle donne* at Ferrara were struggling, as women's musical voices slowly emerged from obscurity and stigma. Gender, class, and musical performance were to be combined with care. In the world of the courtiers, exceptional listeners demanded exceptional music.

FOR FURTHER READING

Burke, Peter, *The Fortunes of the Courtier: The European Reception of Castiglione's Cortegiano,* Penn State Series in the History of the Book (University Park, PA: Pennsylvania State University Press, 1996)

Feldman, Martha, and Bonnie Gordon, eds., *The Courtesan's Arts: Cross-Cultural Perspectives* (New York: Oxford University Press, 2006)

Haar, James, "The Courtier as Musician: Castiglione's View of the Science and Art of Music," in *Castiglione: The Ideal and the Real in Renaissance Culture*, ed. Robert Hanning and David Rosand, pp. 165–90 (New Haven: Yale University Press, 1983)

Kelly, Joan, "Did Women Have a Renaissance?" in *Women, History, and Theory: The Essays of Joan Kelly,* pp. 19–50 (Chicago: University of Chicago Press, 1984)

Marino, Joseph, "A Renaissance in the Vernacular: Baldassare Castiglione's Coining of the *aulic,*" in *Perspectives on Early Modern and Modern Intellectual History*, ed. Joseph Marino and Melinda Schlitt, pp. 145–63 (Rochester: University of Rochester Press, 2000)

Newcomb, Anthony, "Courtesans, Muses or Musicians? Professional Women Musicians in Sixteenth-Century Italy," in *Women Making Music: The Western Art Tradition, 1150–1950,* ed. Jane Bowers and Judith Tick, pp. 90–115 (Champaign, IL: University of Illinois Press, 1986)

Prizer, William F., "Isabella d'Este and Lucrezia Borgia as Patrons of Music: The Frottola at Mantua and Ferrara," *Journal of the American Musicological Society* 38 (1985): 1–33

——, "Una 'Virtù Molto Conveniente a Madonne': Isabella d'Este as a Musician," *Journal of Musicology* 17 (1999): 10–49

Wistreich, Richard, *Warrior, Courtier, Singer: Giulio Cesare Brancaccio and the Performance of Identity in the Late Renaissance* (Aldershot and Burlington, VT: Ashgate, 2007)

Ⓢ Additional resources available at wwnorton.com/studyspace

CHAPTER EIGHT

Josquin des Prez and the "Perfect Art"

In his famous treatise on the melodic modes, the *Dodecachordon* (The 12-String Lyre) of 1547, the Swiss humanist Heinrich Glarean put the music of Josquin des Prez (ca. 1450–1521) at the pinnacle of the craft of composition. Josquin's works, he proclaimed, exemplified "an already perfect art." Glarean's values were both historical and aesthetic. Finding little of merit in the works of his contemporaries, he preferred to look back to the years around 1500 for a golden age that embodied all that was correct in musical art. Glarean's book was not simply about Josquin. As we saw in Chapter 2, his principal aim was to explore the musical modes of Catholic plainsong and their role in shaping polyphonic practice, aligning them with the legacies of classical antiquity while he was at it. But in singling out Josquin from among the many worthy masters whose music was known to him, Glarean articulated something that many others, from the sixteenth century until today, have sensed in Josquin's music.

In recent years, many basic facts of Josquin's life and creative output have been fundamentally reevaluated. There are serious doubts, for instance, about the authenticity of several works long considered Josquin's. And new evidence has emerged from the archives that puts many assumptions about his career in doubt, often with profound implications for our picture of musical style. We could raise similar questions about almost any composer of the Renaissance in light of changing views of biography, reputation, and style. Johannes Ciconia, Guillaume Du Fay, Heinrich Isaac, Pierre de La Rue, Orlando di Lasso, and Luca Marenzio have all undergone major reassessments. The case of Josquin, however, is particularly compelling, since his musical language and claims about his creative life figure importantly in writings about music of the years around 1500, a period of profound stylistic and cultural change.

Poised between the old traditions of cantus firmus, canon, and rigorous counterpoint on one hand, and on the other new concerns for the power of music to declaim, represent, and express the secular and sacred texts it sets, Josquin's works are demanding, moving, and endlessly fascinating. They are hardly unique, however, for we find many of these same tendencies in the works of his contemporaries. We should certainly not ignore the other important masters of the years around 1500 in favor of the outmoded "great man" approach to music history. Yet the challenge of evaluating Josquin's music in relation to his career, and to its reception by his contemporaries and later generations, brings us to the heart of the problem of coming to terms with the music of almost any musician of the period.

PERFECTION IN PRACTICE: JOSQUIN'S
AVE MARIA . . . VIRGO SERENA

At first glance there is much in Glarean's claim of perfection that jibes with received notions about Josquin's music. Listening to a work like his four-voice setting that begins *Ave Maria* (Hail Mary), for instance, we cannot help but be captivated by the sense of balanced variety, clarity, and order that unfolds among the various parts (Anthology 14). There are points of imitation (in which all four voice parts lay equal claim to the same melodic idea in turn), lively contrapuntal duets (first pairing superius and altus, then tenor and bassus), and homorhythmic passages that declaim whole lines of text with compelling intimacy. Josquin's contemporaries often hinted at the effectiveness of his treatment of his chosen texts, whether secular or sacred. For modern writers, their suggestions have opened a long thread of discussions about the rhetorical eloquence of Josquin's approach to words and his emblematic status as a composer whose music gives voice to the humanist currents of the day and their abiding concern for the affective, persuasive dimensions of language.

Ave Maria . . . virgo serena is especially rich in this regard. The sudden turn in the closing moments to chordal textures seems perfectly suited to the private, inner calls for Mary's intercession ("Remember me," the singers intone collectively). But elsewhere Josquin's music is no less effective in its treatment of the form and meaning of the text, amplifying the initial calls of praise ("Ave") with systematic imitation for all four voices, rhyming couplets with parallel duets, and swelling gestures that seem to weave images before our ears. Josquin invented neither these musical devices nor their application to the presentation of texts. Indeed, as we will soon see, they are also to be heard in the varied textures and gestures of works by composers like La Rue and Isaac. Rarely, however, had these elements been brought together with such skill, expressive power, and sheer invention.

Ave Maria . . . virgo serena is by no means the most challenging or novel of the works credited to Josquin. In other pieces we find expansive structures built upon repeating cantus-firmus melodies, like the motet *Miserere mei, Deus* (Have Mercy on Me, Lord), or upon abstract patterns built around musical space itself, as in the *Missa L'homme armé super voces musicales.* Still other pieces look back to prestigious lineages, like the lament *Nymphes des bois/Requiem* (Nymphs of the Woods/Requiem) with a cantus firmus drawn from the Mass for the Dead, in which Josquin mourns the death of the great master Johannes Ockeghem, in part by recalling his fascination with notational riddles (see Chapter 5).

In other secular music, too, Josquin combined literary registers and musical techniques in striking ways, turning old *formes fixes* poems into musical canons or making elaborate polyphony from a fragment of a popular tune, as in *Petite Camusette* (Little Snubnose; see Chapter 3 for Ockeghem's setting of this text). Yet the modest motet *Ave Maria . . . virgo serena* has long been one of Josquin's most admired compositions, as well as one of the most frequently performed and recorded pieces of Renaissance polyphony.

RENAISSANCE IMAGES OF JOSQUIN DES PREZ

How well does our modern image of Josquin's music align with the one imagined by his contemporaries and immediate followers? There is ample evidence that his music was held in the highest esteem during the late fifteenth and sixteenth centuries, and not just by conservative theorists like Glarean. In a series of letters to Duke Ercole I of Ferrara, a courtier named Girolamo da Sestola tried to persuade his patron to hire Josquin as a member of his private chapel. "My Lord," he wrote in August 1502, "I believe that there is neither lord nor king who will now have a better chapel than yours if Your Lordship sends for Josquin. Don Alfonso [Ercole's son and heir] wishes to write this to Your Lordship and so does the entire chapel, and by having Josquin in our chapel I want to place a crown upon this chapel of ours." Appealing to the duke's ambition to outshine other princes, Girolamo held out the promise of Josquin's arrival as a perfecting jewel in what was already among the finest ensembles of the day. According to Girolamo, Josquin was the hands-down favorite of the other singers and the duke's music-loving son.

The duke, however, also heard reasons to hesitate in offering the post to Josquin. Another of his musical recruiters, Gian de Artiganova, argued that

Heinrich Isaac (ca. 1450–1517) would make a better choice for pragmatic reasons. "To me he seems well suited to serve Your Lordship," Gian advised in September 1502, "more so than Josquin, because he is of better disposition among his companions, and he will compose new works more often. It is true that Josquin composes better, but he composes when he wants to, and not when one wants him to, and he is asking 200 ducats in salary while Isaac will come for 120—but Your Lordship will decide."

ISAAC'S COMPETING CLAIM

Based on what we know of Isaac's career, there was some merit to Gian's recommendation. Isaac was undeniably an accomplished composer. Indeed, his musical career is remarkable in comparison to those of Josquin and many other contemporaries for the fact that he was not a cleric (he was married, with children, in fact); nor does he seem to have had duties as a chapel singer (as did Du Fay, Ockeghem, Obrecht, and Josquin). In archival documents Isaac is almost always identified as a composer, and in this capacity he was truly prolific, crafting dozens of mass cycles, hundreds of liturgical, devotional, and ceremonial motets, and many secular compositions in French, Italian, and German.

By 1485 Isaac was in Florence, where he was affiliated with the cathedral, the adjacent baptistry, and the household of Lorenzo de' Medici, gathering place for some of the most important humanists of the day. The poet, priest, magician, and Neoplatonic philosopher Marsilio Ficino (see Chapter 6) was there. So was Angelo Poliziano, the dramatist whose retelling of the Orpheus legend had been performed at the court of Mantua in the 1470s by the improvisatory singer Baccio Ugolino. When Lorenzo died in 1492, Isaac set a humanistic poem by Poliziano in memory of their great patron. Each section of the four-voice motet draws upon a cantus-firmus mass that Isaac composed after Lorenzo's death, *Missa Salva nos* (Save Us Mass), the music reworked in conjunction with various ideas in Poliziano's poem. The second section of the motet begins with the tenor standing silent in mute testimony to the departed Lorenzo. ("Laurus tacet" [The laurel is silent], reads the canonic instruction in Petrucci's 1503 print of the piece.) Meanwhile, the bassus part repeats a fragment of a Latin cantus firmus drawn from the *Salva nos* antiphon plainsong, inscribing the Christian liturgy in the context of a secular, humanistic lament. As if this were not enough, the upper part vividly depicts the animated trace of the lightning bolt ("fulminis") that struck down the metaphorical laurel tree (Ex. 8.1).

By the early sixteenth century Isaac had returned north of the Alps, beginning a period of service at the court of Emperor Maximilian I in Innsbruck. Thanks to his association with this powerful Habsburg monarch, Isaac's music was heard in many places, both on account of his travels and thanks to the circulation of his music in manuscript and print. In 1508 the Cathedral of Konstanz,

Example 8.1: *Heinrich Isaac,* Quis dabit capiti meo aquam?, *mm. 65–71. From* Anthology of Renaissance Music, *ed. Allan W. Atlas (New York: W. W. Norton, 1998), p. 168.*

The laurel by rough lightning
May he rest in peace

near the modern border with Switzerland, commissioned Isaac to compose a complete cycle of Mass Propers (the changing melodies and texts, in contrast to the fixed Mass Ordinary so often used in tenor cantus-firmus settings) for the liturgical year. Eventually printed in the 1550s, long after Isaac's death, the three-volume *Choralis Constantinus* (Choral Music of Constance) is a monument of Renaissance vocal polyphony. Not until the time of William Byrd, in the early 1600s, did another Renaissance composer attempt so complete a set for the Christian Mass (see Chapter 11).

Thus in Heinrich Isaac we see a worthy counterpart to Josquin's "perfect art." He was a prolific composer of deeply expressive music, every bit as comfortable with the latest fashions of humanist verse as with the old traditions of cantus firmus and counterpoint. If Gian de Artiganova was prepared to see Josquin as simply one of several good candidates for the Ferrarese chapel, perhaps we should too, resisting the urge to assimilate him to the ready image of an exceptional figure who stands out from his age in all respects. Yet as it happened, Josquin's aura of prestige won out, and by the spring of 1503 he had taken up a post at Duke Ercole's court.

THE JOSQUIN "BRAND"

Whether the duke really thought of Josquin as the metaphorical, perfecting crown imagined by Girolamo we cannot say. Nor can we say whether Josquin needed much prompting to compose a tenor mass, the *Missa Hercules Dux Ferrarie* (Ercole, Duke of Ferrara Mass), in which the duke's name and title were reworked as a *soggetto cavato*—a melody "carved out" of the text by mapping each vowel onto a corresponding tone from the old solmization system (Ex. 8.2). It must have been considered quite

Example 8.2: *Josquin des Prez*, Missa Hercules Dux Ferrarie, *Kyrie, mm. 1–8. From Josquin des Prez*, Masses Based on Solmisation Themes, *ed. James Haar and Lewis Lockwood, New Josquin Edition, 11 (Utrecht: Koninklijke Vereniging voor Nederlandse Muziekgeschiedenis, 2002), 2.*

Lord, have mercy

an honor to have one's name transformed in this way. When manuscript copies of the mass were prepared—almost certainly without Josquin's knowledge—for presentation to other princely patrons by scribes of the Netherlands Habsburg court during the early sixteenth century, the cantus firmus was deftly rebadged with the names of new recipients: "Philippus Rex Castillie" (Philip the Fair, a Habsburg prince) and "Fridericus Dux Saxsonie" (Imperial Elector Frederick the Wise, an ally of the Habsburg dynasty). No matter that the musical syllables no longer made any sense with respect to the titles; apparently Josquin's music was quite literally a crown worthy of *any* king. (We'll learn more about the manuscript tradition of Josquin's music in Chapter 9.)

For those who lacked the resources to hire Josquin or to commission a personalized copy of one of his compositions, merely associating oneself with his music was irresistible. In Baldassare Castiglione's popular *Book of the Courtier* (1528), which we discussed in Chapter 7, we find a story about the Josquin "brand" as a lesson about the fickleness of aesthetic judgment and the tendency of even the most learned courtiers to rely on the opinions of others as a guide to what was worthy and what was not. "It is not long ago," Federico Fregoso complains,

> that certain verses were presented here as being [Jacopo] Sannazaro's, and they seemed most excellent to everyone and were praised with exclamations and marvel; then when it was known for certain that the verses were by someone else, they at once sank in reputation and were found to be less than mediocre. And a certain motet that was sung before the Duchess [of Urbino] pleased no one and was thought not good until it was known to be by Josquin des Prez. What clearer proof of the weight of opinion could you wish for?

Federico's taunt reminds us of how dependent listeners of the day were on the judgments implied when a work came to them under Josquin's name. Prior to his move to Ferrara, after all, even Duke Ercole could rely only on what his musical advisors told him about the authorship of pieces that came to court. When Bartolomeo de' Cavalieri, Ercole's ambassador to the court of France, wrote to the duke in 1501, he noted that one of the duke's other singers, Johannes Ghiselin, "is sending a new work which he says is by Josquin," who had recently been seen at the chateau of Blois. We, like the duke, must assume that Ghiselin knew what he had, and that he had good reason to make sure that the duke got the genuine article. Things must have been tougher for singers without direct access to Josquin, for Castiglione's imagined courtiers, and for the growing number of music lovers who wanted to draw close to the perfection of Josquin's art.

JOSQUIN, PETRUCCI, AND MUSIC PRINTING

In the years before 1500, Josquin's music would have passed from hand to hand through manuscripts. By the early sixteenth century, printed music books offered another venue for the distribution of music. Not surprisingly, Josquin's music quickly became a selling point and a way for printers to establish credibility with readers. His *Ave Maria . . . virgo serena* took pride of place in Ottaviano Petrucci's very first book of polyphonic motets. Not long afterwards, Petrucci used Josquin's music to inaugurate a new series of polyphonic masses, each devoted to the works of a particular composer. This first set was entitled simply *Misse Josquin* (Josquin Masses), as if prospective buyers would have needed no more than Josquin's name to know what they were getting. Indeed, the very first mass in this new series, the *Missa L'homme armé super voces musicales*, reveals a musical mind of astonishing invention, deeply engaged with the old cantus-firmus tradition and with the great lineage of composers of the fifteenth century who took up the *L'homme armé* tune (see Chapter 5 and Anthology 11).

In addition to Josquin's volume, Petrucci subsequently brought out sets of masses by Ghiselin, Antoine Brumel, Jacob Obrecht, Pierre de la Rue, and Alexander Agricola. But Josquin took a commanding lead in the project: two further sets of masses by him were issued by Petrucci, and all three were reprinted more than any other in the series. The second of the Josquin volumes was issued in 1505, shortly after Ercole's death in June. By that time Josquin had left Ferrara for the Church of Notre Dame at Condé in northern France. The *Missa Hercules Dux Ferrarie* appears in this new set, and it has been suggested that Petrucci meant the book as a public tribute to both the composer and his patron. Over the course of the sixteenth century, musicians came to understand prints like these as important vehicles for the preservation of their intentions. Among Josquin's contemporaries, the entrepreneurial Isaac seems already to have sensed the power of the new medium and the new role of composer it helped to shape (see Chapter 9; for an image of one of Josquin's chansons from Petrucci's very first imprint, see Fig. 9.3). Yet despite the circumstantial connections between Josquin, Petrucci, and the court of Ferrara, we have no evidence to suggest that Josquin authorized Petrucci's prints, nor do we know what he thought of them.

Petrucci's colleagues in the relatively new market for printed music books took a while to return to Josquin's music as a focal point in their publications with the same urgency found in the mass sets. But by the 1530s and 1540s interest in Josquin's music underwent a renaissance. German printers in Nuremberg took the lead in issuing masses and motets, including quite a few works that are unlikely to have been composed by Josquin. The introduction to the *Novum et insigne opus musicum* (A New and Outstanding Musical Work, 1537) puts Josquin's name in capital letters at the head of a short list of old masters that includes Isaac and Ludwig Senfl: "All will easily recognize JOSQUIN as the most celebrated hero of the art of music, for he possesses something that is truly inimitable and divine. Nor will a grateful and honest posterity begrudge him this praise."

The idea of Josquin as the venerable figure of a grateful posterity was also projected in the preface to a large retrospective volume of French secular music, the *Livre des mélanges* (Miscellany), published in Paris in 1560. In dedicating this anthology to King Francis II, the poet Pierre de Ronsard imagined Josquin as the founder of a French school of composition, passed down through "disciples" such as Pierre Mouton, Clément Janequin, Claudin de Sermisy, Pierre Certon, and Jacques Arcadelt (SR 38:302; 3/3:24). (In the expanded 1572 edition of the book, Ronsard added a flowery reference to "the now more than divine Orlando [di Lasso].") No matter that there is almost nothing to show that Josquin ever taught any of these composers, most of whom came of age or were born well after his death in 1521. The point for Ronsard was to hold Josquin up as a worthy "ancient" in the field of music, "because the music of the ancients has always been esteemed the most divine, the more so since it was composed in a happier age, less contaminated by the vices which reign in this last age of iron."

And so Josquin's music came to stand in for the lost music of antiquity, the profound effects of which were plain to read in the writings of the classical authorities that Ronsard and his fellow humanists loved to quote. Through Josquin's works, Ronsard suggested, modern music might measure its own worth. By virtue of its connection with the past, this music in turn could serve as "the sign and the mark of those who have shown themselves virtuous, magnanimous, and truly born to feel nothing vulgar." If modern composers can show their connections to the "ancient" Josquin, Ronsard seems to imply, then modern patrons like King Francis II will reveal themselves as counterparts of the great patrons of antiquity. Thus Josquin, although only tangentially connected with France during his lifetime, held out the promise of perfecting the culture of an entire kingdom. Glarean's nostalgic claim was becoming an established fact 39 years after Josquin's death.

BY JOSQUIN OR NOT?

On closer inspection a good number of the motets ascribed to Josquin in the *Novum et insigne opus musicum* and its companion print, the *Secundus tomus novi operis musici* (New Musical Works, Second Volume), are unlikely to be by him. Whoever put Josquin's name to these pieces must have felt that his style was not really beyond imitation after all. In 1540 the Lutheran physician, composer, and editor Georg Forster recalled "that a certain famous man said that Josquin wrote more compositions after his death than during his life." It has been suggested that the famous man in question was Martin Luther, a close associate of Forster's during the doctor's years in Wittenberg. Luther certainly had much respect for the music of Josquin's generation. But no matter its source, Forster's comment should alert us to the fact that as previously unknown works by Josquin emerged during the mid-sixteenth century, some listeners understood that not everything that bore his name was authentic.

Even during Josquin's lifetime musicians sometimes mistook the works of other composers as his own. The stylistic elements in his music were hardly unique and can be found in motets, masses, and secular pieces by many of the composers noted above. Still others probably sought to imitate Josquin's style; after all, the emulation of notable masters, so much a part of the old *maîtrise* system, was widespread among the new generation of humanistic thinkers who sought to revive the eloquence of ancient literatures and oratory. If Josquin could imitate Ockeghem, then surely another composer might imitate Josquin. And since works often circulated in manuscript copies with unreliable or miss-ing attributions, many works have been ascribed to Josquin on no reliable basis.

The problem was evident even a few years after Josquin's death, and even in a place like the Papal Chapel in Rome, where he once sang and composed. The Venetian composer and music theorist Gioseffo Zarlino recalled in his *Istitutioni harmoniche* (Harmonic Foundations) of 1558 how his teacher Adrian Willaert told of the embarrassment that unfolded when he arrived at the chapel during the second decade of the sixteenth century. Members of the ensemble were in the habit of singing a six-voice setting of the sequence *Verbum bonum et suave* (A Good and Pleasant Word) that was preserved in one of their choirbooks under Josquin's name. But according to Zarlino, when Willaert "pointed out that it was in fact his own, as it indeed was, such was their malice, or rather (to put it more generously) their ignorance, that they never wanted to sing it again." As is the case with many stories told about Josquin and his music, there is no easy way for us to test the truth of the tale, although by the time Petrucci printed the piece in 1519 it was correctly attributed to Willaert. Yet it is revealing as an inversion of the anecdote told by Castiglione's Federico Fregoso. If Josquin's name could bring instant approval, it's plausible from the standpoint of sixteenth-century readers that its sudden withdrawal could be a justification for neglect.

During the last two decades in particular, scholars have become increasingly skeptical about many pieces ascribed to Josquin in manuscripts and prints of the fifteenth and sixteenth centuries. There was always reason to question the authorship of works that appeared uniquely in sources prepared at great dis-tances of time or geography from Josquin. But as the example of Willaert's motet demonstrates, sometimes it is hard to tell a reliable source from an unreliable one: Josquin himself, after all, had once been a singer in the Papal Chapel, and we might reasonably imagine that one of their choirbooks ought to have things right. The numbers are truly daunting, for there survive hundreds of differ-ent sources—manuscripts and prints, vocal and instrumental—offering pieces claiming to be by Josquin. Yet the current scholarly consensus is that less than a third of the pieces can really be by him.

As researchers have worked through the documents, assessing the authority of a scribe, conflicting attributions, and each work against stylistic features in works unassailably by Josquin, some favorite compositions suddenly find themselves no longer part of the Josquin work list. The result has been a steady and almost systematic de-attribution of works once accepted as Josquin's. Among these is the rich and expressive motet *Absalon, fili mi* (Absalon, My Son), in which the biblical King David wishes that he could have died in place of his son, "descending to the depths, weeping." The music poignantly portrays the image described in the text as the four voice parts spin dizzyingly through a series of contrapuntal combinations that force the singers to modulate through musical space to a resting point using D♭s and A♭s (Ex. 8.3). Just as King David imagines himself transported to a distant realm, the listener, too, is carried to an unfamiliar place that stands far beyond the confines of the standard musical gamut as it was understood by theorists of the day.

Example 8.3: *Josquin (or Pierre de La Rue), Absalon, fili mi, mm. 78–85. From Josquin des Prez,* Werken, *ed. A. Smijers et al.,* Supplement *(Amsterdam: Vereniging voor Nederlandse Muziekgeschiedenis, 1969), p. 25.*

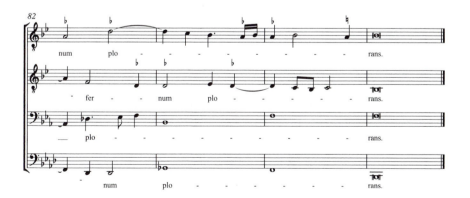

This piece was long cited as an emblem of Josquin's concern to represent and express his chosen texts. Yet scholars now lean toward Pierre de La Rue (ca. 1452–1518) as the more likely author. (As we'll see in Chapter 9, La Rue's music circulated far and wide throughout Europe, largely as a result of his connection with the court of Marguerite of Austria.) The work is certainly no less moving, but we should pause to consider how our understanding of it changes depending on who we believe wrote it. Do we really invest so much in the premise of authorial intent that the work matters only if it is by Josquin? Can we accept that some sixteenth-century musicians took it as Josquin's and held it in higher esteem on this account?

MILLE REGRETS AND THE PROBLEM OF AUTHORSHIP

The four-voice chanson *Mille regrets* (A Thousand Regrets), among the most frequently performed of Josquin's works, offers another test case for the critical and aesthetic problems that swirl around his music. The text draws on a tradition of serious poetry that was fashionable at French-speaking courts around 1500. Josquin set one of these poems by Jean Lemaire de Belges, poet at Marguerite of Austria's court in Brussels. The French music printer Pierre Attaingnant may have been thinking of this poem when he credited *Mille regrets* to "J. lemaire" in an anthology of chansons he issued in 1533 (see Chapter 10). Yet the poem and the setting are plainly not part of this old courtly tradition. The poem is not in one of the *formes fixes* so fashionable throughout the fifteenth century, and the musical style is much more consistently chordal than anything heard in the old repertory, or indeed among Josquin's other French secular songs.

Mille regrets was first credited to Josquin in an intabulation for vihuela (a kind of Spanish guitar) by Luys de Narváez in 1538. The Antwerp printer Tielman Susato issued the now-familiar four-voice version in a chanson album of 1549, where it was followed by his own setting of a poetic "response" that reworked the rhymes and themes of the original poem in a competitive reaction that was fashionable among midcentury composers. Susato also published an arrangement of the chanson for three voices, a favorite texture for domestic music-making in the mid-sixteenth century. In 1546 Pierre Phalèse had arranged it as a lute pavane, which Susato reprinted five years later. Each of these versions was credited to Josquin, although each in its own way reflected fashions of music-making that arose after his death.

Mille regrets has been widely played, recorded, and transcribed in modern editions. But as scholars turned a sharper eye to Josquin's work list, the ascription suddenly seemed less secure. There is no early manuscript or printed source that can be traced to Josquin's orbit, and *Mille regrets* seems quite unlike the chansons for which Josquin's authorship is unassailable. Those pieces typically rely on tunes borrowed from popular urban traditions or other composers active around 1500; *Mille regrets* does not work in this way. Josquin's other chansons bristle with canons, imitative textures, and other contrapuntal writing; *Mille regrets* is characterized by quiet, homorhythmic writing and frequent cadences. Should we view it as a late work that experimented with new fashions? Or as music that was only associated with our composer through a posthumous source tradition?

JOSQUIN DES PREZ OR NOT?

At the same time that scholars interrogated style and sources with new rigor, they also returned to the documentary record of Josquin's life in an effort to understand his development as a composer and his place in music history. This work, too, has resulted in some startling revisions in recent years. Since the publication of an important two-volume study of Josquin's life and work by Helmuth Osthoff in the 1960s, the accepted version of his biography has undergone a number of radical changes. For an eye-opening exercise, simply consider the two very different stories of his life and work lists that appear in the first (1980) and second (2001) editions of the *New Grove Dictionary of Music and Musicians*. Indeed, a recent volume devoted to Josquin's life and works, the *Josquin Companion*, edited by Richard Sherr (2000), contains two biographical chronologies: "Josquin des Prez" and "Not Josquin des Prez." Another new and definitive biography by David Fallows includes two appendices: "Musicians Called Josquin and Cognates" and "Some People Called Desprez or Similar."

At first glance, the broad outline of Josquin's life seems to have changed rather little. He was born in northern France, possibly in or around Condé-sur-l'Escaut, where he also lived for roughly the last 15 years of his life, following his departure from Ferrara in 1504. All of this seems quite secure and beyond dispute. Thanks to new work in the archives, however, the story of Josquin's life between these two poles has changed considerably. For years it was assumed that he was born about 1440; now that date seems to have been too early by a decade or even two. For years, too, scholars assumed that the Josquin mentioned in the pay records of the Cathedral of Milan during the 1470s was our composer, but that seems to have been a case of mistaken identity. Josquin des Prez (he was also called Jossequin Lebloitte) was indeed in Milan, first as a member of the household of Cardinal Ascanio Sforza in 1484–85 and then as a member of the chapel of Lodovico Sforza of Milan for a few years starting in 1489. But he was not a member of the cathedral choir in Milan, nor was he in that city early enough to have been a central figure in the creation of a new musical style heard in works by other composers there in the 1470s, such as Loyset Compère and Gaspar van Weerbeke. As it happens, Josquin's *Ave Maria . . . virgo serena* is a good example of this new style of motet, though it is preserved in a Milanese source only after 1500. It now seems to be a reflection of the musical experiments undertaken there rather than an early example of them. All of this has obliged scholars to step back from received wisdom and question the claims made about Josquin's originality and his place among his contemporaries. It is the sort of insight that requires us to question the stories we tell as historians.

After Milan, Josquin's next regular positions were with the Papal Chapel during the early 1490s and at the court of Ferrara in 1503–1504. Like other singers of the day, Josquin was highly mobile: he was spotted with the French royal court at Blois in 1501 by Ercole's agents, among others. Further archival sleuthing has complicated the accepted picture of Josquin's life in still other ways: news that he was in the household of René d'Anjou in France during the late 1470s; a long series of papal documents connecting him with benefices in churches and territories in northern France; and possible reports of him at the courts of Hungary, Mantua, and the Habsburg Netherlands. Very recently a careful examination of Renaissance graffiti on a long-hidden wall at the Sistine Chapel revealed the name "Josquin," quite possibly scratched there by the composer himself! Something of the same spirit of historical revision now applies to a well-known woodcut portrait published in 1611, nearly a hundred years after the composer's death. Many scholars had serious doubts that it was a very accurate portrayal of the musician it claimed to represent. Careful work in the archives now reveals that it was copied from a prized portrait of Josquin once owned by a priest who lived in Brussels during the first half of the sixteenth century. It may indeed be the closest likeness we have of the composer (Fig. 8.1).

IOSQVINVS PRATENSIS.

Figure 8.1: *Portrait of Josquin, from Petrus Opmeer,* Opus chronographicum *(1611), based on a now lost painting from a Brussels church*

JOSQUIN'S PUPILS, REAL OR IMAGINED?

Despite these discoveries, however, we are still ignorant of many details of Josquin's life and works, including where he had his earliest musical training, who his teachers were, and whether he had any students. The archives are largely silent on these questions, probably for the same reason that they tend to say relatively little about individual works and why they were composed and copied. But over the course of the sixteenth century, musicians started to tell stories about Josquin's character, teachings, and the circumstances behind individual compositions. Scholars have understandably been fairly skeptical about these tales, for they often seem to serve the interests of the teller rather than the reader's need to have the truth of the matter from an independent witness. It seems fairly obvious, for instance, that the list of Josquin's "disciples" offered in Ronsard's preface to the *Livre des mélanges* cannot have been meant in any literal sense of a master–pupil relationship. But its figurative meaning allowed French audiences, above all King Francis II, to see the chansons assembled there as part of a lineage of prestige stretching back to a golden past that eclipsed "this last age of iron."

Still others insisted that their connections with Josquin were genuine and direct. Among them was the Protestant schoolmaster Adrian Petit Coclico (1499/1500–1562), whose *Compendium musices* (Musical Compendium, 1552) was intended for German youth "ignorant of the traditions of music" (see Chapter 2). Coclico wasted no time in establishing his own impeccable credentials by citing an apprenticeship with Josquin whenever possible. "As a mere boy," he relates, "I was entrusted to the protection of the most noble musician Josquin, where, when I had perceived those elementary precepts of our art, incidentally, from no book, I began at once to sing and in singing to observe those things with which today many precepts deal, and to form my song and all my models after his example." It is more than a little ironic that Coclico should have tried to promote a book about how to sing, improvise, and compose by insisting that his own formation took place under Josquin's personal guidance and "from no book." There is nothing in the record of Coclico's or Josquin's lives that would substantiate the connection between them. But Coclico's readers in mid-sixteenth-century Nuremberg would have had no way to know otherwise. Perhaps they allowed themselves to be taken in by Coclico's claims. The idea of joining so noble a tradition would certainly have motivated them to learn.

Coclico's claim both aligns with and contradicts other approaches promoted in Josquin's name. He insisted that Josquin's method stressed practice over concept, and action over premeditation. "My teacher, Josquin des Prez," Coclico recalls, "never rehearsed or wrote out any musical procedures, yet in a short time made perfect musicians, since he did not hold his students back in long and frivolous precepts, but taught precepts in a few words at the same time as singing through exercise and practice." Yet a reader of Glarean's *Dodecachordon* (1547) would have taken away a very different impression of Josquin's working methods, in particular

> his diligence in emending his works. For those who have known him say that he brought his things forth with much hesitation and with correc- tions of all sorts, and that he gave no composition to the public unless he had kept it by him for several years, the opposite of what we said Jacob Obrecht is reported to have done. Hence some not inappropriately main- tain that the one may justly be compared to Virgil, the other to Ovid. (SR 70:430–31; 3/35:152–53)

Glarean makes no claim of personal knowledge of Josquin, although his account bears out the reports of "those who have known him."

RECONSIDERING JOSQUIN'S GENIUS

We might resolve the tension between Glarean's and Coclico's claims in vari- ous ways. Perhaps they were dealing with different aspects of music-making (singing in one case, and distributing written music in the other). Or maybe they were simply two different but equally unreliable witnesses whose stories about Josquin's methods ought to be discounted in the way we now discount so many of the falsely attributed works that appear in sources of the period. But even if they are tall tales, these stories are in some ways revealing of the attitudes of musi- cians who attempted to come to terms with music that seemed too important for them to ignore, yet was almost impossible to explain. To the extent that we suc- ceed in brushing aside such reports in our search for an authentic and unmedi- ated knowledge of Josquin and his music, we risk creating a "truthful" image of the man and his music that would nevertheless be largely unrecognizable to his contemporaries. One music historian has recently put the predicament before us in compelling terms:

> No creative individual can be seen as totally distinct from the attitudes and perceptions of his contemporaries. When it comes to Josquin's per- ception of himself (and this is as "real" a Josquin as one might ever hope to recover) he was, in a real sense, his own contemporary. If others could misremember things about him, if they could expect him to behave in certain ways, if they could revise, rearrange, or miscopy his works, and tell exaggerated but flattering anecdotes about him, then so, of course, could he. Surgically to remove such attitudes and perceptions in pursuit of the ultimate privacy of Josquin's creative mind is to divide the com- poser against his contemporaries, and ultimately against himself.

This insight encourages us to understand the many statements about Josquin as manifestations of viewpoints in which his patrons, listeners, and fellow musicians were themselves inescapably enmeshed. Paramount among these are the ways in which Josquin was portrayed as hard to manage, unpredictable, and transgressive. Gian de Artiganova, we should recall, warned Duke Ercole about the challenges of working with Josquin: He demanded a high salary, was not easy to get along with, and composed according to his own schedule and needs. It is entirely possible that all of these things were true about Josquin. But it is also interesting to note how assumptions about his personal demeanor spill over into assessments of his works. Glarean, for instance, did not hesitate to point out aspects of Josquin's works that made them no less noteworthy as compositions, but revealed a personality that could not quite contain itself.

A canon from Josquin's *Missa L'homme armé super voces musicales* impresses but also disquiets Glarean. As we saw in Chapter 5, the mass is an extraordinary achievement of design in which the basic cantus-firmus melody appears in a succession of transpositions that cycle through all six syllables (*voces*) of the hexachordal system (*ut, re, mi, fa, sol, la*). A canon in the middle section of the Agnus Dei movement, however, omits the cantus firmus and in its place explores multiple dimensions of musical time rather than space (see Fig. 5.1). Here Josquin prefaced a single notated voice part with three different mensuration signs—an imitative canon in which all three parts begin together but unfold at different rates, while nevertheless producing harmonious combinations.

Josquin was neither the first nor the last composer to produce many voices from one in this way. Ockeghem, as Glarean observes, was famous for writing such works. But Glarean nevertheless worried that "in compositions of this kind, to say frankly what I believe, there is more display of skill than there is enjoyment that truly refreshes the hearing." And while he does not criticize Josquin alone in this regard, the theme of excessive artifice, like "the display of skill," was never far from the surface when he was discussing Josquin's music:

> If the knowledge of twelve modes and of a true musical system had fallen to the lot of this man, considering his natural genius and the acuteness of intellect through which he became esteemed, nature could have produced nothing more august, nothing more magnificent in this art. His talent was so versatile in every way, so equipped by a natural acumen and vigor, that there was nothing in this field which he could not do. But in many instances he lacked a proper measure and a judgment based on knowledge and thus in some places in his songs he did not fully restrain as he ought to have, the impetuosity of a lively talent, although this ordinary fault may be condoned because of the otherwise incomparable gifts of the man.

Talk of "natural genius," "impetuosity," and an inability to "fully restrain" one's talents brings us close to the sort of language we would more likely encounter in an account of musical creativity from the middle years of the nineteenth century than from the sixteenth century. But clearly the cultural codes that understood artistic activity as not easily circumscribed were already circulating long before they became a hallmark of Romantic ideology. The sources and meanings of those codes are too big a topic for us to explore here (see Chapter 6). For now we'll simply note that in Glarean's testimony, Josquin's place in the "perfect art" rests paradoxically on his very inability to fit within the category to which his music aspires. We must put his creative life and works in the context of his many equally able peers and predecessors. We must work to recognize, and sometimes question, the assumptions we bring to the task of understanding the distant past.

The example of Josquin, in short, offers some important lessons about the problems of studying creative figures from the distant past. His career reminds us that history is not simply a chronicle of facts. It is an ongoing process of discovery and explanation. In recent decades scholars have unearthed a great deal of new information about Josquin that has radically transformed our vision of his "already perfect art." The same has been done for several of his illustrious contemporaries, including men like Pierre de la Rue and Heinrich Isaac. The challenge is not simply to sort truth from fiction in search of an accurate chronicle. That kind of history would not be very interesting, as Cicero advised his friend 2,000 years ago, and as the Renaissance readers who encountered his letters came to understand. Equally important is the job of recognizing the modes of explanation that give meaning to the facts. For scholars of the nineteenth century and much of the twentieth, the idea of a "great man" and his creative genius were the prevailing model of explanation. They have had a lasting effect on images of Josquin and his music. As we have discovered, the situation is much more complex than this, both as we have learned to measure Josquin's achievements alongside those of his equally accomplished contemporaries, and as we have come to recognize the interpretive assumptions that stand behind all historical work.

FOR FURTHER READING

Fallows, David, *Josquin* (Turnhout: Brepols, 2009)

Higgins, Paula, "The Apotheosis of Josquin des Prez and Other Mythologies of Musical Genius," *Journal of the American Musicological Society* 57 (2004): 443–510

Lowinsky, Edward E., "Musical Genius—Evolution and Origins of a Concept," *Musical Quarterly* 50 (1964): 321–40 and 476–95

Macey, Patrick, "Galeazzo Maria Sforza and Musical Patronage in Milan: Compère, Weerbeke and Josquin," *Early Music History* 15 (1996): 147–212

Meconi, Honey, "Another Look at Absalon," *Tijdschrift van de Koninklijke Vereniging voor Nederlandse Muziekgeschiedenis* 48 (1998): 3–29

Owens, Jessie Ann, "How Josquin Became Josquin: Reflections on Historiography and Reception," in *Music in Renaissance Cities and Courts: Studies in Honor of Lewis Lockwood*, ed. Jessie Ann Owens and Anthony Cummings, pp. 271–80 (Warren, MI: Harmonie Park Press, 1997)

Sherr, Richard, *The Josquin Companion* (Oxford and New York: Oxford University Press, 2000)

Wegman, Rob C., "'And Josquin Laughed . . .': Josquin and the Composer's Anecdote in the Sixteenth Century," *Journal of Musicology* 17 (1999): 319–57

Wilson, Blake, "Heinrich Isaac among the Florentines," *Journal of Musicology* 23 (2006): 97–152

◎ Additional resources available at wwnorton.com/studyspace

CHAPTER NINE

Scribes, Printers, and Owners

Today's music lovers often play the role of producer, compiling lists of favorite songs, assembling them into sets, and sharing them with friends. A generation ago, before cheap cassette tape decks, CD burners, and iPods opened up the possibilities of making one's own "playlists," listeners would simply have taken the sets included on LP albums or sequences heard on radio broadcasts as beyond their immediate control. Similarly, performing instrumentalists take parts (orchestral, solo, chamber) as self-evident, and would certainly not be expected to copy out or arrange music for their own ensemble. These functions are best left to professionals and scholars, so the modern musical workplace holds.

Circumstances were quite different for musicians and listeners in the fifteenth and sixteenth centuries. In this Chapter we will explore what Renaissance music books looked like, what they contained, who had the resources to produce them, and with what purpose. We'll also see how musicians made use of these books and what interpretive skills they implied or demanded. As we'll discover, we still know surprisingly little about how music was written down, distributed, and collected during this period.

Surviving Renaissance music books reveal a culture poised between the old priorities of the handwritten manuscript and the many possibilities inherent in the new medium of print. They also point to changing roles for music as it spread out from churches and aristocratic settings to private domestic spaces. By the sixteenth century it was not enough simply to patronize or study music. Musical literacy was increasingly a matter of civility, a primary means through which aspiring gentlemen and women demonstrated their familiarity with the cultural ideal expounded in Castiglione's *Book of the Courtier*. The changing technology of writing and print emerged alongside—and may even have encouraged—a new consciousness about what it meant to "own" music, for patrons, collectors, and even composers themselves.

HANDMADE BOOKS

For the musical chaplains of fifteenth-century choirs charged with the observance of various ceremonies of church and state, having legible music books at hand was no less important than having the proper robes to wear or candles for light. Parchment and ink had to be purchased, specialist music scribes compensated, bindings prepared, and books kept safe until needed by singers. Wealthier institutions might have a scribe in house, to keep up with the music needed for new endowments and the unpredictable demands of prelates and princes. Simon Mellet was one such man, serving as a copyist at the Cathedral of Cambrai for about 25 years starting in the 1440s. Mellet's work for the cathedral Chapter overlapped with the time that Guillaume Du Fay was a canon there, and he must have been among the first to see some of the composer's new music. When the priest Michel de Beringhen founded a new plainsong service in honor of the Virgin Mary in 1457 (see Chapter 4), it was Mellet who copied out Du Fay's melodies for the service. Cathedral records give remarkably detailed descriptions of still other music Mellet was asked to copy, including some pieces by Du Fay that are now lost.

Such partnerships between scribes and local choirmasters must have been fairly common at larger institutions. Although other archives are rarely as complete as those of Cambrai, some of the great cathedral music libraries were the work of several decades, revealing not only the profound conservatism of the liturgy but also its gradual transformation. The choirbooks of the cathedral of Treviso (near Venice), for instance, were copied over the course of some 50 years, with volumes organized according to genre, function, and calendar: masses, then Vespers hymns and Magnificats, and finally various motets according to their place in the church year. The Basilica of Santa Barbara in Mantua, founded at the request of Duke Guglielmo Gonzaga during the mid-sixteenth century, had a liturgy that remained distinct from that of official Roman practice. Santa Barbara scribes produced their own set of choirbooks for plainsong and polyphony between the 1560s and the 1630s. A collection of some 100 books for this liturgy survives largely intact in Mantuan archives.

Even in Rome the changing demands of the musical liturgy kept local scribes busy producing new books. Polyphonic music had not been a high priority for papal singers during the early fifteenth century. But as the Sistine Chapel ensemble expanded to include as many as 24 singers in the decades around 1500, the institution commissioned a series of books of polyphonic masses and motets for them to use. They were huge volumes, with notation big enough to be seen by the entire ensemble gathered around a lectern. By the middle years of the sixteenth century, the scribe's task could occupy an entire career: Johannes Parvus was chief copyist and music editor at the Sistine Chapel between the 1530s and the 1580s. Similar long-term projects were undertaken at the ducal court of Bavaria at Munich, where Franz Flori was principal copyist from the 1560s until his death in 1588, a period that coincided with Orlando di Lasso's tenure as court composer and chapel master. Across the Atlantic, the calligraphic talents of scribes in New Spain, some of whom were almost certainly from local Amerindian families, were put to use producing books of plainsong and polyphony for the cathedrals of growing imperial capitals like Bogotá, Mexico City, and Guatemala City (see Chapter 13).

Parvus and his Roman colleagues benefited from the papal court's unique position as a cultural crossroads. In books prepared for the Sistine Chapel, we find an unusually broad range of works (chiefly masses and motets) by composers active across Europe, including not only the Italian peninsula but also France and the Habsburg Netherlands. Some of these pieces must have come to Rome in the luggage of the singers recruited for the chapel. Others might have been supplied by contacts among the households of the cardinals in and around the papal curia, most of whom came from Europe's leading aristocratic families. Yet thanks to a remarkable alignment of princely encouragement and a craftsman's bold initiative, music manuscripts produced in the northwest corner of the Continent near Brussels during the late fifteenth and early sixteenth centuries became luxury export goods of unrivaled calligraphic quality and musical importance. (For a pair of facing pages from one of the books produced there, see Fig. 9.1.)

THE ALAMIRE WORKSHOP

The man at the center of this court workshop called himself Petrus Alamire (ca. 1470–1536), a surname that puns on a bit of music theory that would have been familiar to any choirboy: The tone A could function as *la*, *mi*, or *re*, depending on its melodic context in one of the three basic hexachords of the old solfege system. Originally from the craft-rich city of Nuremberg, by the 1490s Petrus attached himself to a series of institutions in the Netherlands as a music scribe and purveyor of musical wares. He provided music books to the pious Confraternity of Our Lady at 's-Hertogenbosch and, later, manuscripts to the Church of Our Lady in Antwerp. But by far the most important coup for the enterprising Alamire was his appointment as music scribe in 1509 at the court of Marguerite of Austria in Brussels. Archival records suggest that Alamire's was a wholly remarkable musical life. He supervised the production of several dozen manuscripts of the highest quality. He composed, traded in musical instruments, played mailman for Erasmus of Rotterdam (who was nevertheless unhappy with the slow service!), visited the influential Augsburg banking house of the Fugger brothers, and served occasionally as diplomat and spy, as seems to have been the case in his dealings with King Henry VIII of England.

Thanks to the dynastic and political connections of his Habsburg employers, the manuscripts produced by Alamire's team were sent to prominent recipients across Europe. Unlike the purely functional books assembled by Mellet and Parvus, these luxury presentation volumes were probably intended for display more than performance. Copied on large-format parchment and expertly decorated with ornate calligraphy, many of them also feature colorful painted heraldic emblems or portraits of their recipients. The production of personalized books for export was a well-established craft in this corner of Europe, but these stand out on account of their peculiar contents. A patron who opened a personalized, pocket-sized book of hours (a book of prayers and psalms intended for private devotion) might be understood to read it with a particularly inward gaze. But what purpose ought we to imagine for individual signs of ownership in a book of polyphonic music? These volumes were not simply princely conversation pieces. And yet, if they were used in daily performance by chapel singers employed by their recipients, we have little evidence of it in the form of corrections, annotations, or the usual wear and tear that would come with regular use.

Of course, it is entirely possible that the books served as both visual and acoustical symbols of their recipients' stature. As we learned in our exploration of Josquin's life and reputation, he once built an entire cyclic tenor mass around the musical syllables suggested by the name of his patron, Duke Ercole I of Ferrara (see Chapter 8). When Alamire's assistants copied out Josquin's mass in books prepared for Habsburg patrons and allies, they simply fitted the cantus firmus with new rubrics in honor of Philip the Fair and Imperial Elector Frederick the Wise. Perhaps Philip and Frederick were content with seeing their names in bright red ink beneath the notes. Perhaps they were simply ignorant of the fact that the tenor tones were punning abstractions of Ercole's title and not their own. Or perhaps they knew, but Alamire wanted to let them pretend that Josquin had composed such a piece just for them. In any case the point is clear: Alamire's manuscripts were carefully crafted and shipped off to particular dedicatees, probably with the active encouragement of his Habsburg employers.

Private interests, too, seem to have shaped Alamire's selections for books prepared by his staff. The wealthy banker Raimund Fugger the Elder apparently

Figure 9.1: (a) *The Kyrie from Josquin's* Missa L'homme armé super voces musicales *(see Anthology 11), a manuscript produced in the scriptorium of Petrus Alamire and once owned by Raimund Fugger of Augsburg, superius and tenor parts, fol. 1ᵛ*

commissioned a pair of beautiful manuscripts from Alamire that were devoted exclusively to Josquin's masses, including the original version of the *Missa Hercules Dux Ferrarie*. It is possible that the Augsburg merchant was trying to fill a hole in his vast collection of music and musical instruments. Alamire added to one of the manuscripts an extra page on which he copied out some tricky

Figure 9.1: (b) *Contratenor and bassus parts, fol. 2ʳ*

resolutions to musical canons found in a book of Josquin's masses that had recently been printed by Ottaviano Petrucci in Italy. Petrucci's three-volume set of Josquin's masses was just the sort of thing Fugger would have wanted for his library, and it makes sense that he would have used his connection with Alamire to commission custom-made manuscripts of these pieces from the finest workshop of his day.

THE PIERRE DE LA RUE CONNECTION

How Alamire managed to get his hands on so much of Josquin's music remains something of a mystery. The riddle is not unique to this workshop; in fact, few of the extant sources of Josquin's music can be traced with any certainty to a time and place where the master himself might have been in residence to supervise their copying. In any case, Josquin was never in the regular employ of any Habsburg patron who could have given Alamire ready access to his music. Quite the opposite is true, however, of Josquin's contemporary Pierre de La Rue (ca. 1452–1518), whose career centered on some of the same institutions that supported Alamire's workshop, including the confraternity at 's-Hertogenbosch in the 1480s and 1490s and especially the Netherlands court of Marguerite of Austria, who ruled as regent on behalf of her nephew, the future Emperor Charles V.

Not surprisingly, La Rue's music is abundantly represented in the books prepared under Alamire's supervision, accounting for roughly a third of the 600 compositions in about 50 surviving manuscripts. Five of the books are given over entirely to La Rue's music, his compositions dominate another five, and many of the anonymous compositions in the albums could well be La Rue's work. His music was doubtless held in great esteem at Marguerite's court, which must have been pleased to have its own prestige projected across musical Europe. Of course, in terms of portability Alamire's limited editions pale by comparison with the cheap prints that began to be produced in the mid-sixteenth century. Alamire's scribes nevertheless made La Rue's music available to the finest musical chapels of the day. Recently, thanks to attentive scholarship and fine singing, La Rue's work has recovered some of the international reputation it enjoyed in the prime of Alamire's workshop.

La Rue and Alamire were equally ready to provide music for local consumption. There must once have been much music on paper, such as leaves of single compositions or gatherings of small sets, informally copied down for use by singers and instrumentalists at Marguerite's court. But Marguerite also owned two deluxe chanson albums that can still be seen in the Royal Library in Brussels. One of them, prepared for her by Alamire's scribes, was filled with music and poetry she knew well from her youth at the court of France, as well as much that was written expressly for her. The album is decorated with painted borders featuring garlands of daisies, or "marguerites." On the first two pages of the book, above the opening of La Rue's *Ave sanctissima Maria* (Hail Mary Most Holy), Marguerite's portrait appears opposite that of the Virgin Mary (see Fig. 4.1).

Other works with Latin texts point toward pious remembrances that must have been dear to Marguerite: a lament on the death of her father, Emperor Maximilian I, and a chanson with a tenor that refers to "the death of my brother Philip." Several of the three dozen chansons presented here can also be tied to Marguerite in one way or another: a setting of her own poem *Pour ung jamais* (For One Never); La Rue's settings of poems by the French court poet Octavien de St. Gelais that were in turn written to console her when the French king Charles VIII refused to marry her as promised in 1493; and settings by La Rue and Josquin of poems by Marguerite's own court poet, Jean Lemaire de Belges. The theme of lamentation runs throughout the chansonnier, a pattern that several scholars have interpreted as representing the conventions of mourning appropriate to a woman once rejected and twice widowed.

CHANSONNIERS AND CHOIRBOOKS: FORMATS AND PURPOSES

As we saw in Chapter 3, the manuscript chansonnier was a distinct type of book in the fifteenth century. Its format, contents, and function were quite different from those of the mass and motet choirbooks made for cathedrals and court chapels. Chansonniers and choirbooks alike presented the various polyphonic voice parts separately, unlike the modern multipart scores we use today. But here the similarities quickly end. The choirbooks were massive, upright volumes in which each voice part was situated in its own sector of the page. With the book on a huge lectern and open to a pair of facing pages, each singer could see his part clearly even in a group of two or three to a part: superius and tenor were on the left-hand page, while the altus and bassus were on the right-hand page. Page turns had to be coordinated among the voices, sometimes with verbal reminders such as "Verte folium" (Turn the page). We can see books like these in images of church choirs throughout our period: Figure 3.2 shows the Burgundian court chapel ensemble of the fifteenth century, and Figure 11.2 is an image of the Bavarian court choir at the time of Orlando di Lasso's service there in the sixteenth century.

Chansonniers, in contrast, were often more modest in size, in keeping with the domestic settings for which they must have been intended. Here music would be performed with one musician to a part, or even fewer (recall that virtuosos like Pietrobono were renowned for their ability to sing and play two lines at once). As in choirbooks, each voice appeared in its own particular space upon the page: in three-voice pieces, the superius was on the left-hand page, often above extra poetry for the successive stanzas typical of the texts set to music in this repertory. The tenor and contratenor were piled together on the right-hand page of the opening spread, often with only basic indications of text. (See Figures 3.3 and 4.1 for samples of what these books look like. Many others are available in the online resources accompanying this text. We'll have more to say about the format of partbooks in the section on owners and collectors later.)

This physical evidence might seem to suggest mixed instrumental and vocal performance of the chanson, but in practice the options must have been quite broad, and a few sources are careful to include text for the tenor as well as the superius. If singers were familiar enough with poems to figure out how to perform successive stanzas with the superius part, they surely could have coordinated the words on the left-hand page with the music of the tenor or even contratenor part on the right. In any case, competent musicians of this period were expected to bring considerable interpretive skill to bear on their performances of chansons in particular, supplying necessary *musica ficta* (unwritten accidentals) and finding an appropriate way of fitting words with tones, all while navigating the tricky back-and-forth page turns demanded by some of the formal schemes of the poems. (See Anthology 4 and 5 for discussions of *musica ficta* and text underlay in Du Fay's *Par le regart* and Busnoys' *Ja que li ne s'i attende*, respectively.)

Marguerite's chanson albums stand at the end of a long tradition of manuscripts prepared for highly literate musical readers and recipients. Johannes Tinctoris (ca. 1430–1511) was probably involved in the planning and production of a high-quality book for Beatrice of Aragon, the daughter of his employer, King Ferrante of Naples (see Fig. 3.3 for an image of pages from this source). Like Marguerite's albums, the Mellon Chansonnier presents a mix of secular songs and devotional motets. Where did the repertory come from? We lack convincing evidence that any one of the surviving books was copied directly from another, leading scholars to assume the existence of some kind of reference copies, now lost or destroyed through constant use. Another possibility is that the models were not full books at all but instead small gatherings or fascicles of pieces, not unlike the "signatures" that were assembled to make the books in the first place. And while none of these survive either, we know from scattered references in archives that music often circulated in this way—passed from singer to patron's agent, folded into a letter, rolled into luggage.

As noted in Chapter 3, a letter that Guillaume Du Fay wrote in 1456 to Piero and Giovanni de' Medici hints at the epistolary trade in poetry and music that swirled among leading centers in the path of Du Fay's musical travels. "I have felt encouraged to send you some chansons," he reported, referring to pieces that he had composed at the request of royal officials when he was in France with the duke of Savoy. There is other new music, he explained to the Medici brothers, some set to texts sent to him from the court of Naples. "If you do not have them, be so kind as to let me know and I shall send them to you" (SR 41:311–12; 3/6:33–34). We cannot be sure that patrons like the Medici ever took Du Fay up on the offer to send more music. But it is hard not to imagine that after collecting enough of the separate quires or sheets, the natural thing to do would be to have a local scribe recopy your favorite pieces into a practical and perhaps beautiful album. Poetry certainly circulated in this way. Given the need for legible copies or arrangements suited to the requirements of local ensembles, there is every reason to think it could have been the norm for musical works, too.

MUSIC IN PRINT

The ability to write music down, send it, and assemble it into unique albums was fundamental to the culture of musical manuscripts in the fifteenth century. Such patterns persisted well into the sixteenth century, whenever competent singers and instrumentalists needed to put their ideas down on paper. But even as Alamire's scribes worked on beautiful, one-of-a-kind chansonniers and choirbooks for rich patrons, others sought to create music books for wider distribution by the new means of movable type.

OTTAVIANO PETRUCCI

In 1498 an entrepreneur named Ottaviano Petrucci (1466–1539), whom we met in Chapter 7, was granted a privilege of protection by the Venetian Senate for what he called a "new method" of music printing. Petrucci's projects, which appeared over the course of two decades beginning in 1501, are now heralded as radical innovations. They did in fact inaugurate a new conception of a "book" of printed polyphony, as opposed to a textbook illustrated with music. In many respects, however, the books' format, appearance, and even function emulated those of manuscripts, just as the Bibles printed from movable type by Johannes Gutenberg in Mainz starting in the 1450s tried to look like handwritten texts. The best copies of these Bibles were printed on parchment, and those who could afford it subsequently sent their copies out for illumination by the same specialists who decorated the finest manuscripts with decorated initials that mimic handmade decoration (Fig. 9.2). To be sure, even these deluxe prints cost far less than a comparable handwritten book.

Petrucci's work reflected equal virtuosity. Using techniques employed in the printing of liturgical books in two colors, he devised a way to print mensural polyphony from movable type in multiple impressions: first the staves, then the notes, and finally the text. Later the process was combined into double-impression printing, although this still required no less impressive craftsmanship for its accuracy and legibility. The books emerged in a series of distinctive sets. *Odhecaton A* (One Hundred Songs [Book] A), *Canti B* (Songs [Book] B), and *Canti C* (Songs [Book] C) were large collections of three- and four-voice chansons and a few motets, often minimally texted, representing the fashion for polyphony by northern composers as it had been cultivated in courts like Milan, Mantua, and Ferrara. (Figure 9.3 shows a page from *Odhecaton A*.) There were sets of masses—including, as we have seen, three entire books devoted to Josquin alone—plus albums of motets and lamentations.

Each collection was issued in "partbooks," an affordable format that made good use of expensive paper by sequestering each vocal line in its own printed volume. Large-format choirbooks of printed polyphony were extremely rare throughout the sixteenth century, no doubt on account of the acres of paper they consumed around relatively sparse musical notation. Partbook format was also convenient for domestic performance, suggesting that thanks to Petrucci's new mechanical medium even liturgical genres like masses were sung, heard, and studied in contexts far beyond the courts and churches where such music was originally crafted.

Perhaps the most interesting and influential books to come from Petrucci's musical press, however, were the 11 volumes of frottole he issued between 1504

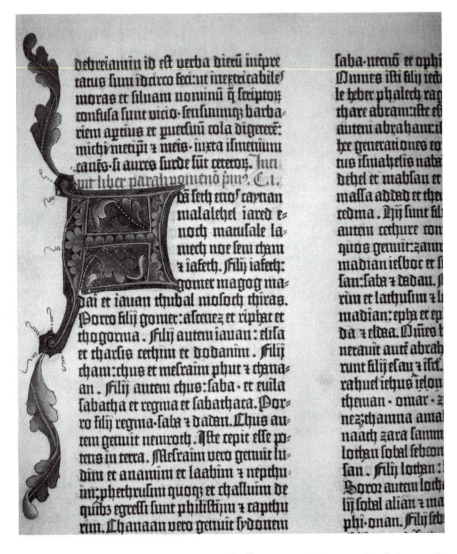

Figure 9.2: *Detail from the Gutenberg Bible (1455), printed on vellum, and with decorated initial*

and 1514. They drew on the literary and musical fashion for Italian song at the music-loving courts of patrons like Isabella d'Este in Mantua. Petrucci's frottole probably appealed to the tastes of amateur singers and players for music of modest difficulty and great lyrical charm. They were easily adapted to different performing forces and ensembles. Some of the books were issued in versions for four voices. (See Figure 7.3 above for a page from one of these volumes.) He also issued three volumes of frottole as solo pieces with lute ac-

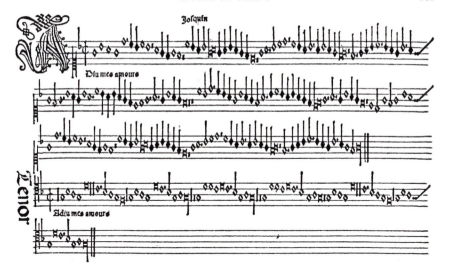

Figure 9.3: *Josquin des Prez,* Adieu mes amours *from Ottaviano Petrucci's* Harmonice musices Odhecaton A *(Venice, 1501), fol. 16ᵛ, showing superius and tenor voice parts*

companiment, with the original altus part omitted and the tenor and bassus parts condensed into instrumental tablature. Somewhat like modern guitar tabs, such notation solves tricky problems of mensural polyphony simply by encoding the music in terms of strings, frets, and fingers, thus providing a shortcut to musical literacy. (Figure 9.6 shows a later set of tablature for lute.) In short, Petrucci's books were designed to appeal to Italian noblemen of the sort presented in Castiglione's *Book of the Courtier* (see Chapter 7), who favored this performance practice for their domestic displays.

When Petrucci applied to the Venetian Senate for a patent to protect his planned investment in type fonts and other materials for his new music books, he had good reason to be anxious. The Venetian book trade was busy and highly competitive. By 1500 some 150 print shops were active in the city, enterprises that by some estimates had already produced over two million books of all types. Even the wealthy citizens of the Venetian republic could not have afforded to buy all of these books, so we must assume that through book fairs, traveling students, and speculators the market for music extended to other cities in Italy and beyond the Alps. In Venice itself, Petrucci's patent barred others from publishing polyphonic music until 1520. Soon both the demand for and the supply of music expanded in Europe's great commercial centers at a remarkable pace. By the 1540s there were active music presses not only in Venice but also in Antwerp, Lyons, Nuremberg, and Paris.

PIERRE ATTAINGNANT AND OTHERS

Each printer seems to have both measured and helped to create a market for his wares by cultivating local literary tastes and by tapping local church or court chapels for repertory. Like Petrucci, they also appealed to local authorities for protection from competition. The earliest privileges were a form of copyright that ensured exclusive authority to print polyphonic music. Although printers surely paid for and benefited from their privileges, the official proclamations, often reproduced in the books themselves, presented these commercial monopolies as a form of public good. "Having received the humble supplication of our well-loved Pierre Attaingnant, printer-bookseller dwelling in the University of Paris," King Francis I in 1531 proclaimed that for the next half-dozen years Attaingnant would have the exclusive right to print all sorts of music by movable type: "masses, motets, hymns, chansons, as well as for the said playing of lutes, flutes, and organs, in large volumes and small, in order to serve the churches, their ministers, and generally all people, and for the very great good, utility, and recreation of the general public" (SR 46:331; 3/1:53).

Armed with his new patent, Attaingnant used the medium of movable type to bring out dozens of music books. There were books of motets arranged in liturgical or thematic sets, volumes of masses, and modest collections of fashionable chansons, just as Venetian printers brought out affordable collections of madrigals and popular villanelle. The chansons appeared both in all-vocal versions for three or four parts and in arrangements for solo voice and lute. (See Chapter 10 for more on Attaingnant's songbooks.) Single-impression printing was now the norm, using type fonts made up of tiny segments of music staff, each with a single note indicating rhythm and pitch. Text underlay also became quite exacting, perhaps reflecting the market among amateur singers for books in which they needed make only a few interpretive decisions of their own. The success of a publication hinged on the technical skills and taste of the music editor. Some of these new print entrepreneurs were musicians, while others hired professionals to select music and proofread the publications.

Later in the sixteenth century, many other musicians took part in commercial ventures like these, often partnering with more-experienced printers in order to bring out works they thought might fill a niche or turn a good profit. Some of the music they sought to publish was new, but often it seemed safer to reissue well-known compositions. The *First Book of Madrigals* of Jacques Arcadelt (? 1507–1568), first issued in Venice in 1538, was a perennial favorite. Over the following 100 years, it was reprinted nearly 50 times by 25 different printers. The Venetian organist and composer Claudio Merulo (1533–1604) took his turn at editing the madrigals for his partner Giorgio Angelieri.

Merulo and his fellow editors rarely explained their craft. But in a preface to his first independent publishing venture in 1566—a republication of a pair of madrigal books by Philippe Verdelot that had originally appeared in the 1530s—Merulo explained how his editorial interventions undid layers of errors introduced by sloppy printers. "Each of you, benign readers, knows that in the frequent printing and reprinting of a work, various grave errors occur." The madrigals of Verdelot, he continued, "have suffered such obvious blemishes that they give indigestion even to mediocre musicians." Merulo set about correcting parallel fifths and octaves, notating *musica ficta* and other accidentals for beginners who might not know how to do so properly, and even adjusting counterpoint by moving some notes from one voice to another. In making these silent corrections, Merulo blurred the boundaries between scribe, editor, composer, and performer. He sought to establish credibility with his readers by claiming to have swept aside errors, "honoring the compositions of Verdelot" even as he made them accessible to musicians of moderate experience.

But how could Merulo claim to know Verdelot's intentions? And was he not simply imposing his own interpretive priorities on behalf of readers who formerly had to take responsibility for decisions about *musica ficta* and other questions of performance practice? Printed texts provide no guarantee of authenticity, despite Merulo's claims to the contrary. Yet faith in the durable, repeatable medium of print prompted Pope Gregory XIII to commission Giovanni Pierluigi da Palestrina (1525/26–1594) and his colleague Annibale Zoilo (ca. 1537–1592) in 1577 to purge the Catholic plainsong liturgy of the "barbarisms, obscurities, contrarieties, and superfluities" that had accrued "as a result of the clumsiness or negligence or even wickedness of the composers, scribes, and printers" (SR 61:375; 3/26:97). Palestrina and Zoilo were unable to complete the project, though it eventually appeared in 1614 as the so-called *Editio Medicaea* (Medicean Edition; see further discussion of this project in Chapter 11). Their efforts remind us that the new medium of print was not only a commercial matter but also an agent of change and authority.

OWNERS AND COLLECTORS: PRINCES, PRIESTS, AND BANKERS

Exactly who bought and used any of these books is a subject of ongoing investigation. In the case of printed books dedicated to a particular patron, we can safely assume that a copy was presented to him or her by the composer or printer. Palestrina, for example, is depicted on the title page in the act of presenting his book to the pope (Fig. 9.4). With markets for new works often untested, and good paper relatively expensive, it made sense to rely on the largess of a wealthy patron to underwrite the cost of publication. Yet we know that by the middle years of the sixteenth century press runs for books of chansons, madrigals, and motets would normally total 500 copies. The churches, as Attaingnant's privilege suggests, might have purchased his collections of sacred music. Archives also offer occasional glimpses of the literate urban officials and tradesmen who wandered into the shops of printer-sellers in search of music books. At the time of his death in 1544, for instance, the personal library of Jean de Badonvillier, a Parisian official, contained a printed collection of masses, two of Attaingnant's chanson anthologies, and printed books of motets by Claudin de Sermisy and Johannes Lupi. The account books of the Florentine bookseller Piero di Giuliano Morosi tell us that in the 1590s his music-buying clients included a customs officer, a leather worker, and a local priest. There must have been many similar customers in places like Antwerp, Lyons, Nuremberg, and the other great commercial centers of Renaissance Europe.

Wealthy merchants often assembled impressive libraries. In Augsburg, not far from Munich, members of the Fugger banking dynasty amassed an impressive collection that included many music prints. Many of these eventually passed into the library of the dukes of Bavaria and subsequently into the present-day Bavarian State Library in Munich. The Augsburg patrician merchant Hans Heinrich Herwart similarly put together a fabulous collection of printed music, including a nearly complete set of the chanson volumes issued by Attaingnant. Such books could have been obtained directly from the publisher with the help of an agent. We also know that books were sold at fairs such as the one held at Frankfurt, where European publishers still regularly converge. Yet individual titles could sometimes linger on shop shelves for decades. Morosi and his Florentine colleagues complained that the flood of inexpensive books from Venice remained in their stockrooms for much longer than they cared, and that customers nevertheless preferred them to the new books they had issued themselves.

Although these books were public offerings, they were destined in many instances for domestic enjoyment, as imagined in an Italian painting of the late sixteenth century, showing a serious family gathered around music books as they sing and play (Fig. 9.5). In Paris, Nicolas du Chemin's chanson series of the 1550s, for example, was printed with pairs of voices on facing pages of each of two partbooks. The design naturally lends itself to use on opposite sides of a small table, with superius and tenor parts facing one side and altus and bassus facing the other. Other sets were issued in four or five

Figure 9.4: *Giovanni Pierluigi da Palestrina presents a book of masses to Pope Julius III, from* Missarum liber primus *(Rome, 1554)*

Figure 9.5: *Leandro da Ponte Bassano,* The Concert *(ca. 1590). Bassano was active in and around Venice during the last quarter of the sixteenth century.*

individual partbooks, but there were also formats that put four voices, sometimes with lute accompaniment, into a single book that could be read from four directions at once when it was open on a table. Figure 9.6 shows music by the English composer John Dowland with parts for voice and lute on the left-hand page, and parts for various viol players arrayed in different directions on the right-hand page.

The wide circulation of printed music books is unimaginable without the basic musical skills to read the works they contain. The legacy of Attaingnant's chansonniers stimulated sufficient public demand to justify the publication of music primers such as Claude Martin's *Elementorum musices practicae* (Fundamental Practices of Music, 1550) or Maximillian Guilliaud's *Rudiments de musique practique* (Foundations of Practical Music, 1554). There were also lute tutors, with instructions on tuning and tablature. And, as we will see in Chapter 12, there were printed how-to books on every aspect of the aspiring amateur's craft, from basic notation to the arts of embellishment and composition. These modest treatises shed some light on the habits and competencies of the readers who used them. Such skills doubtless afforded a point of entry into urban society, as we saw in Chapter 2 in connection with Thomas Morley's *A Plaine and Easie Introduction to Practicall Musicke* of 1597.

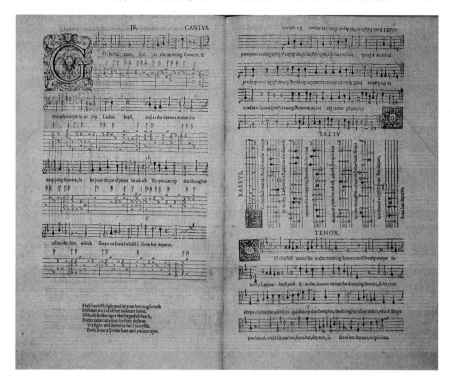

Figure 9.6: *Lute tablature and vocal parts in a single book designed for use around a table, from John Dowland,* First Booke of Songes *(London, 1597)*

COMPOSERS, PRINTERS, AND PUBLICS: WHO OWNED MUSIC?

From the standpoint of modern musicians, it seems self-evident that composers would jump at the chance to publish their works, but the situation for sixteenth-century composers was much more complex. Having one's music printed was not a way to make easy money, in part because authors and composers did not enjoy a clear right of ownership over intangible goods like literary or musical works. (The concept of intellectual property rights wasn't codified in law until the nineteenth century.) They could, of course, sell their work to printers or editors. However, privileges and grants of copyright like those held by Attaingnant and his colleagues were intended to protect the printers' commercial interests as makers of new copies, not the right of authors to determine how a musical work might be presented.

Composers were rarely involved in seeking or receiving a privilege to print their music during the first half of the sixteenth century. In 1538 Costanzo Festa (ca. 1485/90–1545) was granted a privilege by Venetian officials protecting his music from unauthorized publication for a period of ten years. As it happens, only a single book was ever published under this privilege, in circumstances that suggest Festa's powers to have been more narrow than broad: The print in question was issued in Rome rather than in Venice and was prominently emblazoned with his own emblem, suggesting that it was produced on commission and under Festa's direct supervision. In 1544 the Spanish master Cristóbal de Morales (ca. 1500–1553) made a contract with a printer in Rome to publish a book of his polyphonic masses. The composer and printer, according to the contract, were to divide the print run of 525 copies between them. Clearly, this was a commercial venture. The same could be said of the partnership between English composers Thomas Tallis and William Byrd that began in the 1570s, when financial hardship prompted them to petition Queen Elizabeth for a royal patent on the production of printed music books and even ruled music paper. (For more on the spiritual context of their work together, see Chapter 11.)

No composer of the sixteenth century seems to have been more keenly aware than Orlando di Lasso (1532–1594) that print had the power to put reliable musical texts into the hands of performers. The composer of over 1,300 works in every imaginable genre, Lasso collaborated with a long string of prominent music printers in Antwerp, Paris, Nuremberg, Munich, and Venice. By the end of his life, he also enjoyed unprecedented rights that gave him legal authority over the publication of his music in France and in the German-speaking lands ruled from Vienna by the Holy Roman Emperor. Lasso was a long-time employee of the dukes of Bavaria, serving as the master of one of the finest musical chapels of its day (see Fig. 11.2 for an illustration of him directing the ensemble). His reputation as a composer stretched far and wide. During the 1560s and 1570s, a great deal of his French music was issued by the firm of Le Roy and Ballard, official printers to the French royal court. Lasso visited the court briefly in 1571; not long afterward, King Charles IX granted the composer a special authorial privilege that gave him exclusive control over the printing, distribution, and sale of his compositions in France.

It seems likely that Charles IX granted this privilege in the hope of enticing Lasso to leave the Bavarian court and accept a lucrative position with the French royal establishment. The chief effect of his proclamation, however, was to reinforce the independence of composer and printer from the royal household. Now free to choose whichever printer he saw fit, Lasso could assume a new level of control over the distribution of his music—indeed, a new kind of ownership of his works—without ever leaving the comforts of Munich. His experience reflects the changing professional status of the composer, as he (or in exceptional cases she) was transformed from a skilled contrapuntist who was simply the maker of musical materials to the owner of the intellectual content they embodied. This process had its origins nearly a century before, in the generation of Josquin des Prez, Heinrich Isaac, and Pierre de La Rue, when printed music was new.

As we have seen, the rapid development of music printing in the sixteenth century had profound effects on musical life, but it certainly did not make handwritten books obsolete. Musicians in ecclesiastical chapels, courtly chambers, and private households still made their own albums and adapted music for their own needs. But the new medium of print helped to create a burgeoning market for musical ideas. It contributed importantly to the spread of developing genres like the chanson and madrigal. The availability of inexpensive partbooks promoted musical literacy among a growing segment of city dwellers who found in music new modes of entertainment and a measure of their aspiration to the ideals of cultural refinement set forth in Castiglione's influential *Book of the Courtier*. In providing a technical means to present literary or sacred texts in close coordination with musical notes, printing encouraged a new awareness of music as an intellectual property and of the possibility of controlling its effects and purposes. Through figures like Lasso, we can begin to gauge the complex history of the idea of a musical work and what it meant to create, collect, or own one.

FOR FURTHER READING

Alden, Jane, *Songs, Scribes, and Society: The History and Reception of the Loire Valley Chansonniers* (New York: Oxford University Press, 2010)

Bernstein, Jane A., "Financial Arrangements and the Role of Printer and Composer in Sixteenth-Century Italian Music Printing," *Acta musicologica* 63 (1991): 39–56

Brooks, Jeanice, "Jean de Castro, the Pense Partbooks and Musical Culture in Sixteenth-Century Lyons," *Early Music History* 11 (1992): 91–149

Carter, Tim, "Music-Selling in Late Sixteenth-Century Florence: The Bookshop of Piero di Giuliano Morosi," *Music & Letters* 70 (1989): 483–504

Haar, James, "Orlando di Lasso: Composer and Print Entrepreneur," in *Music and the Cultures of Print*, ed. Kate Van Orden, pp. 125–62 (New York: General Music Publishing Co., 2000)

Meconi, Honey, "Margaret of Austria, Visual Representation, and Brussels, Royal Library, Ms. 228," *Journal of the Alamire Foundation* 2 (2010): 11–36

Shephard, Tim, "Constructing Identities in a Music Manuscript: The Medici Codex as a Gift," *Renaissance Quarterly* 63 (2010): 84–127

ⓒ Additional resources available at wwnorton.com/studyspace

PART IV

After 1500

The political, intellectual, and technological transformations put in motion in the years around 1500 were keenly felt throughout the ensuing century. For literary critics like Pietro Bembo in Italy and Joachim du Bellay in France, writing in the vernacular could be every bit as eloquent as the classical Latin of Cicero, Horace, or Quintilian. Experimenting with new forms and genres, writers of the sixteenth century cultivated a new self-consciousness about style—how to find just the right word or turn of phrase for the job. Dozens of poets imitated the language of the fourteenth-century Tuscan poet Petrarch. Others, like Giovanni Battista Guarini, broke down barriers between tragedy, comedy, and the pastoral.

Musicians responded to these new attitudes with an equally bold set of experiments. Some mixed the sonic hallmarks of different genres, as when the popular three-voice villanella was joined to the serious five-voice madrigal. Others developed new musical resources that seemed to fit the vibrant moods and statements of the poetry they set. As we will discover in Chapter 10, their musical response to these lyrics could be deftly contrapuntal, strikingly chromatic, or so declamatory as to obliterate the border between speech and song.

Musicians who practiced their craft in the service of religion were also confronted with new constraints and choices. When Martin Luther posted his 95 theses in 1517, arguing against the papal tradition of selling indulgences that would deliver the souls of donors from purgatory, he sought to reform established Christian practice, not to break with it. Yet over the next two decades he was obliged to do just that. The Catholic hierarchy first demanded that he recant his critiques, then excommunicated him when he refused. Protestant reformers like Luther and Jean Calvin often differed sharply on particular points of doctrine. But they were united in their emphasis on the vernacular: they saw to it that the Bible and other religious texts were translated into German, French, or English, and in general sought to empower congregants to participate in religious services through the singing of hymns in those languages. Popular piety had always been an important component of spiritual practice in Europe; now it was a Protestant priority. During the middle decades of the century, musicians gradually filled the void, producing books of monophonic hymns for use in church and modest polyphonic settings for use at home.

The Council of Trent, an ecumenical gathering of cardinals and Catholic theologians from across Europe that lasted from 1545 to 1563, promulgated a series of stern rulings that tried to bring all aspects of worship into line with official doctrine. The movement they started is known as the Catholic Counter-Reformation. Composers who worked in Catholic chapels were admonished to attend carefully to the sacred texts they set, and to present important articles of creed in ways that would be clear for all to understand. The Latin motets and elaborate polyphonic masses they produced might seem far removed from the intimate congregational hymns crafted for Protestant worshippers. But, as we will learn in Chapter 11, there is often more that unites the spiritual aims of these musicians than divides them.

Meanwhile, the sixteenth century witnessed an explosion of printing that transported music across boundaries of geography, class, and context with dizzying speed. The availability of printed music books both encouraged and depended on new musical literacy, especially among amateurs. Enterprising professionals produced all kinds of books that helped aspiring amateurs read music, master an instrument, improvise, and even compose, as discussed in Chapter 12. Through their efforts music moved rapidly from one context to the next: Italian madrigals by composers like Luca Marenzio were fashionable in English households; the chansons and motets of Orlando di Lasso were known throughout France, even though Lasso himself rarely left the Bavarian court in Munich. The result was a new sense that individual composers had something unique to say. One could imitate, adapt, and rework their music, but it preserved their authorial stamp.

As European conquest extended through the New World, Africa, and Asia, musical horizons expanded still further. As we will discover in Chapter 13, the encounter with different cultures prompted many to reflect on the purposes and meaning of music, both at home and abroad. Musical expression could be taken as a sign of civility. It could also be taken as a sign of *incivility*, and thus was enlisted as an agent of acculturation and conquest. Arriving at last at the chronological endpoint of our study, we will pause in Chapter 14 to examine some radical experiments of the years around 1600. In examples by Carlo Gesualdo, Claudio Monteverdi, and Claude Le Jeune, we will discover how musicians tested the limits of the idioms they inherited, even as they looked back on the history that made them possible.

CHAPTER TEN

Music and the Literary Imagination

L ove, in all its varied forms, is the prevailing subject of the vernacular poems set to music during the sixteenth century. These lyrics present a variety of poetic themes, forms, and language. How different composers responded to the poems tells us a great deal about their habits as readers. In situating these songs in the wider story of Renaissance humanism and its abiding concern for language and expression, we will focus on a small selection of French chansons and Italian or English madrigals by composers like Claudin de Sermisy, Clément Janequin, Jacques Arcadelt, Adrian Willaert, Orlando di Lasso, and Luca Marenzio. We will explore the relationship of rhyme and phrasing, repetition and refrain, and the ways in which music represents the ideas, images, and conditions suggested by the poetry. These works are especially rich in musical ideas. They are also important for what they reveal about the relationships among composers, performers, and audiences for secular vocal music in a period of profound cultural change.

PIERRE ATTAINGNANT'S SONGBOOKS

The French chanson of the second quarter of the sixteenth century offers a good place for us to begin. Chanson composers of the later fifteenth century, as we learned in our discussion of Princess Beatrice's chansonnier (Chapter 3), normally confined themselves to the courtly *formes fixes*, with their highly conventionalized language and elaborate refrain schemes. Composers of the sixteenth century were no less bound to a set of literary and musical conventions than their predecessors, but their works are nevertheless notable for the strong contrast with approaches of the past. Their chosen lyrics carefully avoid the complicated refrains of the formes fixes, instead following simple pairs of rhymed verses arranged in poems of four, eight, and sometimes ten lines. The music for these lyrics is also a model of clarity in comparison with the older chansons, featuring balanced, parallel phrasing for rhymed lines and tuneful, often syllabic melodies. Musical textures are often homorhythmic, and while there are no refrain forms per se, there is often a formal economy to the music, with the same phrase or two being used to support successive pairs of rhymed lines, or perhaps brought back to round out the song at the end.

As we saw in Chapter 9, the sixteenth-century chanson is also notable for the ways in which it was mediated by the relatively new medium of print. Like poems, music often circulated in albums consisting of many independent works. Scribes had often played the role of editor in the production of chansonniers for individual users, as in the case of Beatrice's songbook and the albums produced for the court of Marguerite of Austria around 1500. With the advent of music printing in the early sixteenth century, the role of editor took on new importance in the formation of tastes among an anonymous public. The Parisian printer Pierre Attaingnant (ca. 1494–1551/52) was among the most important of these new makers of musical readership, particularly for the chanson. Over two decades, beginning almost simultaneously with the founding of the firm and its receipt of a royal patent of commercial protection in 1528 (quoted in Chapter 9 in a version from 1531), Attaingnant and his colleagues produced several dozen chansonniers—sets of neatly printed partbooks of two or three dozen songs each.

Attaingnant's output is often closely identified with the so-called Parisian chanson, a light and lyrical four-part composition typified by *Jouissance vous donnerai* (Pleasure I Will Give You, Ex. 10.1) by Claudin de Sermisy (ca. 1490–1562). In fact, Attaingnant's chansonniers are far more varied than the stereotype would allow. There are older works as well as new ones, pieces from the provinces no less than from Paris, and works by composers active at cathedrals and as professional arrangers as well as by those who worked for aristocratic patrons. Each collection contained some 30 chansons by composers associated with the royal court like Sermisy and Pierre Certon, men from cathedrals of provincial France like Guillaume le Heurteur from Tours, and even composers like Nicholas Gombert and Pierre de Manchicourt, associated with the courts and churches of the Habsburg Netherlands.

Example 10.1: *Claudin de Sermisy,* Jouissance vous donnerai, *mm. 1–7. From* The Oxford Book of French Chansons, *ed. Frank Dobbins (Oxford: Oxford University Press, 1987), p. 36.*

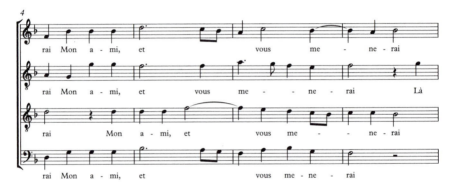

Pleasure I will give you, my beloved, and you will take

Institutional affiliation and geography certainly bear some relation to musical style in this repertory. The works of northern composers like Gombert and Manchicourt are in general much more contrapuntal than those by composers active at the French royal court. But in other respects the conventional dichotomy between the Parisian and Franco-Flemish schools of composition is too simplistic. This view of style largely ignores an equally important repertory of chansons published in Lyons, which reveals a preference for longer poems than those typically found among the Attaingnant prints. Perhaps more important, the conventional view of the "'Parisian'" chanson glosses over special generic conventions dictated by literary topic, poetic language, prosody, and verse form. Two pieces from Attaingnant's collections will help us measure the range of possibilities and the responses they engendered.

MILLE REGRETS AND THE SOUNDS OF LOVE SICKNESS

The text of *Mille regrets*, which appeared in an Attaingnant collection of 1533, is brief and to the point. In essence, it says: "I'm filled with pain now that you're gone. I'm going to end it all." Renaissance physicians would have said that the speaker is suffering from "erotic melancholy," a condition of physical suffering, even the urge to flee from life itself, that was brought on by an absence. It's the memory of the beloved that caused the problem, they would explain, as signaled by the insistent repetition of the falling "tear motive" (see Chapter 6).

Mille regrets de vous abandonner
Et d'élonger votre face amoureuse;
J'ai si grand dueil et peine douloureuse
Qu'on me verra brief mes jours déffiner.

A thousand regrets in leaving you,
And in losing sight of your loving look;
I have such great sorrow and sad pain
That one can see how my days are numbered.

Poems like this were fashionable around 1500, and the language would probably have seemed a little dated to Attaingnant's French readers in the 1530s. As we discovered in Chapter 8, some modern scholars have serious doubts about Josquin des Prez's authorship of the piece. Whoever the composer was, he or she sought clear alignment of rhythm, prosody, and musical line, with each line of poetry corresponding to a melodic phrase. Countless Renaissance chansons begin with the dactylic rhythmic motto (long-short-short), often on repeated notes, that serves as a hallmark of the genre. This stereotypical opening probably reflects the composers' compulsion to observe the medial coupe, or pause, that divides the first segment of four syllables from the second segment in ten-syllable (decasyllabic) French verse of the day. In many of these French chansons, composers preferred to treat the opening segment of the line syllabically, then allow the second segment more musical room, with a melismatic flourish culminating in a syncopated cadence. The composer of *Mille regrets* has taken the opposite approach: it's the first segment that carries the expansive weight of each line, while the second segment is more syllabic and declamatory. As it happens, this "inversion" of the usual sort of lyrical profile fits nicely with other aspects of the piece, with its obsessive deferral and delay of closure. The style and form accord perfectly with the speaker's inner condition. (See Anthology 15 for a more detailed discussion.)

JANEQUIN'S *MARTIN MENOIT* AND THE SOUNDS OF DESIRE

Serious songs like *Mille regrets* had a long history, expressing the sufferings of unrequited love in its noblest forms. The serious musical idiom of the chanson was even capable of expressing chastity no less than desire, as we will discover in our discussion of *Susanne un jour* in Chapter 11 and Anthology 23. Yet already in Attaingnant's album readers could find pieces that take as their subject matter the exploits of ill-suited lovers, buffoons, and errant priests. Inverting just about all of the conventional conceits of serious love, these poems portray an upside-down world that echoes the scenarios of French satire and *fabliaux* (oral tales, both moral and funny) of the period. Avoiding the closed formal designs and long lyrical lines favored by Sermisy and Certon, composers who set these lighter texts preferred a style that was declamatory, animated, and full of rapid shifts of energy.

With its imitations of everyday speech, crude noises, and busy, repetitive melodic motives, *Martin menoit* by Clément Janequin (ca. 1485–1558), printed by Attaingnant in 1535, fits the type perfectly. The text by the French court poet Clément Marot is far removed from the idealized love-longing of his serious lyrics. It is the story of a peasant couple, Martin and his beloved Alice, as they walk their pig to market. She proposes a quick fling, and soon the pastoral scene degenerates into a bawdy roll in the grass. Tying the prized pig to her leg for safekeeping—in the sixteenth century it was a peasant's most valuable possession—Alice is quite literally "carried away" as she and Martin mate.

Martin menoit son pourceau au marché
Avec Alix qui en la plaine grande
Pria Martin de faire le péché
De l'ung sur l'aultre, et Martin luy demande:
"Et qui tiendroit nostre pourceau, friande?"
"Qui," dist Alix, "bon remede il y a."
Lors le pourceau a sa jambe lya
Et Martin juche qui lourdement engaine
Le porc eut peur et Alix s'escria:
"Serre Martin, nostre pourceau m'entraine."

Martin was taking his pig to market
With Alice, who when right in the open
Begged Martin to commit the sin
Of lying one with another, but Martin asked:
"And who will hold onto our pig, my dear?"
To which Alice replied, "There's an easy solution."
Then she tied the piglet to her leg.

But when Martin mounted and was heavily engaged
The pig took fright and Alice cried:
"Push, Martin, our piglet is dragging me off."

Love is here reduced to its elemental physicality, in contrast to the emotional or spiritual pangs that courtly poetry rehearses. Janequin's musical response likewise attends more to what we hear and see than to anything felt or thought. Martin's question in line 5 of the text, for instance, is clearly set off from the line before it, with which it rhymes. Even before he can finish his question, moreover, Janequin has Alice eagerly interrupt him with her simple solution (Anthology 16).

For Janequin and other composers of the mid-sixteenth century, the narrative themes and exclamatory dialogue found in this kind of poetry suggest a style that tends toward contrast and animation for convincing effect. These chansons are dramatic in their tendency to imitate both the energy of narrated action and the recitational profile of speech. Turning away from the old priorities of linear counterpoint and flowing melodic lines, such compositions reflect a new awareness of the rhythms and sounds of the spoken word. Thanks to Janequin's polyphony, we hear the assurance in Alice's simple solution, and her shrieks as the pig pulls her away.

In putting music to work in the representation of the sounds of spoken dialogue—and not just in the form or expressive content of a poem—songs like *Mille regrets* and *Martin menoit* take on a new persuasive urgency. Through them singers could try out different modes of speech, from the elevated to the crude, and experiment with their effects. It hardly seems coincidental that these possibilities for joining text and tone emerged in tandem with the relatively new medium of music printing and its exceptional capacity to link words and music in exacting ways across many copies of the same book. Skilled scribes were certainly capable of aligning words and music with care, but the text underlay was bound to vary slightly from one copy of a piece to the next. With the help of an expert typographer, however, a composer could exert a new level of control over his works. This must have been especially important for Janequin, a man whose career was remarkable among his contemporaries for the fact that he never was a member of a major court or ecclesiastical chapel. In some important ways, then, books such as Attaingnant's are more than the containers of this new aesthetic; they are also its principal means. Print technology and the humanist's love of language were put in close alliance.

MADRIGALS AND THE ART OF PLEASING VARIETY

When the Elizabethan composer and music theorist Thomas Morley (1557/58–1602) turned in his *Plaine and Easie Introduction to Practicall Musicke* of 1597 to consider the claims of genre on the craft of composition, he spelled out a clear hierarchy of types. Motets and other sacred music were at one end of the spectrum, dance music and other instrumental forms at the other. The Italian madrigal and its allied genres of secular vocal music occupied a broad space between these extremes. The madrigal was a mixed genre in which the composer might demonstrate contrasting moods. "If therefore you will compose in this kind," Morley wrote,

> you must possesse your selfe with an amorus humor (for in no composition shal you proue admirable except you put on, and possesse your selfe wholy with that vaine wherein you compose) so that you must in your musicke be wavering like the wind, sometime wanton, sometime drooping, sometime graue and staide, otherwhile effeminat, you may maintaine points and revert them, use triplaes and shew the verie uttermost of your varietie, and the more varietie you shew the better shal you please.

Morley's account is clear enough about the techniques that the madrigal might draw from the world of the motet, with its sedate points of imitation and contrapuntal inversions. But what of the strategies to be gathered from the "lighter" forms of Italian music, as he called them? A change of mensuration, from the prevailing duple meter of most motets to the "triplas" of dance music, is one possibility. Others, Morley implies, are to be found as we descend the ladder of musical and literary genres, from motet to madrigal to canzonetta and so on. What might this varied musical landscape sound like? Let's consider a pair of works by Jacques Arcadelt (?1507–1568) and Adrian Willaert (ca. 1490–1562), two Flemish composers active in Italy during the middle years of the sixteenth century whose settings of Italian lyrics were especially prized by sixteenth-century musicians.

ARCADELT'S SWAN SONG

Thanks to an accident of its history in print, Arcadelt's *Il bianco e dolce cigno* (The White and Gentle Swan) is perhaps the most famous madrigal of the sixteenth century (Anthology 17). It took pride of place at the outset of his *First Book of Madrigals*, a publication that enjoyed a remarkably long life, being reprinted nearly 50 times between its first appearance in about 1538 and 1654. The secret of the piece's appeal is perhaps to be found in the delicate balance between melodic and contrapuntal interest, here arrayed in the restrained representation of the text. The poem dwells on the contrast between two "deaths": the "disconsolate" death of the swan and the metaphorical "happy" death of the poet, presumably in sexual release (according to the lightly coded language of the sixteenth century):

Il bianco e dolce cigno
cantando more. Et io
piangendo giung' al fin del viver mio.
Stran' e diversa sorte,
ch'ei more sconsolato
et io moro beato.
Morte che nel morire
m'empie di gioia tutt' e di desire.
Se nel morir' altro dolor non sento
di mille mort' il dì sarei contento.

The white and gentle swan
dies singing. And I,
weeping, approach the end of my life.
Strange and different fate,
that he dies disconsolate
and I die happy.
Death that in dying
fills me with complete joy and desire.
If in dying I feel no other sorrow,
A thousand deaths a day would content me.

What matters about Arcadelt's madrigal, however, is not so much the content of the lyrics as the ways in which his music helps us hear them. In this instance, it is not just the swan who is singing but the poet, too. As a result, Arcadelt's setting blurs the presumed difference between the two figures and the paradoxical opposition of the two deaths. He manages this feat by presenting the poem in ways that might not occur to us when reading it on the page. The text unfolds as a series of rhymed verses of either 7 or 11 syllables: **abbcddeeaa**. However, Arcadelt's polyphony emphasizes these poetic divisions only when they align with units of grammatical meaning. Sometimes he manages to undercut the pattern of rhyme with irregular or equivocal cadences, breaking up poetic lines *against* their place in the rhyme scheme in order to exaggerate and then conflate his two "singing" subjects. Elsewhere there are striking detours through chromatic extremes and sudden resolutions.

Arcadelt was a northerner by birth, one of the many singer-composers who came to Italy in the late fifteenth and early sixteenth centuries to become members of church choirs and private musical households. He emerged on the Italian scene in a public way via his *First Book of Madrigals*, which was published in Venice by one of the many printing presses that thrived in that commercial and cultural center (see Chapter 9 for the place of this book in the story of music printing of the sixteenth century). Yet Arcadelt himself sang and composed mainly in Florence, where he was a member of the household of Duke Alessandro de' Medici during the 1530s, and then in Rome, where through Medici connections he eventually found a position in the Sistine Chapel during the 1540s and 1550s. Arcadelt's patrons in both Florence and Rome seem to have preferred the restrained, lyrical style of madrigals like *Il bianco e dolce cigno* and his many chansons. The two genres had much in common during the decades in question. Meanwhile, elsewhere in the Italian peninsula musicians and musical thinkers were imagining still other ways to combine polyphony and vernacular poetry of both the serious and light-hearted varieties.

WILLAERT'S MADRIGALS, SERIOUS AND NOT

Madrigals by Willaert are also often held up as examples of the serious aspirations of the genre at midcentury. This aspect of his work is most plainly heard in his *Musica nova* (New Music, 1559), a printed album that includes both motets and madrigals for five voices. Here, both kinds of pieces share a preference for imitative counterpoint, nuanced melodic writing, and, above all, a subtle understanding of the stresses, meaning, and syntax of the texts. Sonnets are the norm for the madrigals, many of them by the great fourteenth-century Florentine poet Petrarch. Petrarch's poetry had been a subject of intense discussion since the late fifteenth century, as humanists debated the respective merits of classical Latin and vernacular Italian verse as stylistic models.

Petrarch's poetry appears among Arcadelt's Florentine madrigals, including his setting of a moving sonnet, *Hor che 'l ciel e la terra* (Now that the Heaven and the Earth, from the *Third Book of Madrigals* of 1539), that became a favorite text of madrigalists of the sixteenth century. In the 1540s the literate gentlemen of Venice's many private academies took up the problem of language and style, prompted by the discussion in Castiglione's *Book of the Courtier*. Reading, understanding, and imitating Petrarch's Italian was the surest road to eloquence, according to critics like Pietro Bembo (1470–1547), himself an editor of and character in Castiglione's treatise, and author of an influential book on Italian literary style, *Prose della volgar lingua* (published in 1525). The new, motet-like madrigals of the circle of musicians and patrician amateurs assembled around Willaert would thus seem to be part of a self-conscious effort to draw secular music into a central project of Renaissance humanists, for whom language and the arts of persuasion were of great value and importance.

No matter the precise reasons behind Willaert's musical innovations, he was certainly a highly influential figure. As master of the musical chapel at the Venetian Basilica of San Marco, he was teacher to musicians like Gioseffo Zarlino, whose theoretical writings frequently cite Willaert's authority in matters of counterpoint and especially text-setting. "Thus Adriano has taught us," Zarlino observed in describing how best to translate the expressive values of poetic texts into musical terms in *Le istitutioni harmoniche* (The Harmonic Foundations, 1558; SR 71:459; 3/36:181). Individual works by Willaert and other composers in his Venetian orbit, like the Flemish master Cipriano de Rore, eventually became touchstones of the genre. Like Arcadelt before him, Rore (1515/16–1565) set Petrarch's *Hor che 'l ciel e la terra* in 1542. His five-voice settings of other Petrarchan texts were imitated, quoted, and reworked by dozens of madrigalists throughout the century. Morley's readers in Elizabethan London, too, felt the weight of Willaert's and Rore's innovations when they were advised that the madrigal was closely bound to "sonnets of Petrarcha." A famous account by Morley of how aspiring composers ought to use melodic and harmonic intervals as ways of representing the meaning of their poetic texts was taken almost word for word from Zarlino's treatise.

IN A LIGHTER VEIN

Even for Willaert, however, the Petrarchan sensibility of the madrigals assembled in the *Musica nova* was only one thread in a complex tapestry of literary and musical genres. He was equally at ease with texts of a very different sort, like the first stanza (two lines of verse) and the refrain (four lines of verse) of the following villanella, published in 1545:

Madonna mia famme bon'offerta	*Lady, make me a good offer,*
Ch'io porto per presente sto galuccio.	*So I'll give you this fat rooster.*
Che sempre canta quand'è dì,	*He's always crowing to tell the hens*
	it's day,
Alle galline e dice: chi-chir-chi.	*"Chi chir chi," he'll always say.*
E tanto calca forte la galina,	*And so hard he presses the hen,*
Che li fa nascer l'ov'ogni matina.	*That she lays an egg each morning.*

The style of the piece is almost uniformly homorhythmic—all four voices move in simultaneous syllabic presentation of the text. The stanzaic design of the poetry, with its crowing refrain ("Che sempre . . ."), calls out for the reuse of the same music from one strophe to the next (Anthology 18). But in Willaert's setting, whole lines, and even parts of lines, are repeated in a patchwork of short formulaic ideas. The song, and especially the refrain, seem surprisingly crude coming from the pen of a composer who crafted the sophisticated counterpoint of the madrigals and motets in *Musica nova*.

Fortunately, Morley's account of the hierarchy of musical and literary genres offers some clues that help us hear *Madonna mia famme bon'offerta* with new understanding. In the pieces he calls canzonettes and *canzoni alla napoletana* (Neapolitan songs), Morley notes that repetition was the norm, much as it is in Willaert's piece (see SR 75:480; 3/40:202). Such compositions are also, by implication, homorhythmic or chordal, since in these works imitative counterpoint is only "lightly touched." Chordal writing is also a hallmark of the pieces Morley calls villanelle, in which even the most primitive parallel fifths or octaves are not forbidden: "for in this kind they think it no fault (as being a kind of keeping decorum) to make a clownish music to a clownish matter." Willaert's piece does not have many parallel fifths, but its manner fits the characterization perfectly.

Morley's characterization of villanelle as "country songs" is perhaps reasonable as a literal translation of the word. But Willaert and his fellow composers of the mid-sixteenth century were not trying to write peasant tunes in any folkloric sense of the term. Some of the earliest examples of the genre appear in collections printed in Venice during the 1540s, where they are called *canzone villanesche alla napolitana* (or simply *napolitane* or *villanesche*). Although they were written in Neapolitan dialect, they were the work of church composers, not popular singers or players. Such pieces were certainly simple: a tuneful melody in the canto (as the superius is often called in Italian sources), a tenore (the tenor) to shadow it in parallel thirds or sixths, and a basso (or bassus) part making thirds and fifths with the main melody. As Morley notes, villanelle self-consciously avoided any hint of the learned style.

Soon Willaert and others arranged such pieces for four voices, putting the original superius tune in the tenor, allowing for the sort of counterpoint we heard in *Madonna mia famme bon'offerta*. Their printers also often retouched the texts to align them with Italian as it was spoken and read in the north. As an employee of Neapolitan aristocrats during the years around 1550, the young Flemish singer and composer Orlando di Lasso (1532–1594) similarly adapted three-voice villanesche as the foundation of his own four-voice compositions. They were subsequently included in his very first solo publication, issued in 1555 by his Antwerp printer-partner Tielman Susato. All of these pieces were published in a variety of formats for vocal ensemble and for solo voice and lute.

Rather than understanding villanelle as folklore, we should instead see them as fashionable amusements, for they were often collected and performed by the same Venetian patricians who took part in the heady discussions of the learned academies. Indeed, Lasso's patron Giovan Battista d'Azzia was a founder of the Neapolitan Accademia dei Sereni (Academy of the Serene Ones), whose members included the church composer Domenico da Nola and noblemen skilled in music, like Fabrizio Dentice and Giulio Cesare Brancaccio. They acted in comedies performed in patrician palaces and were ready to sing villanesche and villanelle in the streets at Carnival time, their real identities protected by masks. As we learned in Chapter 7, the true gentleman must never risk confusion with the role of the mere professional. So perhaps the strutting calls of villanesche like *Madonna mia famme bon'offerta* should be understood more as a bit of temporary theater for those in the know than as "popular" music in the literal sense of the term.

This perspective also suggests another reading of Willaert's opening phrase: it transposes the expressive swooning heard in serious madrigals like Arcadelt's *Il bianco e dolce cigno* into the strut of a barnyard rooster, not the heartfelt cry of a dying swan. Our patricians were apparently quite prepared to poke fun at the very elevated styles with which they spent so much time. Francesco Berni, a Florentine humanist and poet at the court of Pope Clement VII, specialized in burlesques of this sort—parodies, echoes, and transformations of fashionable Petrarchan sonnets and other serious material. An entire literary subgenre has been dubbed in his name: the "Bernescan," in counterpoint to the "Petrarchan." Given how important serious verse was in musical circles, we should perhaps not be too surprised that this sort of parodic verse turns up in musical settings from time to time.

MADRIGAL PARODIES

In the polyphonic madrigal comedy *L'Amfiparnaso* (Amphiparnassus, 1597) by Orazio Vecchi (1550–1605), the fumbling Doctor Gratiano, a stock figure from the commedia dell'arte tradition, tries to serenade his new fiancée with a madrigal. It's a parody of one of the most famous—and serious—madrigals of the century, *Ancor che col partire* (Even Though in Parting), a four-voice setting by Cipriano de Rore, itself already the subject of many instrumental arrangements and elaborations (Ex. 10.2). Vecchi retains the original canto (superius) part—Gratiano is supposed to be singing to his beloved while accompanying himself on the lute—but replaces the remaining three voices with four newly composed ones (Ex. 10.3). The parody text does away with the refined Tuscan language of

Example 10.2: *Cipriano de Rore,* Ancor che col partire, *mm. 1–10. From Cipriano de Rore,* Opera Omnia, *ed. Bernhard Meier, 8 vols.,* Corpus Mensurabilis Musicae, *14 ([Rome]: American Institute of Musicology, 1969), 4:31.*

Example 10.3: *Orazio Vecchi, parody of Rore's* Ancor che col partire, *mm. 1–10. From Orazio Vecchi,* L'Amfiparnaso. A New Edition of the Music with Historical and Analytical Essays, *ed. Cecil Adkins (Chapel Hill: University of North Carolina Press, 1977), p. 70.*

the original poem in favor of a crude Bolognese dialect that that sounds familiar but comes out all wrong. Here is the original poem as set by Rore:

Ancor che col partire	*Although in parting*
Io mi sento morire,	*I sense myself dying,*
Partir vorrei ogn'hor, ogni momento	*I wish to leave every hour, every moment,*
Tant'è il piacer ch'io sento	*So much is the delight I feel*
De la vita ch'acquisto nel ritorno.	*Of life recovered upon returning.*
E così mill'e mille volt'il giorno	*And so, a thousand times a day*
Partir da voi vorrei	*I should like to part from you,*
Tanto son dolci gli ritorni miei.	*So sweet are my returns.*

And here is Dr. Gratiano's mangled version:

Ancor ch'al parturire	*Though on giving birth*
Al se stenta a murire	*One feels that one is dying,*
Patir vorrei agn'or senza tormiente.	*I should like to give birth all the time without torment,*
Tant'è'l piacer Vincenze	*So overpowering is my joy.*
L'acqua vita m'ha pist'e pur ai torne	*The brandy has given me such a turn,*
E così mille mele al far del zorne	*And so a thousand apples at break of day*
Padir agn'or vurrei	*I'd like to digest at every hour,*
Tanto son dolci i Storni ai denti miei.	*So sweet the starlings are to my teeth.*

The original text is not by Petrarch, nor is it a sonnet. But in its elegant Tuscan idiom, and in its pointed oppositions of life and death, separation and return, it plays out many of the themes on which Petrarch's poetry often turns, and which were so ably explored in the music of the midcentury Venetian madrigal. As we will discover in Chapter 12, the instrumental variations on Rore's madrigal emulate the piece in one way, playing upon sounds of the original polyphonic parts and harmonies as vehicles for all sorts of skillful embellishment. The parodic version in Vecchi's *L'Amfiparnaso* plays upon the original in still other ways, finding words that sound very much like the originals but mean something quite different. Sound and sense here play off each other to hilarious effect.

Vecchi's madrigal comedy was not a dramatic work in the strict sense, with audience, stage, and performers. It was instead meant for the enjoyment of the performers themselves as they sat around a table with partbooks before them. As such, it was the perfect inside joke for patricians steeped in discussions of style and proper language. (See Chapter 13 for a discussion of Vecchi's ethnic stereotyping.)

LUCA MARENZIO AND THE MADRIGAL OF THE LATE SIXTEENTH CENTURY

Vecchi's scenario illustrates that the genres outlined by Morley were not wholly high or low cultural property. They were instead part of a shared landscape of aesthetic alternatives, each linked to distinct traditions that could nevertheless be combined with great persuasive force. If Morley advocated self-conscious variety as the surest means for a composer to please his performers or listeners, the union of motet-like polyphony with the melodic and textural clarity of the villanella was an array ideally suited to the task. Of all the composers who explored this mixed style during the second half of the sixteenth century, none did so more ably than the Italian madrigalist Luca Marenzio (1553/54–1599). Indeed, the first piece in his very first album of published madrigals, *Liquide perle* (Liquid Pearls, 1580), relies precisely on this style as a musical counterpart to the rich palette of literary images at work in the poem it sets (see Chapter 1).

Liquide perle Amor da gl'occhi sparse	*Liquid pearls Love brought from my eyes*
In premio del mio ardore;	*As reward for my desire;*
Ma lass'ohimè, chè 'l core	*But alas, my heart*
Di maggior foco m'arse.	*Burned me with greater fire.*
Ahi, che bastava solo	*Ah, if only the first searing pain*
A darmi morte il primo ardente duolo.	*Had been enough to cause my death.*

Marenzio responded to these lines with an incredibly varied array of musical ideas. Some, like the lively descending patterns that open the madrigal, paint the text as an image in sound. Such imagistic approaches to literary texts have earned the scorn of a few modern critics, who called them "madrigalisms" as a mark of contempt. But if we are willing to be persuaded by Morley's advocacy of variety as an aesthetic virtue, there seems little to criticize in gestures like these, especially once we put them in context with the remainder of the piece. (For a detailed reading of the many nuances of this madrigal, see Anthology 1.)

Marenzio's music was in any case immensely popular in its own day, and is much beloved by modern listeners and performers, too. *Liquide perle* was repeatedly republished in various forms: in reissues of his debut madrigal album; in arrangements for lute; transformed into a religious piece, with a new text, as *Fiamme di vero amore* (Flames of True Love), by the Roman priest Giovenale Ancina in 1588; and translated into English as *Liquid and watery pearls* in *The First Sett, of Italian Madrigalls Englished*, prepared by the London printer Thomas East in 1590. Indeed, Marenzio's madrigals and villanelle were important models for English composers of the late sixteenth and early seventeenth centuries. To cite a pair of examples, Thomas Morley's *Miraculous love's wounding* (Anthology 3) and John Wilbye's *Draw on, sweet Night* (Anthology 12) are unimaginable except against the backdrop of Italian music, especially that of the prolific Marenzio.

MARENZIO AND THE AVANT-GARDE POETS

Of course, Marenzio was not the only brilliant madrigalist to emerge during the last quarter of the sixteenth century. He was thoroughly familiar with the famous Petrarchan texts that Willaert and Rore had helped to establish in the repertory, but he was no less at home with the popular villanelle (also called canzonettas by this point), of which he published some 300 in all. It's worth noting that among the masters whom Morley suggests as models for aspiring composers, only Marenzio figures in the lists for serious and light forms alike.

Marenzio was also among a vanguard of composers to set some of the latest poetry by Battista Guarini, including texts from his tragicomic pastoral play *Il pastor fido* (The Faithful Shepherd), and Torquato Tasso, including excerpts from the epic-romance *Gerusalemme liberata* (Jerusalem Liberated). The work of these poets is notable for the ways in which it bends conventions of genre, much as Marenzio and composers like Giaches de Wert, Luzzascho Luzzaschi, and Claudio Monteverdi had been doing with music (see Chapters 12 and 14). Settings of texts by Guarini and Tasso can be found among Marenzio's earliest books of madrigals. His expansive treatment of Guarini's *Tirsi morir volea* (Tirsi Wished to Die) takes its place alongside *Liquide perle* in his *First Book of Madrigals* of 1580, where we also find an equally moving setting of Tasso's *Ohimè dov'è il mio ben* (Alas, Where Is my Beloved). But Marenzio's most extensive explorations of these fashionable lyrics came later: the *Sixth Book of Madrigals* for five voices (1594) features a number of poems from *Il pastor fido*; and madrigal cycles based on multi-stanza poems by Tasso appear in the *Fourth Book of Madrigals* for five voices (1584) and in the *Sixth Book of Madrigals* for six voices (1595).

Exactly how Marenzio came to know and set these texts is something of a musicological mystery. During the 1580s he was a member of the extended household of Cardinal Luigi d'Este, a wealthy and cultured member of the famous Ferrarese ducal family for whom Tasso worked. Luigi's visits to Ferrara brought Marenzio into the orbit of that remarkable court and its equally remarkable musical chamber ensemble, the singing virtuosos known as the *concerto delle donne* (see Chapter 7 and the discussion of Marenzio's *O verdi selve* in Chapter 12). Marenzio's pursuit of a new and luxuriant style of vocal ornamentation and his parallel interest in Tasso's poetry certainly bear witness to Ferrarese tastes. But he probably did not get his poetry directly from the author. Indeed, surviving letters and other documents suggest that composers were often guided in their poetic choices by literate patrons and acquaintances who might send them a poem in a letter, suggest a book to read, or otherwise encourage a particular line of thought. It is clear that during the 1590s Marenzio's new interest in texts from Guarini's *Il pastor fido* came through some of his Roman patrons, notably Cardinal Cinzio Aldobrandini, who took a special liking to the pastoral drama.

Marenzio's career reminds us that composers and poets rarely operated in a vacuum and were often not at liberty to collaborate out of earshot of their patrons. Their choices were in many ways shaped by the tastes of the influential patricians for whom they worked, and to whom they looked for protection in an artistic landscape that was frequently buffeted by intense debates about style. As we'll see in Chapter 14, during the last decades of the sixteenth century, even as Marenzio and others crafted polyphonic madrigals of great intensity and beauty, some writers wondered whether polyphony was altogether the wrong medium for the persuasive presentation of literary texts. For them, it was time to imagine a new kind of music to suit a new expressive aim.

Marenzio, Janequin, and the other composers we've encountered in this Chapter were adept readers of literary texts. In their works we can see new combinations of textures, rhythms, and harmonies put to work in the service of those texts in various ways. Viewed from a wider cultural vantage point, these developments in the chanson and madrigal can also be linked to the broader story of Renaissance humanism and its abiding concerns for the persuasive power of language and speech. Through works like these we can sense the competing modes of literary expression in the vernacular (refined and coarse, high and low) that were enlisted in the larger project and its self-consciousness about style and tone. Now music, too, was a place to try out the imaginary alternatives with one's literate peers. The combination of music and poetry was the perfect medium for the job.

Throughout this exploration of music and the literary imagination, we have also stressed the importance of music printing, both as a technical innovation that could support new aesthetic possibilities and as a medium of new social exchange around musical works. This new means of reproduction of musical texts did not foreclose the possibility of interpretation on the part of performers, of course. But it allowed composers to exert an authorial presence that extended far beyond the households and church choirs where they practiced their trade. For men like Janequin and Marenzio, who spent much of their careers outside the usual institutions of patronage, the musical press became an important channel through which their works might reach players and singers on a truly Continental scale. In an age acutely concerned with the persuasive power of language, music in these printed collections of chansons and madrigals could become an important point of entry into the imaginary spaces of sound and idea.

FOR FURTHER READING

Bizzarini, Marco, "Marenzio and Cardinal Luigi d'Este," *Early Music* 27 (1999): 519–32

Brooks, Jeanice, "Ronsard, the Lyric Sonnet and the Late Sixteenth-Century Chanson," *Early Music History* 13 (1994): 65–84

Fromson, Michele, "Themes of Exile in Willaert's *Musica nova*," *Journal of the American Musicological Society* 47 (1994): 442–87

Mace, Dean T., "Pietro Bembo and the Literary Origins of the Italian Madrigal," *Musical Quarterly* 55 (1969): 65–86

Macy, Laura, "Speaking of Sex: Metaphor and Performance in the Italian Madrigal," *Journal of Musicology* 14 (1996): 1–34

McClary, Susan, *Modal Subjectivities: Self-Fashioning in the Italian Madrigal* (Berkeley and Los Angeles: University of California Press, 2004)

Owens, Jessie Ann, "Marenzio and Wert Read Tasso: A Study in Contrasting Aesthetics," *Early Music* 27 (1999): 555–74

Perkins, Leeman L., "Toward a Typology of the 'Renaissance' Chanson," *Journal of Musicology* 6 (1988): 421–47

Tomlinson, Gary, *Monteverdi and the End of the Renaissance* (Berkeley: University of California Press, 1987)

Ⓢ Additional resources available at wwnorton.com/studyspace

CHAPTER ELEVEN

Music and the Crisis of Belief

The story of sacred music in the sixteenth century has often been told as a series of stark contrasts between the rival claims and practices of two sharply divided faiths. To be sure, Protestant reformers like Martin Luther and Jean Calvin reimagined music to suit the needs of their communities. Congregants were expected to participate in singing hymn tunes and simple harmonies that carried spiritual messages made immediate in languages used in daily life. Music for Catholic services was very different, consisting of elaborately contrapuntal settings of Latin motets and masses that were best left to professional choirs maintained at the leading cathedrals and courts.

However, music can be understood as a bridge between faiths no less than as a marker of profound theological difference. Protestant and Catholic thinkers alike worried about the emotional power of music and how to maintain what they felt to be its sacred purity. Musicians of both faiths were also deeply interested in the relationship between words and tones, an extension of the preoccupation with language and textual traditions so deeply ingrained in the humanist debates of the day. In fact, many Christian humanists, such as Desiderius Erasmus, Marsilio Ficino, and Johannes Reuchlin, turned to ancient sources in Hebrew, Greek, or Latin as they grappled with important matters of faith, doctrine, and interpretation. As we'll see, Catholics like Bishop Bernardino Cirillo Franco were no less worried about the role of music in relation to belief than were Protestant reformers like Luther and Calvin. And so even as we recognize the ways in which music was embroiled in the crisis of belief, we should also be ready to see how the malleable medium of music might bridge faiths in ways that the conventional narrative would be hard pressed to convey. Our encounter with sacred music of the sixteenth century will begin and end with a joint project that can serve as an emblem of this hopeful role for music.

SACRED SOUNDS FOR A NATION OF DIVIDED FAITHS

In 1575 the English composers Thomas Tallis (ca. 1505–1585) and William Byrd (ca. 1540–1623) joined forces with the London printer Thomas Vautrollier in issuing a set of partbooks, the *Cantiones, quae ab argumento sacrae vocantur*, that stands at the unlikely intersection of patronage, commerce, and belief (Fig. 11.1). Dedicated to Queen Elizabeth I, the *Cantiones* were the first books issued under a new patent that the queen had recently granted Tallis and Byrd. The title seems to dance around the status of the works: "Songs, Which by their Subject Matter Are Called Sacred." Why not simply *Cantiones sacrae* (Sacred

Figure 11.1: *Thomas Tallis and William Byrd, title page from* Cantiones . . . sacrae *(London, 1575).*

Songs) or motets? Elizabethan readers would have been familiar enough with the latter term. Two decades later, when Thomas Morley dedicated his *Plaine and Easie Introduction to Practicall Musicke* to Byrd, he was quick to link the motet with the sacred. For him it was a kind of music causing "most strange effects in the hearer . . . for it will draw the auditor (and speciallie the skilfull auditor) into a devout and reverent kind of consideration of him for whose praise it was made."

We'll never know what prompted Tallis, Byrd, and Vautrollier to use such elevated language in their title, and to be so indirect about the status of the music they printed here. One reason could have been an attempt to appeal to musicians who were themselves divided from each other by faith. Tallis began his career in the service of a Catholic monastery, then played a formative role in the creation of music for the Anglican liturgy, as a succession of English monarchs formalized the break with papal authority in Rome that King Henry VIII had precipitated in 1534. Given the priority of English anthems and simple hymns over Latin motets, Tallis had good reason to equivocate on the status of the music he brought out under the protection of a queen who embodied the English national church. His younger partner Byrd also had reason to be guarded about the Latin music in the *Cantiones*: he was a Catholic, a member of a minority obliged to hide their religious practices from public view. As for Vautrollier, he was a French Protestant who, like many others in the print trades, had sought refuge in London following the bloody sectarian violence that swept French towns during the religious wars of the 1560s.

All of this invites us to ask some basic questions about the place of music in the religious life of the sixteenth century. What spiritual values did Catholics and Protestants of various denominations attach to music? How might music be enlisted in the service of their religious views and practices? And how, in a landscape torn by religious violence from all quarters, might music transcend seemingly incompatible differences of creed?

FROM THE *CANTIONES* TO BYRD'S *GRADUALIA*

By the time Byrd formed his promising partnership with Tallis in 1575, he was already a leading figure in English music. Still only in his thirties, in 1572 he had risen to the post of gentleman in the highly regarded Chapel Royal, where he remained for many years. His success seems all the more noteworthy in light of his steady commitment to Catholicism. Catholic "recusants" (so-called when they refused to take part in Anglican services or forswear allegiance to the pope in Rome) were subject to fines, exclusion from office, and possibly torture or execution. It probably did not help when Byrd set some stanzas of a poem ("Why do I use my paper, ink, and pen") written to protest the death of Edmund Campion, a Jesuit priest who was publicly and horribly executed by the state in 1581.

By 1593 he had retreated to the Essex home of the Catholic Sir John Petre. It was here that Byrd composed music for the Catholic service: three masses and some 200 motets that later were published as two volumes of *Gradualia* (1605 and 1607). The latter books, like the modern gradual, were compendia of sacred music organized according to the liturgical year. This time there was no need for ambiguity about the character of the publication: *Gradualia, ac cantiones sacrae* (Gradualia, and Sacred Songs).

Byrd's preface to the *Gradualia* reveals much about his intentions for the music and his reaction to the liturgical texts. "In the very sentences," he wrote of his compositional process, "there is such hidden and concealed power that to a man thinking about divine things and turning them over attentively and earnestly in his mind, the most appropriate measures come, I do not know how, as if by their own free will, and freely offer themselves to the mind that is neither idle nor inert." Whether music really came to him by its own "free will" is probably unknowable, but his emphasis on the mysterious power of sacred texts calls out for further inquiry. It's not enough simply to read them; only when "turning them over in his mind" can the right form in which to present them at last emerge. Perhaps this is what Byrd's pupil Thomas Morley meant when he defined the motet as a genre that might cause "most strange effects" in auditors, but especially in "skilful" ones. If composing for Byrd was a way of making thoughts audible, perhaps Morley's skillful listeners were those prepared to listen to the thoughts of others, entering (as Morley put it) "a devout and reverent kind of consideration" of the divine.

The *Gradualia* thus fulfills two complementary functions: liturgical and devotional. On one hand, the organization by liturgical calendar suggests music to be used in the observance of religious ritual. On the other, Byrd's statements on the origins of the material suggest not ritual but commemoration. Consider one of the most famous of his works, his four-voice setting of *Ave verum corpus* (Hail, True Body; Anthology 19). Taken in the context of the *Gradualia* in which it was first published, the work was intended for the Feast of Corpus Christi: "Here is the true body of Christ" is its basic message.

We ought to remember, however, that in the context of Catholic practice in late-sixteenth- and early-seventeenth-century England, Corpus Christi was unlikely to have been observed with all of the public spectacle it was afforded in many places on the Continent, or even as it had once been throughout England until the Reformation. So if it was not intended to accompany the procession of the Feast of Corpus Christi, what purpose might such a motet serve? One clue is to be found in the crushing cross-relation as the singers intone "verum" (true) in the opening line of the text, where the F♯ in the superius is followed immediately by an F♮ in the bassus. In stressing the word "verum" rather than the more obvious "corpus" (body), Byrd may have been hailing not the Body of

Christ but the Eucharist, which miraculously *is* the Body. The declamation "Ave *verum* corpus" makes a doctrinal point of great importance to Catholics of Byrd's time, who were locked in controversy over the issue of transubstantiation. And perhaps it is not too abstruse to suggest that by echoing this false relation later in the piece—at "O dulcis, o pie," "o Iesu," and mostly at "miserere mei"—Byrd meant to keep the Eucharist more clearly before our eyes than the text itself manages to do.

This insight chimes with a small but significant variant in the text that was common in books of hours and other volumes intended for private devotional use. Unlike the liturgical version of *Ave verum corpus*, Byrd's ends with a personal supplication, "miserere mei" (Have mercy on me). We've seen this kind of individual statement voiced through the collective vehicle of polyphony in works of the fifteenth century like Du Fay's *Ave regina celorum* (Chapter 4) and Josquin's *Ave Maria . . . virgo serena* (Chapter 8). But its use by an embattled community of believers for whom ritual was increasingly internalized seems especially poignant. Perhaps Byrd's polyphony had the power to help Catholics contemplate in sound what they could not celebrate in public.

THE REEVALUATION
OF CATHOLIC MUSIC

Catholic composers active on the Continent during the second half of the sixteenth century worked in less perilous circumstances than Byrd and his co-religionists. But their concern for the proper relationship between text, tone, and doctrine was no less acute, especially as Protestant and Catholic theologians vied with each other over questions of what to believe and how to behave. Music, with its ineffable power to move listeners in one way or another, needed to be watched with care. In a public letter to a colleague published in 1549, Bishop Bernardino Cirillo Franco complained about the spiritual corruption of Masses built on secular melodies like *L'homme armé* or the syllables of Duke Ercole of Ferrara's name (see Chapters 5 and 8). "What numbers, what intervals, what sounds, what motions of the spirit, of devotion, or piety can be gathered from them," he asked, "and how can music agree with such subjects as the armed man or the duke of Ferrara?" Music also needed to present sacred texts in an intelligible way, "framed to the fundamental meaning of the words, in certain intervals and numbers apt to move our affections to religion and piety" (SR 59:370–71; 3/24:92–93).

Cirillo Franco's comments are often cited by historians in the context of the Council of Trent (1545–1563), a long set of discussions involving Catholic cardinals, bishops, and other officials and centering on questions of doctrine and practice. Cirillo Franco was not, in fact, a regular member of the council, although his views on the importance of subordinating music to sacred texts accord with its deliberations. It has been suggested that the clerics assembled at Trent came close to banning polyphony altogether and that the Roman composer Giovanni Pierluigi da Palestrina (1525/26–1594) was somehow singlehandedly responsible for "saving" church music from their overzealous reforms. The story has little basis in fact, but it was frequently repeated and wildly elaborated by subsequent writers.

Nevertheless many Catholic musicians and clerics working in the Italian peninsula shared Cirillo Franco's interest in purifying music and linking it to sacred texts. In this respect, the edicts of the Council of Trent were often explicitly acknowledged. When in 1570 the Milanese chapel master Vincenzo Ruffo (1508–1587) published a set of masses for use at the cathedral of Milan, whose cardinal, Carlo Borromeo, was a central figure in the discussions at Trent, he recalled having written music "in accordance with the decree of the sacred Council of Trent" that would avoid "everything of a profane and idle manner in worship." So there would be no doubt about the message, he restrained the polyphony "so that the numbers of the syllables and the voices and tones together should be clearly and distinctly understood and perceived by the pious listeners." For Ruffo as well as Cirillo Franco, it was important to purge music of ill-defined impurities and put it to work in the service of intelligible sacred texts (Ex. 11.1).

Palestrina, too, was caught up in the movement to purify polyphonic music in the service of the sacred. Together with his Roman colleague Annibale Zoilo (ca. 1537–1592), he was commissioned by Pope Gregory XIII in 1577 to take on a huge project of musical and liturgical reform that sought to bring plainsong in line with official practice. The language of Gregory's charge to the two musicians reveals much about the new and pressing concerns of the Catholic hierarchy to control the slippery but powerful effects of sound through correct texts. "It has come to our attention," the pope wrote, "that the Antiphoners, Graduals, and Psalters that have been provided with music for the celebration of the divine praises and offices in plainsong (as it is called) since the publication of the Breviary and Missal ordered by the Council of Trent have been filled to overflowing with barbarisms, obscurities, contrarieties, and superfluities as a result of the clumsiness or negligence or even wickedness of the composers, scribes, and printers" (SR 61:375; 3/26:97).

Although the pope's language may sound excessive, his reform project reflects a profoundly humanist outlook. Textual criticism, after all, was a distinctly humanist enterprise, as central to the exegesis of religious texts as it was to the exploration of ancient philosophy and literature. The job of cleaning things up was greater than Gregory could have imagined. In fact, it was not completed until 1614, well after Gregory, Palestrina, and Zoilo were all dead, with the

Example 11.1: *Vincenzo Ruffo, Missa Quarti toni, Credo, mm. 10–17. From Vincenzo Ruffo, Seven Masses, ed. Lewis Lockwood, 2 vols., Recent Researches in the Music of the Renaissance, 32–33 (Madison, WI: A-R Editions, 1979), 2:10.*

All things visible and invisible

publication of the *Editio Medicaea* (Medicean Edition), a book that remained the foundation of the Catholic liturgy until the nineteenth century.

Palestrina seems to have internalized this spirit of change. When he dedicated one of his own books of motets for five voices to Pope Gregory in 1584, he turned his back on settings of erotic or carnal love lyrics as unworthy of a true believer: "I blush," he confessed, to have been one of those who set songs "alien to the name and profession of Christian." This book was a public act of contrition in favor of spiritual or divine love. "I have changed my purpose," Palestrina wrote:

> Therefore I have both already labored on those poems which have been
> written of the praises of our Lord Jesus Christ and his Most Holy Mother
> the Virgin Mary, and at this time chosen those which contain the divine
> love of Christ and his spouse the soul, indeed the Canticles of Solomon.

I have used a kind of music somewhat livelier than I have been accustomed to use in ecclesiastical melodies, for this I felt that the subject itself demanded.

The motet book of 1584 consists entirely of lyrics drawn from the biblical Song of Solomon, also known as the Song of Songs. Ironically, the language of this poetry is on its surface anything but spiritual, describing as it does the frankly erotic longing of two lovers. However, Rabbinic commentators had for generations understood these poems as allegorical expressions of the longing of the Jewish people for the divine. As noted in Chapter 4, Christian thinkers appropriated the poems according to their own needs—for example, as expressing the "divine love" (as Palestrina's preface put it) of Christ for the human soul. No wonder Palestrina felt that these lyrics required a "somewhat livelier" idiom than one might otherwise want in the setting of sacred texts.

PALESTRINA'S *MISSA NIGRA SUM*

The spiritual and the sensual have often existed side by side in music, despite Palestrina's apparent repudiation of the possibility and Bishop Cirillo Franco's thumping protests. Consider, for instance, a section of a mass that Palestrina based on a motet by Jean Lhéritier (ca. 1480–after 1551). Lhéritier was a French composer active for many years at San Luigi dei Francesi in Rome, the church attended by many of the city's French-speaking residents. His motet, published in 1532, takes as its point of departure the text of a plainsong melody sung in honor of the Virgin Mary, *Nigra sum, sed formosa* (I Am Black, but Comely), which in turn uses verses from the biblical Song of Songs.

The idea of musical borrowing, and in particular of building a cyclic mass on some other musical work, was not new, as we saw in Chapter 5. But by the middle of the sixteenth century the technique centered on adaptations of models that were themselves polyphonic, and not just individual lines, as had been the habit of composers before Josquin des Prez and Pierre de la Rue. The motet that Palestrina took as his model comes from the generation of composers active right after Josquin's death in 1521. Like many of the sacred pieces composed in the 1530s and 1540s, Lhéritier's is overwhelmingly contrapuntal, imitative, and continuous in its texture (Anthology 20). The approach to dissonance is very controlled, and there are no strong breaks in the fabric for simultaneous declamation of any part of the text. In this respect, its musical profile probably would not have offended listeners like Cirillo Franco, no matter what the character of its text.

Yet Lhéritier's conclusion to the work is both striking and unexpected: he repeats the words and music for the last line of the text, then suddenly turns to weave a long series of descending scales for the very last words of the motet, which describe the beloved's entry into the royal bedchamber. We cannot be certain exactly what Lhéritier had in mind. Perhaps he meant to evoke the sense of movement implied by the text: the idea of being drawn into a royal chamber could well be understood as the worldly equivalent of the movement of the soul toward heaven, for instance. In any case, Palestrina was ready to adapt the motet and its memorable closing gesture to his own needs in the context of the mass, and the Credo in particular. (See Anthology 21 for a detailed exploration of the relationship between the Credo and its model.)

The first challenge must have been to sort out how to adapt a motet with only three short lines of text to a long liturgical formula with many breaks, as well as many important points of doctrine. The Credo is a core statement of Catholic faith, including affirmations of the Holy Trinity, the story of Jesus's miraculous conception, crucifixion, and resurrection, and the unity of the Catholic Church itself. Palestrina's solution is to present the music of the motet twice, borrowing from strategic points at the beginning, middle, and end in ways that aligned with important parts of the Credo text. Most tellingly, he uses the striking cascade of descending lines from the end of *Nigra sum* for a vivid depiction of two descents described in the Credo: of the Holy Ghost from heaven, and of Jesus into the tomb. Perhaps Palestrina was inviting his listeners to hear the musical descent into the royal chamber of *Nigra sum* as a prototype of ideas fundamental to the Christian creed of his day.

LASSO AND COUNTER-REFORMATION MUNICH

Music historians have often written about music from Catholic courts and churches of late-sixteenth-century Europe as if it were monolithic in its austerity and spiritual restraint. The reality was probably not so neat. Many musicians and musical thinkers were intent on discovering the right spiritual sounds, but there was little unanimity on what these might be. Palestrina, as we have just seen, allowed himself a "more lively" idiom in approaching the Song of Songs motets he dedicated to Pope Gregory XIII. In contrast, in a book of masses dedicated to King Philip II of Spain in 1567, he stressed the great care and restraint with which he approached works destined for one who guarded "the purity of the orthodox religion most ardently" (SR 60:374; 3/25:96).

Not to be outdone by Habsburg patrons like Philip, the sponsors of Orlando di Lasso (1532–1594) at the ducal court of Bavaria in Munich also fashioned themselves as protectors of Catholic faith locked in struggle with nearby Lutheran towns. Duke Wilhelm V used the annual Corpus Christi procession to demonstrate his piety in a public way. Beginning in the 1570s the Munich Corpus Christi observances became ever larger, eventually involving well over 3,000 participants out of a total population of about 15,000. At one point it took 200 pages of chronicle just to describe the event. Guilds and religious confraternities were there, members of the local nobility were compelled to take part by ducal decree, and the ducal household took pride of place just behind the Eucharist itself: ducal trumpeters cleared the way for both of them.

A famous musical legend is associated with the Corpus Christi procession in Munich. Just as things were about to get under way in 1584, a thunderstorm threatened to disrupt the ritual. But when court officials called for the choir, then under the direction of Lasso, to sing one of his four-voice motets, *Gustate et videte* (Taste and See), the skies suddenly cleared. The music quickly became an annual feature of the procession, and court chroniclers insisted that no matter what the weather, the skies became even brighter as soon as Lasso's motet was heard. Court officials had every reason to repeat the tale, given Wilhelm's exaggerated image of his role as protector of the Bavarian Catholic Church. The court chapel choir, under Lasso's able direction, was a vanguard of the duke's self-appointed role. He saw to it that lavishly illustrated manuscripts were copied for the group, complete with images that made the ensemble look every bit as impressive as it must have sounded (Fig. 11.2).

CROSSING CONFESSIONAL BOUNDARIES

A six-voice motet that Lasso composed around the time he first joined the Munich court chapel in the 1560s draws together still other strains of Catholic piety that circulated during the Counter-Reformation of the sixteenth century. *Infelix ego* (Unhappy Am I) is filled with striking musical gestures—sonorous blocks of sound in staggered entries, dramatic pauses and changes of texture built around various cadence types, and above all a rich palette of harmonies and poignant dissonances. All of this is put to work in the service of the Latin text, for *Infelix ego* is filled with reflective questions and appeals for divine help. It culminates in a quotation from Psalm 50 (which corresponds to Psalm 51 in Protestant Bibles): "Miserere mei, deus, secundum magnam misericordiam tuam" (Have mercy on me, Lord, according to your great mercy; Ex. 11.2).

Infelix ego is also remarkable for the origins of its text: it comes from the pen of Girolamo Savonarola, a Dominican friar from Ferrara who by the 1490s had risen to a position of great power and influence in Florence. As the popularity of his preaching grew, he became increasingly critical of the ruling Medici family, and after the death of Lorenzo de' Medici and the political exile of his heir, Piero II, Savonarola became the most powerful voice in the republic. With significant popular support, he imposed a severe theocratic government on the city. He was eventually ousted, excommunicated by the pope, arrested, tortured, and burned at the stake in May 1498.

During his imprisonment and torture, Savanarola wrote poignant meditations on two of the Penitential Psalms, numbers 30 and 50, which were promptly

Figure 11.2: *Lasso and his choir in the Bavarian court chapel. From an illuminated manuscript prepared by Hans Mielich between 1565 and 1570.*

smuggled out of jail, printed, and widely read by Catholics and Protestants alike. The court of Ferrara, where Savonarola's father had once lived, cultivated his teachings with particular enthusiasm. Indeed, perhaps at the request of his

Example 11.2: *Orlando di Lasso,* Infelix ego, *mm. 132–36. From Orlando di Lasso,* The Complete Motets *5, ed. Peter Bergquist, Recent Researches in the Music of the Renaissance, 109 (Madison, WI: A-R Editions, 1997), p. 274.*

employer, Duke Ercole I d'Este of Ferrara, Josquin des Prez composed a setting of Psalm 50 that appropriates the form of Savonarola's meditation as the cue for a slow-moving cantus firmus in repeated stepwise transpositions over the course of the motet. Other composers with connections to Ferrara, including Adrian Willaert and Cipriano de Rore, paid homage to this motet throughout the sixteenth century.

Lasso's *Infelix ego* comes not from Savonarola's main meditation on Psalm 50, but rather from the introduction to that exercise, which helps us to understand why it ends with the opening words of the psalm. This introductory text had been set by Willaert and Rore, who appreciated the Ferrarese interest in Savonarola's writings. But Lasso's motet remains musically independent of those pieces, and so we cannot say with certainty how he was drawn to the text. Perhaps it was suggested to him by one of his new patrons at Munich, who were quite interested in musical developments at the Ferrarese court. On the other hand, perhaps Lasso was prompted to set the text by Melchior Linck, a wealthy patrician from the nearby town of Augsburg to whom the composer had dedicated the motet book in which the work first appeared in 1566. Unfortunately, we do not know enough about Linck to do more than guess about his reactions to Lasso's *Infelix ego*. Was he aware of Savonarola's authorship of the text? Did it matter to him that Savonarola's bitter critiques of the Catholic clergy of late-fifteenth-century Italy were in part responsible for his excommunication from the church and sympathetic readings his life and work were given in some Protestant circles? We'll probably never know.

In any case, Linck's Augsburg was the perfect place for this musical and confessional boundary-crossing. The ground for such dialogue was prepared by the controversial Augsburg Interim of 1548, an agreement forced upon Protestant princes of various German towns by Holy Roman Emperor Charles V, a staunch Catholic. It allowed Lutherans a certain degree of autonomy over practices like the distribution of Communion and the marital status of priests, in the hope that the newly convened Council of Trent would soon reunite Christians who had been sharply divided following Luther's break with papal authority in 1517. Solutions from Trent, however, were slow in coming and often more polemical than conciliatory toward Protestants. With the intransigent Charles V about to abdicate, in 1555 German princes went ahead with their own compromise, the Religious Peace of Augsburg, in which they agreed that individual rulers and towns could decide their own religious affiliation. In many locales, thousands of families were forced to emigrate, but in free imperial cities like Augsburg, which were under the emperor's direct rule, there was official coexistence.

PROTESTANT VERSUS CATHOLIC IN MUSIC

The apparent presence of Protestant sympathies in works like Lasso's *Infelix ego* as it circulated in Melchior Linck's patrician world, which included wealthy Catholic families like the Fuggers and Herwarts, illustrates the ability of sound to transcend religious barriers. However, music more often demonstrated differences rather than commonalities. Immediately after the Augsburg Interim was proclaimed, agitators on both sides began printing propaganda that took their messages into the streets and houses of German towns. Protestants produced

ANTICHRISTVS.

Figure 11.3: *The pope and priests selling indulgences. Woodcut from the studio of Lucas Cranach, from Philipp Melanchthon's anti-Catholic pamphlet* Passional Christi und Antichristi *(1521).*

mocking images of popes and priests: Figure 11.3 shows them selling indulgences that promised purchasers a speedy trip through purgatory. Catholics countered with derisive cartoons of Luther himself: in Figure 11.4, his head has been transformed into the devil's bagpipes. There were also pamphlets attacking different theological positions, and outright resistance to political and religious authority.

Polemical songs of various kinds played an important role in stirring up conflict. Especially common were parodies of the psalms and *contrafacta*, in which new texts were grafted onto familiar hymns or popular tunes. No doubt some of these pieces were sung out loud by citizens who could read the words and music for those who could not. But once learned by the illiterate, these tunes took on lives of their own as they entered the popular imagination. Nor was musical propaganda confined to humble folk. Middle-class burghers, craftsmen, and theologians must also have pored over the posters, with their acrostic poems, Latin puns, and occasional polyphonic arrangements meant for performance around a table rather than in the street. Sometimes Catholic

Figure 11.4: *Luther as the devil's bagpipes, from an anonymous woodcut of the sixteenth century*

musicians shot back with their own musical polemic, such as the motet *Te Lutherum damnamus* (We Condemn Thee, Luther), a paraphrase of the *Te Deum laudamus* (We Praise Thee, Lord), an old hymn from the Latin service. It was probably crafted by Maistre Jhan, a composer active at the court of Ferrara during the 1530s, where Protestant thinkers, poets, and musicians from France had sought refuge from oppression and violence under the protection of a sympathetic French duchess, Renée de France.

In a culture ready to enlist music in struggles over faith and practice, we should perhaps not be surprised to discover composers and music teachers occasionally taking part in the fray. In the midst of instructing young students on the basics of music, for instance, the Lutheran pedagogue Martin Agricola (ca. 1486–1556), choirmaster of the Protestant Latin school in Magdeburg, could not resist a defamatory swipe at the moral failings of Catholic clergy. "Do not be eager to become a papist priest," he warned in his *Musica instrumentalis deudsch* (Instrumental Music in German) of 1545. "They scorn marriage and are always chasing after whores; they are also the most evil blasphemers of God, as is generally observed in all of them." Lasso, too, took his turn poking fun at the clergy. His chanson *Un jeune moine* (A Young Monk), a musical representation of the outrageous exploits of a monk who tries to seduce a nun, joined a long tradition of anticlerical songs that dated back to the popular tales retold in Boccaccio's *Decameron*, Chaucer's *Canterbury Tales*, and other medieval sources. When Lasso's friend and printer Adrian Le Roy demonstrated the piece for King Charles IX of France in January 1574, Le Roy reported that the king found it "as agreeable as it was marvelous." Even a Catholic king could laugh at the clergy's expense.

CONGREGATIONAL HYMNS AMONG THE PROTESTANTS

Such works, popular and professional alike, were only one side of a complicated story. Far more important for our understanding of the crisis of belief in sixteenth-century Europe are the uses of music in Protestant churches and homes, and by the theologians who framed the Protestant movement. Perhaps the best place to take up the story is with the writings of Martin Luther (1483–1546) and Jean Calvin (1509–1564), thinkers whose ideas profoundly shaped the character of musical practice in reformed religious communities in German- and French-speaking lands during the sixteenth century.

First and foremost, we ought to recognize that although Luther eventually broke with Rome over various questions having to do with the Eucharist, prerogatives of priests, the status of the saints in the context of prayer, and other fundamental issues, his initial attempts at reform were intended as changes *within* Catholic practice, and not as a radical rejection of it. At the time of his earliest writings he was still a practicing monk, and he carried over many elements of the Latin Mass into his model for worship. New emphasis, however, was placed on prayer in German and on congregational participation through strophic devotional songs. For this material Luther turned to Johann Walter (1496–1570), the choirmaster to the tolerant Catholic elector of Saxony, Friedrich the Wise. In his preface to Walter's *Geistliche gesangk Buchleyn* (Little Sacred Songbook), a collection of about 40 four-part songs in both German and Latin that was printed in Wittenberg in 1524, Luther gave clear voice to his ideal of popular piety expressed through music: "As a good beginning and to encourage those who can do better," he wrote, "I and several others have brought together certain spiritual songs with a view to spreading abroad and setting in motion the holy Gospel which now, by the grace of God, has again emerged" (SR 55:361; 3/20:83).

Luther did not give a name to the "spiritual songs" assembled in Walter's little book, but they quickly became essential to congregational worship in many German towns that took up Luther's reforms. In successive editions of the book,

Walter and others helped craft a complete repertory of harmonized tenor tunes for various functions throughout the sacred calendar—strophic melodies that we now call chorales. The texts and tunes had varied sources. Some were taken from the hymns that Luther and others translated into German. *Komm, Gott, Schöpfer, heiliger Geist* (Come, God, Creator, Holy Ghost), for instance, was based directly on the old Gregorian hymn *Veni, creator spiritus* (Come, Holy Ghost, Creator; Fig. 11.5). Others joined new poetry with familiar secular tunes. Still others were newly composed, text and music alike. But their purposes were singular and clear: to make religious ideas more comprehensible and to elevate everyday sounds with a spiritual component.

Spiritual songs of the sort prepared by the musicians associated with Luther and Calvin were destined for domestic use no less than for congregational worship. When the French Protestant composer Claude Goudimel (1514/20–1572) published some of his psalm harmonizations based on the tunes of the Calvinist hymnal in the 1550s and 1560s, he explained that his polyphonic settings were offered "not to induce you to sing them in church, but that you may rejoice in God, particularly in your homes. This should not be found an ill thing, the more so since the melody used in church is left in its entirety, just as though it were alone" (SR 58:368; 3/23:90). And when Thomas Tallis crafted an array of simple four-part hymns for the Anglican clergyman Matthew Parker's *The Whole Psalter Translated into English Metre* (1567), the printer added a brief note explaining how these modest arrangements might be used: "The tenor of these partes be for the people when they will syng alone. The other parts put for greater queers [choirs], or to suche as will sung or play them privatelye." (See Anthology 22 for a discussion of Tallis's *Why fumeth in sight*.)

LUTHER AND THE "WONDROUS WORK OF MUSIC"

For these sixteenth-century reformers, the true aim of music was to be found in its moral force. Already in Walter's *Geistliche gesangk Buchleyn* Luther imagined that such harmonized tunes would help with the proper formation of the young. They "should and must be trained in music and in other proper arts," he insisted, in order to "learn wholesome things and thus yield willingly, as becomes them, to the good" (SR 55:362; 3/20:84). This call to draw German youth "to the good" through the right kind of music was promptly taken up by musicians and printers, who produced a long line of teaching manuals and practical collections of polyphonic music for use at school and at home. In Nuremberg, the music master Seybald Heyden's *De arte canendi* (The Art of Singing) of 1540 presented the basics of musical notation and offered examples "to make the art of singing as easy and expeditious as possible for young students." Agricola, as we've seen, dispensed anti-Catholic vitriol while teaching boys about music

Figure 11.5: *Martin Luther,* Komm, Gott, Schöpfer, heiliger Geist, *chorale hymn based on* Veni, creator spiritus, *in an illustrated edition from Martin Luther, Konrad Ameln, and Valentin Babst,* Das Babstsche Gesangbuch *(Leipzig, 1545), fols. 27ᵛ–28ʳ*

in a series of Latin and German primers he brought out during the 1540s and 1550s. At about the same time, a friend of Luther, the physician and amateur musician Georg Forster, edited a series of collections containing hundreds of German songs, *Frische Teutsche Liedlein* (New German Songs, 1539–1556).

As we saw in Chapter 9, the help of master printers was essential to all of this work, for without them students and burghers would hardly have been able to afford the music that was seen as essential to their moral education. The Wittenberg printer Georg Rhau was by far the most important; he issued congregational hymnals, including an expanded edition of Walter's *Geistliche gesangk Buchleyn*, teaching manuals, compendia of German songs, and collections of two- and three-part songs of the sort that Heyden advocated. He also published large collections of liturgical music drawn from the works of the best composers of earlier generations, including Obrecht and Josquin.

Rhau's work reminds us that Lutheran musicians did not discard the Catholic music around them; they appropriated and interpreted it according to their needs. In his preface to Rhau's *Symphoniae iucundae* (Pleasant Harmonies, 1538), a collection of Latin works by Josquin, Isaac, and others, Luther offered moving testimony to the value of polyphony: "But when learning is added to all this," he wrote, "and artistic music which corrects, develops, and refines the natural music, then at last it is possible to taste with wonder (yet not to comprehend) God's absolute and perfect wisdom in his wondrous work of music."

The "wondrous work of music" and its remarkable power over human emotion had long been part of European thought. Plato had made music a cornerstone of aesthetic legislation in his vision of the ideal republic (SR 1:9–19; 1/1:9–19); St. Augustine had worried about the power that music seemed to hold over his spiritual sensibilities (SR 13:132–33; 2/5:22–23). So, too, Protestant reformers wanted to rein in music for what they understood as moral ends. In the first printed edition of the Geneva Psalter in 1542, Calvin wrote of music that "it has a secret and almost incredible power to move our hearts in one way or another." Yet along with his recognition of the spiritual potential of music came a simultaneous concern about its sensuous effects and how to control them. To ignore the problem would be to run the risk of "giving free rein to dissoluteness or of our making ourselves effeminate with disordered pleasures." The solution, it seems, was to be found not in discriminating the effects of one sound from another, but instead in making their potentially salutary effects dependent on the verbal texts to which they were bound. In this way Calvin hoped "to moderate the use of music to make it serve all that is of good repute" (SR 57:366; 3/22:88). The challenge for the reformers was not, as Bishop Bernardino Cirillo Franco had worried, how to distill pure from impure sounds. It was how to find the right words to suit a medium that was in some profound sense *already* sacred.

VAUTROLLIER AND THE SPIRITUAL CORRECTION
OF SECULAR SONGS

This takes us back to Thomas Vautrollier, the French Protestant printer who joined forces with the Catholic William Byrd and the Anglican Thomas Tallis in Elizabethan London. Originally from the great paper-making city of Troyes in eastern France, Vautrollier found his way to London and its growing population of French Protestants, or Huguenots, whose ranks increased quickly after the terrible St. Bartholomew's Day Massacre perpetrated by Catholic forces in France in the summer of 1572. Thousands perished in Paris alone, including Claude Goudimel, the most famous Huguenot musician of his day. On hearing news of the slaughter, Pope Gregory XIII organized a public procession of thanks to God, with singing of the customary *Te Deum*. Vautrollier must have been appalled at the news.

Vautrollier's work in his new home was by no means exclusively musical; he also issued editions of Calvin's and Luther's writings, Protestant martyrologies, and how-to books on learning English and French. But his music prints matter for what they reveal about the mediating role imagined by those who hoped to overcome sectarian intolerance through sound. As we have seen, in the preface to their first great collaborative venture under the new royal patent they received from Elizabeth, Tallis and Byrd carefully avoided specifying the spiritual purposes of the Latin music they offered the queen. Vautrollier certainly saw the wisdom of the gesture. But a set of music books he brought out five years earlier gives us a glimpse of what he might have said about the music of Talllis and Byrd had he been bold enough to speak up at the time.

Vautrollier's book was the *Recueil du mellange d'Orlande de Lassus* (Selections from the Miscellany of Orlando di Lasso, 1570), closely modeled on a collection of Lasso's settings of French secular poetry issued by Lasso's friend and printer in Paris, Adrian Le Roy, earlier that year. Vautrollier's purpose, however, was not simply to make a quick profit by pirating the Parisian print. He "corrected" the secular texts by changing their sometimes outrageously erotic or otherwise impious language. In Vautrollier's words, Lasso's music was "joined with serious texts and removed from all impurity."

The production of such spiritual *contrafacta* was a minor musical industry among Protestants and some Catholics in sixteenth-century France. Whether the families who sang through them at home ever really forgot the original lyrics is hard to say. But in principle such publications provided Protestant readers with pious domestic entertainment—something like parental control for Renaissance music. Certain Catholic editors undertook similar projects, not only with Lasso's music, but also with Italian madrigals by Marenzio and others. In the process, an expressive vocabulary developed especially in connection with profane poetry in French and Italian became associated with spiritual registers in French, Italian, and Latin. Mundane music became transcendent through its connection with the correct sorts of texts.

In fact, not all of the music by Lasso that Vautrollier chose to reprint needed spiritual retouching. Lasso's interpretation of one of the best-known spiritual poems of the sixteenth century, the Protestant preacher Guillaume Guéroult's *Susanne un jour* (Susanna One Day), found its way into the *Recueil du mellange* unchanged. The poem relates a story told in the Book of Daniel, in which the pious Susanna was unjustly accused of adultery by two elders who had threatened her with rape. Her fortitude and chastity, through which she was eventually redeemed, were clearly meant as a model of proper behavior. Lasso's setting has a long and admirable history: It takes its tenor part from a still more famous version from the 1540s by the Protestant musician Didier Lupi Second. Lasso's setting in turn engendered further echoes: He composed a polyphonic mass using his own five-voice chanson as a model. The instrumental virtuoso Giovanni Bassano published a wildly ornamented version of Lasso's chanson (see Anthology 23; further on Bassano in Chapters 12 and 13). And the song later turned up in English translation in Nicholas Yonge's popular collection of "transalpine" music, the *Musica transalpina* (Music from Beyond the Alps) of 1588.

Exceptional works like *Susanne un jour* notwithstanding, the fact that Lasso's music was subject to such correction bears testimony to the power of his compositional voice, and its potential to convey spiritual messages. For Vautrollier's readers in England, Lasso's music also served social ends. Alluding to the metaphysical harmony that exists among the various parts of a well-ruled state like his adopted England, Vautrollier compared such social agreement to the concordant union of polyphonic parts in a motet ("despite the differences," he observed, "among them they make no discord at all"). Such humanist speculation about the parallels between musical and social harmony recalls the views that Plato expressed in the *Republic* on the connection between ideal aesthetic and political forms. Vautrollier doubted that there was "more excellent music than that of Orlande de Lassus." Indeed, he was of the opinion that had Lasso's music been around when Plato lived, the philosopher surely would have illustrated his "political harmony" with "works of one such as Orlande." Perhaps Vautrollier's former partners Tallis and Byrd would have wanted their own music to play a similar role.

Music was the site of all sorts of claims by Christians of the sixteenth century. For Protestant communities, it was an essential part of congregational worship, emphasizing an accessible, participatory piety through hymns in the vernacular. Catholic institutions, in contrast, continued to sponsor elaborate Latin choral polyphony that often depended on professional ensembles. But these rival uses nevertheless had much in common. Both Catholic and Protestant musicians were anxious to discover and preserve some divine essence in music. Members of both camps were keen to regulate that sacred power through the careful alignment of text and tone, in the process associating themselves with the same concerns for oratory and persuasion that stand at the root of many humanistic writings of the day. Listeners discovered the divine in worldly sounds familiar from chansons and madrigals, much as they had discovered the means to share inner longings of love in the secular genres they knew so well. At times, music itself was imagined as the means to restore harmony to a continent torn by religious strife. Perhaps men like Vautrollier expected too much from music. But surely his world needed all the moderation it could get.

FOR FURTHER READING

Crook, David, "A Sixteenth-Century Catalog of Prohibited Music," *Journal of the American Musicological Society* 62 (2009): 1–78

Garside, Charles, "Calvin's Preface to the Psalter: A Re-Appraisal," *Musical Quarterly* 37 (1951): 566–77

Levy, Kenneth J., "'Susanne un jour': The History of a 16th Century Chanson," *Annales musicologiques* 1 (1953): 375–408

Macey, Patrick, *Bonfire Songs: Savonarola's Musical Legacy* (Oxford and New York: Oxford University Press, 1998)

——, "Savonarola and the Sixteenth-Century Motet," *Journal of the American Musicological Society* 36 (1983): 422–52

McCarthy, Kerry, *Liturgy and Contemplation in Byrd's Gradualia* (New York: Routlege, Francis and Taylor, 2007)

Monson, Craig A., "Byrd, the Catholics, and the Motet: The Hearing Reopened," in *Hearing the Motet*, ed. Dolores Pesce, pp. 348–74 (New York and Oxford: Oxford University Press, 1997)

——, "The Council of Trent Revisited," *Journal of the American Musicological Society* 55 (2002): 1–37

Nugent, George, "Anti-Protestant Music for Sixteenth-Century Ferrara," *Journal of the American Musicological Society* 43 (1990): 228–91

Oettinger, Rebecca Wagner, *Music as Propaganda in the German Reformation*, St. Andrews Studies in Reformation History (Aldershot and Burlington, VT: Ashgate, 2001)

Palisca, Claude V., "Bernardino Cirillo's Critique of Polyphonic Church Music of 1549: Its Background and Resonance," in *Music in Renaissance Cities and Courts: Studies in Honor of Lewis Lockwood*, ed. Jessie Ann Owens and Anthony Cummings, pp. 282–91 (Warren, MI: Harmonie Park Press, 1997)

Ⓢ Additional resources available at wwnorton.com/studyspace

CHAPTER TWELVE

The Arts of Improvisation, Embellishment, and Variation

M odern performers are accustomed to scores in which composers carefully spell out the directions for realizing their works, but musicians of
the fifteenth and sixteenth centuries were much more on their own. For those
trained in the manuscript tradition of the years before 1500, knowing how to
align words and music, how to apply the rules of unwritten accidentals called
musica ficta (false music), and other routines of performance practice was an
important measure of one's professional expertise. In a world where composers,
performers, and listeners were frequently part of the same closed circle, it was
considered both unnecessary and unworthy to specify too clearly how and what
to play or sing.

As we saw in our discussion of the lost art of improvisatory counterpoint in
Chapter 2, professional musicians depended on their knowledge of these unwritten conventions to flesh out scores. But with the advent of music printing in the
sixteenth century, these interpretive instructions could be disseminated for a
growing readership of amateur performers who often had no direct contact with
the artisans who produced their books or the composers who imagined the music.

Even as the roles of creator and interpreter became more sharply differentiated, the skills that separated amateur from professional musicians were becoming increasingly available to all. Instrumental and vocal genres alike were in rapid flux as a result of these developments, as musicians adapted and reworked conventions, forms, and expressive possibilities in a new creative mix.

THE SINGING LADIES OF FERRARA

In 1628, Vincenzo Giustiniani (1564–1637) sat down to write a memoir in the form of an anonymous letter to an unnamed young nobleman. He offered all sorts of advice: how to manage a household, how to travel, and how to take part in a hunt. He also included "discourses" on painting and music. Giustiniani benefited from his privileged position as a member of an important noble family in Rome and brother of a prominent cardinal, connections that afforded him ready access to the finest that Italian culture had to offer. He knew and supported the painter Caravaggio and amassed an extensive collection of antique art. His *Discorso sopra la musica de' suoi tempi* (Discourse on the Music of his Times) is imbued with the courtier aesthetic, being based "on the little experience I have acquired while I was conversing in houses where there was no gambling but rather delightful occupations, particularly music, performed without assistance of paid performers by divers gentlemen who took pleasure and delight in it through natural inclination."

Perhaps not surprisingly, Giustiniani's recollections favor developments in singing and playing over technical discussion of counterpoint or harmonic proportion. But in stressing these aspects of musical life in Rome and other cities, his *Discorso* reveals much about how men like him perceived the deep connection between performance and composition. Nowhere was this connection more evident, in Giustiniani's memory, than in some formative moments in the 1570s and 1580s, when musical practice changed rather suddenly. Light three-voice textures from the popular urban villanelle were combined with the polyphonic designs of five-voice madrigals (see Chapter 10); multi-voice pieces were composed in imitation of solo songs with instrumental accompaniments.

Most memorable of all were new styles of singing. The virtuoso bass Giulio Cesare Brancaccio, whom we met in Chapter 7 in connection with the ducal court of Ferrara, thrilled listeners with a thundering range of nearly three octaves. Court composers Giaches de Wert in Mantua and Luzzasco Luzzaschi in Ferrara both taught and learned from highly skilled performers. They were "in charge of all the music of the dukes of those cities," Giustiniani recalled, men who took delight in gathering many important gentlewomen and gentlemen to play and sing excellently. So great was their delight that they lingered sometimes for whole days in some little chambers they had ornately outfitted with pictures and tapestries for this sole purpose. There was a great rivalry between the women of Mantua and Ferrara, a competition not only in the timbre and disposition of their voices but also in ornamentation with exquisite runs joined opportunely and not excessively. (SR 54:353; 3/19:75)

Giustiniani's remarks are revealing on a number of accounts, for they describe a world in which social and musical practices from distinct registers came together in a spirit of creative play. Only the composers were paid professionals. Their pupils, in contrast, were members of the nobility. As we saw in Chapter 7, when talented young ladies of good families like Laura Peverara, Livia d'Arco, and Anna Guarini were recruited for the *concerto delle donne* (consort of ladies, as Giustiniani's "women" were known at the court of Ferrara), local noblemen were quickly rounded up to be their husbands. For the Renaissance noblewoman, singing in public or for money risked the serious stigma of being identified as a courtesan. Brancaccio could not bear the thought that he might be confused with a mere professional, and soon left Ferrara in a huff. But performing as a dilettante among one's peers was a different story. According to Castiglione's *Book of the Courtier* (1528), solo singing to the accompaniment of the lute was among the best means to demonstrate one's studied carelessness, or *sprezzatura*. And according to Giustiniani, the singing of the *concerto delle donne* was not to be missed:

There was competition even more in moderating or enlarging the voice, loud or soft, attenuating it or fattening it as was called for, now drawing it out, now breaking it off with the accompaniment of a sweet interrupted sigh, now giving out long runs, distinct and well followed, now turns, now leaps, now long trills, now short ones, now sweet runs sung quietly, to which sometimes one suddenly heard an echo respond; and more still in the participation of the face, and of the looks and gestures that accompanied appropriately the music and conceits of the poetry. (SR 54:353–54; 3/19:75–76)

Giustiniani seems to pass over the contributions that composers made to this remarkable display of virtuosity. For him the interpreters *were* the piece, insofar as their gestures, dynamic inflections, and embellishments were in keeping with the "conceits of the poetry." The preoccupation with the proper relationship between text and tone, and their combined effect upon listeners, has been a recurring theme in this book. What is striking in this instance is the extent to which these expressive connections were forged by accidents of interpretation. Stranger still seems the possibility that such virtuosity could thrive in a landscape of *collective* embellishment practiced by a trio of female performers.

COURTLY IMPROVISERS, COURTLY AUDIENCES

We would like to know more about who contributed what to the extraordinary performances heard in the *musica secreta* (private music) of the Ferrarese court during the 1580s and 1590s. What relationship did the three "singing ladies of Ferrara" bear to the long and largely unwritten tradition of solo singing in Italy in the fifteenth and sixteenth centuries? Or to the experiments with solo singing and dramatic representation undertaken in the late 1500s by Giulio Caccini and Jacopo Peri in Florence (see Chapter 14)? Our sense of mystery about the improvisatory scene in Ferrara is compounded by the veil of secrecy imposed around the *concerto delle donne* by the ducal court, which was keen to protect its musical treasure from common ears and the taint of uncourtly professionalism. Admission to the *musica secreta* was reserved for nobility and visiting dignitaries. It was expressly forbidden to copy or distribute the music sung by the ladies. Even those works by ducal composer Luzzascho Luzzaschi that we know to have been written for the *concerto delle donne* were not published until the early seventeenth century, following the deaths of the singers' noble patrons.

Yet as word of the marvelous singing ladies spread, prominent composers from other households began to write for them. Thanks to the close dynastic alliance between the ruling families of Ferrara and Mantua, for instance, Giaches de Wert had access to the ensemble, as recounted in the dedication of his *Eighth Book of Madrigals* (1586), in which he gushed to Duke Alfonso d'Este over "the marvels, art, character, voice, grace, disposition, memory, and the other abundant and rare qualities of the three most noble young Ladies of Her Serene Highness, the Duchess of Ferrara." Wert's book includes a number of works that capture the luxuriant style of simultaneous embellishment for which the singers were known. Entire collections of madrigals, such as *Il lauro verde* (The Green Laurel, 1583), prepared under the editorial supervision of the Ferrarese court poet Torquato Tasso, were published in honor of Laura Peverara, featuring contributions by an array of leading composers. Luca Marenzio (1553/54–1599), active mainly in Rome, was represented in these honorific books and continued to reach out to meet Ferrarese tastes in the years ahead. Dedicating his *Sixth Book of Madrigals* (1595) to the presiding patron of the *concerto*, Duchess Margherita d'Este, he was careful to feature poetry by Tasso, her favorite court writer, and to include among the various polyphonic lines music written to suit the agile voices of the three ladies, who sang alone in duos, trios, and larger ensembles. As we noted in Chapter 7, men like Giulio Cesare Brancaccio also took part in these performances; no doubt other musicians did, too.

MARENZIO'S *O VERDI SELVE*: A MADRIGAL FOR THE *CONCERTO DELLE DONNE*

In *O verdi selve* (O Verdant Woods), Marenzio capitalized on the twin fashions for new poetry and elaborate vocal ornaments in the same work. The poem takes its place in a long line of echo lyrics, texts in which successive lines are bound in a chain of sonic puns: starting in line 6, the last syllables of one line are repeated as the first syllables of the next (as in *fortuna/Una*). Answering its own questions by replaying sounds just heard with new meanings, Tasso's pastoral poem invites musical treatment that pits one voice or group of voices against another.

O verdi selve, o dolci fonti, o rivi,
O luoghi ermi e selvaggi,
Pini, abeti, ginepri, allori e faggi;
O vaghi augelli, semplici e lascivi,
Eco, e tu che rispondi al mio lamento,
Chi può dar fine a sì crudel fortuna?
– Una. – Dunque sol una
È la cagion del mio mesto concento?
– Cento. – Non son già cento, e pur son molte
In bella festa accolte.
Come una potrà dunque il mal fornire?
– Ire. – Per ira mai nè per dispetto
Non avrà fine amor nel nostro petto.

"O green woods, o sweet springs, o river banks,
O places lonely and wild,
Pines, firs, junipers, laurels, and beeches,
O pretty birds, simple and full of desire,
Here, you who answer my lament,
Who can put an end to such cruel fortune?"
"One [lady]." "Then is only one
The cause of my sad harmony?"
"One hundred." "Perhaps not yet one hundred, but there are many
Gathered together in merry-making.
How will one be able to cause misfortune?"
"Anger." "Never through wrath or spite
Will Love have an end in our heart."

Marenzio seizes on the idea of repetition to showcase the "exquisite runs" that Giustiniani found so fascinating in his account of the luxuriant Ferrarese style. The ornaments animate the pastoral landscape with busy turns, scales, and

Example 12.1: *Luca Marenzio,* O verdi selve, *mm. 1–7. From Luca Marenzio,* Opera Omnia, *ed. Bernhard Meier and Roland Jackson, 7 vols.,* Corpus Mensurabilis Musicae, *72 (Neuhausen-Stuttgart: American Institute of Musicology, 1983), 6:217.*

upward runs that imitate the movement, or even specific sounds, imagined in the text at "dolci fonti" (sweet springs), "rivi" (river banks), "abeti" (spruces), and "vaghi augelli" (pretty birds; Ex. 12.1). A wide range of musical textures also helps to display the abilities of the singers, since Marenzio often breaks down the six-part ensemble into smaller groups: trios (distinguished by the lively rhythms of the secular genre that Giustiniani identified with villanelle), duets, and solos.

O verdi selve must have been as much fun to sing as it was to hear. But we need to look further to understand the connection between a work like Marenzio's, with its careful control of ornament, texture, and timing, and the impromptu embellishments, expressive nuances, and physical movements that Giustiniani recalled in the performances of the *concerto delle donne*. Was Marenzio transcribing something done on the spot by smart ensemble singers? Was he attempting to imitate the character of music that was originally extemporized? In short, did the new compositional styles celebrated by noble dilettantes like Giustiniani arise from the innovations of performers, or should we instead understand the male composers as attempting to rein in the unwritten and unpredictable performing habits of the mainly female singers?

LEARNING THE ARTS OF EMBELLISHMENT FROM A PAPAL SINGER

Giustiniani had nothing but praise for the judicious embellishments of the singing ladies of Ferrara, but he wrote less glowingly about other improvising performers. A certain "Giovanni Luca" of Rome, he noted, usually erred in his altogether excessive application of embellishment. Giustiniani was almost certainly thinking of Giovanni Luca Conforti (ca. 1560–1608), a virtuoso falsettist, or male soprano, in the Papal Chapel in Rome. Conforti specialized in applying unwritten florid ornaments (which he and others called *passaggi*, "diminutions," or "divisions") to vocal works, and brought out various publications to show others how it was to be done. In his *Breve et facile maniera d'essercitarsi a far passaggi* (Quick and Easy Way to Execute Ornaments, 1593), he proudly announced that, thanks to his new manual, the techniques of ornamentation otherwise heard "only in great cities and at the courts of princes" could be sung and heard by any who wished.

Breaching a cordon of exclusivity consciously cultivated by Giustiniani, and especially by the Ferrarese patrons of the *musica secreta*, Conforti would surely have been perceived as threatening the status quo. But even a quick look inside the covers of the *Breve et facile maniera* is enough to make us wonder whether Giustiniani's criticism was justified. Conforti takes students systematically through all the melodic combinations they were likely to encounter, illustrating almost every imaginable pattern that might be used to embellish a given melodic interval (Fig. 12.1).

Cadences are a major site of embellishment, and in this respect Conforti was in agreement with a long line of improvisers. Because cadences were designed to emphasize the syntactic divisions of sacred and literary texts, the practice of ornamenting long notes with rapid passagework for rhetorical emphasis in these places could appeal to Scholastic and humanist thinkers alike. Conforti next offers a tour of melodic intervals and the ways they might be decorated: leaps are filled in, while scales are broken up with turns and other figures, to the point that the original melody is drowned in a flood of energetic ornament.

Figure 12.1: *Illustration of melodic ornaments to be applied to a descending second, from Giovanni Luca Conforti,* Breve et facile maniera d'essercitarsi a far passaggi *(Rome, 1593), p.5.*

To modern ears, what is most important about manuals like Conforti's is the overwhelmingly rhythmic character of the ornaments. These are not the slurred roulades of nineteenth-century vocal or instrumental styles, but rather figures founded on the symmetrical division of longer note values into a string of detached notes. Such "divisions" serve as melodic accents and, in the case of the tutors aimed at players of recorders, viols, or keyboards, are well suited to the limited dynamic range of these instruments. Singers were less constrained in terms of volume, but to judge from books like Conforti's, vocal technique was similar in terms of its preference for division over lyrical phrasing when it came to embellishment.

EMBELLISHMENT FOR EVERYONE

Conforti was not alone in promoting melodic embellishment through printed instruction manuals intended for amateur musicians, for whom the largely unwritten traditions of ornamentation practiced by professionals remained otherwise inaccessible. "Divisions have two effects," the Venetian recorder virtuoso Silvestro Ganassi observed in his *Regola rubertina* (Robertean Rules; the title refers to the dedicatee, Ruberto Strozzi) of 1542. "First, they embellish the composition or enhance the counterpoint, and secondly, they are pleasant to listen to, especially when the ornamentations are varied and well phrased." Indeed, while Giustiniani complained of the indiscriminate application of diminution to a melodic line, the examples of embellished compositions he adduces from treatises by Italian players are remarkably varied, subtle, and surprising. Giovanni Bassano's divisions on the superius line of Orlando di Lasso's spiritual chanson *Susanne un jour*, discussed in Chapter 11, are a case in point (see Anthology 23).

Bassano (ca. 1560/1561–1617) was an accomplished wind player and composer active in churches in and around Venice, one of a number of men who wrote ably in a rich tradition of music for multiple choirs of voices and instruments heard at the Basilica of San Marco. (See Chapter 13 for a discussion of Bassano's unusual family heritage.) In the 1580s and 1590s he published instruction manuals like those issued by Ganassi and Conforti, with suggestions for how to decorate cadences and melodies with diminutions and *passaggi*. In his *Motetti, madrigali, et canzoni francese di diversi eccellentissimi autori* (Motets, Madrigals, and French Canzonas by Various Most Excellent Composers) of 1591, he offered fully ornamented versions of Lasso's chanson and other well-known pieces. The music is filled with the usual pyrotechnics—flashy scales, patterned division of long notes, and other tricks of the virtuoso's trade—and Lasso's musical ideas are compressed, echoed, and put through sequential treatment. But Bassano's embellishments are not merely pleasant to listen to; they have been described as "controlled improvisations" that seem spontaneous and reflective at the same time.

The techniques promoted for the recorder by Bassano and Ganassi take their place alongside those presented in many how-to books aimed at amateur viol players. Musicians active in Italy took the lead. Girolamo dalla Casa (?–1601) was, like Bassano, a permanent member of the instrumental ensemble at the Basilica of San Marco in Venice; his two-volume treatise on ornamentation appeared in 1584. Diego Ortiz (ca. 1510–ca. 1570) was a Spanish musician active in Naples, which had been ruled by Spanish kings since the fifteenth century; his *Trattado de glosas sobre clausulas* (Treatise of Elaborated Cadences, 1553) was published in both Spanish and Italian versions. The title of Ortiz's book suggests a work devoted to the elaboration of cadences, but he also shows ensemble players how to engage in simultaneous diminution, much as the *concerto delle donne* would later attempt to such compelling expressive effect.

The tutors also reveal that sixteenth-century musicians were ready to adapt polyphonic vocal music—sacred motets no less than secular chansons and madrigals—for a wide range of performing forces. Lasso's *Susanne un jour* was a frequent choice. So were several other "hits" of the sixteenth century, including Jacques Arcadelt's *O felici occhi miei* (O My Happy Eyes) and Cipriano de Rore's *Ancor che col partire* (Even Though in Parting; see Chapter 10 on the place of these composers in the story of secular music of the sixteenth century). Motets like Palestrina's *Vestiva i colli* (Clothed the Hills), too, were taken up as models for embellishment and variation. The practice should not surprise us: Dalla Casa, Bassano, and Conforti were members of ecclesiastical establishments. With respect to diminution, instrumental and vocal idioms and repertories were deeply intertwined, but also subject to constant borrowing and adaptation. Ganassi and Dalla Casa show how the superius part could be played or sung while the remaining parts were played by a lutenist, a practice that anticipates the solo textures of the early seventeenth century. When the bassus part is embellished by a viol player, Ortiz and Bassano warn, it is important that a harpsichordist simultaneously play the original, undecorated line.

The busy clash of simple and ornamented parts suggested by Ortiz and Bassano might strike us as incongruous, but sixteenth-century musicians found it perfectly natural. When the Italian music theorist Nicola Vicentino (1511–1576) turned to the question of diminution in his *L'antica musica ridotta alla moderna prattica* (Ancient Music Adapted to Modern Practice, 1555), he acknowledged the prevalence of embellishment by church musicians of the day. But since "diminution always causes the loss of numerous consonances," Vicentino was of the opinion that it should be used only in the performance of compositions with more than four voices, presumably because the need for doublings of consonant tones in larger textures would ensure that essential harmonic proportion was maintained. On this premise he actually encouraged choristers to bring instrumentalists into church in order to play the undecorated lines while the vocalists performed the same parts with *passaggi*. To us, the resulting heterophony might sound more confused than proportionate, but for the theoretical mind, the idea that sensation would override the requirements of reason was unthinkable.

BORROWED MELODIES, "ITALIAN TENORS," AND THE ART OF INSTRUMENTAL VARIATION

Improvising amateur instrumentalists had still other opportunities to put their fast fingers to work. In addition to his suggestions for decorating cadences and vocal compositions, for instance, Ortiz offered pointers on how to improvise against a cantus firmus and against dance tunes known as "Italian tenors," as well as how to improvise from one's own imagination, which he called the art of *fantasía* (see below).

By "Italian tenors" Ortiz meant any of the various standard musical patterns used to accompany dance. The *recercada* presented in Anthology 24 corresponds to a scheme later known as *La folia* (literally, madness, referring to the wild, erotic overtones of the original dance). Other types represented in Ortiz's book include forms of the passamezzo antico and passamezzo moderno, and the romanesca, which is shown in Example 12.2. Like the other patterns in this section of Ortiz's manual, this one unfolds as a series of paired phrases (in our modern transcription each phrase corresponds to 16 measures). Each phrase consists of four stages in a progression (each two measures long) defined by the contrapuntal movement between the lowest part of the accompaniment (which

Example 12.2: *Diego Ortiz,* Recercada settima *(romanesca), mm. 1–15. From Ortiz's* Trattado de glosas sobre clausulas *(Rome: Dorico, 1553), as printed in an edition otherwise identical in musical content, but with all of the prefatory and textual commentary in Italian:* Nel qual si tratta delle glose sopra le cadenze *(Rome: Dorico, 1553), fols. 58ᵛ–59ʳ.*

leaps from B♭ to F, then G to D) and a corresponding motion in the tenor register (moving stepwise from D to C to B♭ to A; it is seen most clearly in the keyboard accompaniment, but is heard in an ornamented version in the solo voice, too). Together they make alternating thirds and fifths, then cadence at the octave to make a convincing close at the end of the paired phrase.

The very same pattern can be heard in an anonymous *galliarde* (a fast-paced dance in triple mensuration) published in Paris during the late 1520s by Pierre Attaingnant in a book of dances and preludes for solo lute (Ex. 12.3). Attaingnant's piece takes only eight bars in our modern transcription, but the paired phrases and basic counterpoint match precisely the model presented by Ortiz: B♭ to F, then G to D in the lowest register, paired with a linear descent (D, C, B♭, A) in the middle register. The formula is repeated, this time with a solid cadence to G. What is more, in both this *galliarde* and in Ortiz's romanesca we can also see how the melodic descent heard in the middle part of the texture

Example 12.3: *Anonymous,* Galliarde *(romanesca),* mm. 1–8. From Preludes, Chansons, and Dances for Lute Published by Pierre Attaingnant, Paris *(1529–1530),* ed. *Daniel Heartz (Neuilly-sur-Seine: Société de musique d'autrefois, 1964), p. 99.*

is joined by parallel motion in yet another line. In the lute part and in Ortiz's keyboard accompaniment this parallel motion starts a sixth above the middle voice (that is: Bb, A, G, F♯). In Ortiz's ornamented solo line these tones are also heard prominently a third *below* the main descent previous described.

Patterns like these were dear to instrumentalists, but singers and composers knew them too, particularly since they provided a ready way to make counterpoint in three voices while avoiding forbidden successions of parallel fifths between any two of them. Indeed, we can hear the contrapuntal formula just described in *Mille regrets* (Anthology 15, where it is put to work in the service of the ideas behind the text) and in Du Fay's *Supremum est mortabilis* (Anthology 9, where it is used to give special emphasis to the name of one of the piece's dedicatees, King Sigismund of Hungary). Patterns like those presented in Ortiz's manual also had a long afterlife, emerging in the seventeenth century as part of the ground bass, or basso ostinato, tradition. They also point the way to chordal harmony and to-nality, inasmuch as they depend on regular phrasing and strong pairings of what modern musicians would hear as tonic and dominant functions. Musicians of the fifteenth and sixteenth centuries certainly recognized the practical utility of this kind of counterpoint, but the concept of triadic inversion so fundamental to later theories of harmonic tonality was not part of their explanatory vocabulary.

As Ortiz's treatise confirms, these tunes were well known to Italian musicians. What is more, Ortiz tells us that the ornamented melody and accompanying bass lines are to be taken as a mere outline. The harpsichord player needs to fill in the intervening span with consonances and counterpoint, much as continuo players were expected to do in the seventeenth and eighteenth centuries. Apparently, such skills were already part of the training of young organists in the sixteenth cen-tury. Manuals such as the *Arte de tañer fantasía* (The Art of Playing Fantasia, 1565), by the priest Tomás de Sancta María of Madrid, offer a glimpse of how this largely unwritten tradition was taught and practiced. Keyboardists learned to pair successive consonances (for example, alternating thirds and fifths) against a given fragment of melody or bass line. Building up longer structures by "playing in consonances" in a chain of contrapuntal patterns (as we can see in Ex. 12.2), Spanish organists like Tomás and his teacher Antonio de Cabezón, the blind court organist to Charles V, were able to apply these templates in a variety of contexts, including not only Ortiz's Italian tenors from the world of social dance, but also the accompaniment of liturgical falsobordones (see Chapter 2) and the "art of *fantasía*."

Italian tenors such as Ortiz's seventh *recercada* (excerpted in Ex. 12.2) and the improvised tradition of playing in consonances exerted a profound influence on sixteenth-century composers. The practice reappears in music for popular dances, not only in Italian sources, but also in sixteenth-century pieces from north of the Alps that feature other forms and steps, such as the sedate duple-meter pavane and the lively triple-meter galliard. The *galliarde* published by Attaingnant in 1529 (see Ex. 12.3) would immediately have been recognized by anyone familiar with Ortiz's Italian tenors.

Through manuals like Ortiz's and collections of dance pieces of the sort brought out by Attaingnant and other northern printers, music that had once been the exclusive domain of professional players took on new purposes. As accompaniment to social dancing, it continued to be played by professional ensembles practiced in the unwritten arts of embellishment and variation. Thanks to didactic manuals and albums of improvised arrangements, however, such music could now be studied, elaborated, and enjoyed for its aesthetic qualities. Through these books we can also trace the emerging sense of specialized genres, and in particular the kinds of soloistic display that would figure centrally in the development of idiomatic instrumental music beginning in the seventeenth century.

FANTASÍA: PLAYING FROM IMAGINATION

Ortiz refrains from describing the "art of *fantasía*" except in general, strategic terms: it is distinguished from other kinds of music by its independence from a cantus firmus or a dance tune. "The *fantasía* one cannot demonstrate," he writes, "because everyone plays it in his own way." When viol and harpsichord players attempt it together, he allows, there ought to be a certain give and take: the harpsichord provides "consonances" while the viol plays diminutions. But if the latter pauses on long notes, it is time for the keyboardist to make imitative "fugues" in the matter of vocal counterpoint. Ortiz makes no attempt to realize the resulting extemporized polyphony, preferring instead to offer just the viol part for each of several model ricercars. The "secrets" of this way of playing, he continues, are best discovered through practice.

Fantasía remained an aural manifestation of the musical imagination in the conception of sixteenth-century musicians for quite some time. When the

influential Venetian priest and music theorist Gioseffo Zarlino (1517–1590) considered the basic rules of unwritten counterpoint, he assured his readers that
the same premises applied no matter whether one was singing "upon a subject"
or "di fantasia." In the first instance he was referring to the old practice of making counterpoint against a notated melody. But what about the kind that comes
"di fantasia"? The plain sense of the text might seem simply to mean "out of one's
own head." Certainly this seems to be the way Thomas Morley (1557/58–
1602) understood the term when he described "fantasy" as an opportunity
for a musician to take "a point [of imitation] at his pleasure . . . making either
much or little of it according as shall seeme best in his own conceit."

Fantasy and imagination were not simply creative abilities, however; they
were physical structures of the mind. Sixteenth-century thinkers held something
"fantastic" or "imaginary" not simply as "made up," but as the delivery in sound
of figures already inscribed in the mind's eye. The art of "playing *fantasia*" was
not simply playing "what one liked"; it was a conscious act that translated temporary figures of the musical imagination for all to hear. Thus when the Spanish
instrumentalist Luys Milán (ca. 1500–ca. 1560) brought out his instruction book
El maestro (The Master, 1536) for vihuela de mano, a six-string fretted instrument
plucked by hand, he explained that any work called *fantasía* earned its title "in the
sense that it only proceeds from the fantasy and industry of the author who created it." The art of *fantasía* is the ability to recall those mental "images" of themes
and motives and put them in order according to the needs of the moment. As such,
fantasía has strong affinities with the orator's arts of imagination, memory, and
delivery as they were understood by fifteenth- and sixteenth-century writers.

The concept of *fantasía* as more process than form might also help us
to understand the complex history of the works of Francesco da Milano
(1497–1543), a lute virtuoso active especially in Rome during the second quarter of the sixteenth century. Francesco was renowned above all for his skills
as an improviser, so we should perhaps not be too surprised that his written
works, with their successions of imitative points, contrapuntal duos, and evoca-
tions of fauxbourdon technique, give the impression of having been transcribed
from performance. As Francesco's works were copied and reprinted by successive
generations of players long after his death, they were continuously reworked
according to need. The art of playing *fantasía* could begin as a transcription of
a mental image, but once written down it invited reassembly according to the
imaginative faculties of each new player.

FABRIZIO DENTICE'S SOLO LUTE FANTASIAS

Not many amateur lutenists could aspire to create fantasias as subtle or compelling as the professional Francesco. But Fabrizio Dentice (?1539–1581) apparently did. Born into an old aristocratic family of Naples, he played and

composed the most demanding music for lute, both embellished interpretations of well-known vocal music and original fantasias of his own. Like Francesco da Milano's music, his compositions for lute reveal a commanding technical skill as a player, and also a sophisticated understanding of form, counterpoint, and melodic invention, reconfiguring a few basic contrapuntal ideas in a variety of musical combinations. These musical "images" move before our ears in ways that permit listeners to follow Dentice's mental *fantasía* (Anthology 25). Yet his was not simply music for public display. Following the prescriptions discussed in our exploration of music and the ideal courtier (Chapter 7), Fabrizio was careful to confine his music-making to settings in which his amateur (and therefore noble) status would not be in doubt. His music was never published during his lifetime, but was instead preserved in private manuscripts for use by fellow gentlemen.

For the swelling ranks of amateur lutenists, keyboardists, and recorder players who purchased the method books by Ganassi, Bassano, and others, the way to music was eased by various conveniences. The music of Dentice and Francesco is notated in tablature, a practical encoding of music that is in essence a shorthand image of the lute fingerboard. Such diagrams give the reader exact information on where to put the fingers on the fingerboard with one hand, and when to pluck the individual strings with the other. Detailed understanding of vocal notation was not necessary, nor was an understanding of *musica ficta*, since all such alterations were already encoded for the player. Lutenists could play directly from the tablature without needing to interpret abstract mensural signs on staves (see Fig. 9.6).

More-advanced students might be called upon to make their own lute "intabulation" of a vocal piece for private performance or to accompany a solo singer. The variety of practical advice on this process of arrangement and transcription is revealing in and of itself. In his treatise *Fronimo* (1568), the Florentine theorist Vincenzo Galilei tells his pupil repeatedly that each and every note of a given vocal model must be put into the intabulation, with the result that some instrumental transcriptions have chords or combinations that are physically unplayable. Another Italian lutenist, Cosimo Bottegari (a gentleman and a longtime resident at the ducal court of Bavaria in Munich), took a different and much more pragmatic approach. In his adaptations, multiple voices have been combined in order to support a solo singer on another line. They preserve the broad sense of the original polyphony but frequently omit notes and details. Their goal was to provide suitable material for players of limited skill who wanted to make things sound and appear more difficult than they actually were. It was a classic example of the *sprezzatura* that every courtier needed to display.

Vocal embellishment, as we have seen in the case of the music for the *concerto delle donne*, opened new possibilities for the representation of literary texts, highlighting the concern for language and expression so long a part of sixteenth-century culture. Diminutions as proposed by writers like Ortiz, Ganassi, and Vicentino also served to introduce new contrapuntal dissonance that anticipates the harmonic innovations of the seventeenth century. Variation patterns like the romanesca, too, point toward instrumental genres and forms central to seventeenth-century idioms and their focus on virtuosic display.

Improvisers and composers, as we have often observed, had much to teach each other. The social dimensions of improvisation, embellishment, and variations are also significant. Printed tutors of the sixteenth century helped to spread knowledge of unwritten practices previously reserved for professionals among a rapidly growing group of amateur musicians who sought new recreational and aesthetic purposes in music. A broad process that differentiated new roles for composers, performers, and listeners was under way, with profound implications for the history of music.

FOR FURTHER READING

Brown, Howard Mayer, *Embellishing Sixteenth-Century Music* (London: Oxford University Press, 1976)

Butler, Gregory G., "The Fantasia as Musical Image," *Musical Quarterly* 60 (1974): 602–15

Horsley, Imogene, "Improvised Embellishment in the Performance of Renaissance Polyphonic Music," *Journal of the American Musicological Society* 4 (1951): 3–19

Polk, Keith, "Voices and Instruments: Soloists and Ensembles in the 15th Century," *Early Music* 18 (1990): 179–98

Roig-Francolí, Miguel A., "Playing in Consonances: A Spanish Renaissance Technique of Chordal Improvisation," *Early Music* 23 (1995): 461–71

Stras, Laurie, "Recording Tarquinia: Imitation, Parody and Reportage in Ingegneri's 'Hor che 'l ciel e la terra e 'l vento tace,'" *Early Music* 27 (1999): 358–63

Ⓢ **Additional resources available at wwnorton.com/studyspace**

CHAPTER THIRTEEN

Empire, Exploration, and Encounter

M usic teaches us much about the European encounter with other cultures during the first century of exploration following Columbus's journey of discovery. As early explorers and missionaries witnessed performances and rituals during their travels in the Americas, Africa, and Asia, their reports reveal as much about the values of the authors as they did about the cultures they attempted to chronicle. Protestant writers in the New World often regarded oral native cultures with suspicion, considering their elaborate ceremonies as offensive as Catholic ritual. Catholic missionaries, from Dominican monks in New Spain to Jesuit preachers at the court of China, similarly heard native musical cultures as echoes of their own anxieties about popular traditions in Europe.

Both Catholics and Protestants used their own music as the vanguard of a vast project of religious conversion that went hand in hand with patterns of colonization and conquest that unfolded almost anywhere Europeans arrived in the name of monarch and church. The same stories that the Renaissance humanists told themselves about their cultural superiority to the "Middle Ages" also convinced them of the inferiority of almost any non-European civilization they encountered on the newly expanded globe. The effect was as plain to them in sound as it was in matters of religious custom, foodways, or even clothing.

VENICE AND THE WORLD

Poets, chroniclers, engravers, and musicians of the fifteenth and early sixteenth centuries were frequently called upon to celebrate the virtues of dynastic rulers with works that marked treaties, victories, and coronations. Now the celebration of colonial expansion and empire was added to these obligations. During the late 1530s, Venice, a powerful maritime city-state, formed a Holy League with Pope Paul III and Holy Roman Emperor Charles V against the Ottoman sultan Süleyman the Magnificent, whose own empire extended through much of the Balkan peninsula and threatened Venetian trading posts in the Aegean. The conflict culminated in a great naval battle at Lepanto in the Gulf of Corinth in October 1571, when hundreds of ships under the command of Don Juan of Austria defeated an even larger force from the Ottoman navy, sinking hundreds of ships and freeing thousands of Christian galley slaves. The event was heralded throughout Europe as the triumph of united Christendom over Islam and the Ottoman Empire. The Battle of Lepanto was celebrated in poems, paintings, and religious ceremony (Fig. 13.1). Inasmuch as the date (October 7) coincided with a feast in honor of Saint Justina of Padua, military commanders of the day credited her with the victory. Eventually the day was observed as Our Lady of Victory, and then (in 1573, following a decision by Pope Gregory XIII) the Feast of the Blessed Virgin Mary of the Rosary; it is still a part of the Catholic liturgy.

Among the musicians who contributed to the celebrations was Andrea Gabrieli (1532/33–1585), organist at the great Basilica of San Marco in Venice from the 1560s through the 1580s. His madrigal *Asia felice* (Happy Asia) offers the reactions of Asia, Africa, and Europe to the good news of the victory (Ex. 13.1). "After glorious ordeals," Europe sings, "now under a true God, not a false Jove, I shall have the reins of the world again." (According to an anonymous chronicler, during the Carnival season of 1572 the work was sung by three groups of four singers, each costumed according to the continent they represented: Turkish garb for Asia, Moorish for Africa, and silk in the Italian manner for Europe.) The celebratory rhetoric of conquest in the name of God and king is bound to be repugnant for modern listeners. Yet considered in the context of Venetian regional politics, the text of Gabrieli's madrigal is hardly surprising. This was a theater of state and church imagined on a worldwide scale.

GREEKS AND MOORS

Gabrieli and his fellow musicians nevertheless understood the world to be a more complex and diverse place than such Eurocentric pieces as *Asia felice* might lead us to believe. Among the hundreds of madrigals he wrote in the course of his long career are nearly 20 *greghesche*—settings of a kind of poetry popular in

Figure 13.1: *Paolo Veronese,* Allegory of the Battle of Lepanto, 7 October 1571

Venice during the 1560s that took its cue from the *lingua greghesca* spoken by Greek mercenaries in the service of the Venetian Republic. Their dialect, with its many borrowings from Greek, was lampooned in theatrical comedies of the day and taken over into parodic verse by writers like Antonio Molino. Gabrieli, the organist Claudio Merulo, and the great San Marco teacher and choirmaster Adrian Willaert set quite a few of these poems as sophisticated polyphonic works for four, five, and even seven voices.

Example 13.1: *Andrea Gabrieli, Asia felice, mm. 1–12. From Andrea Gabrieli,* Complete Madrigals 2: Madrigali a 4. Greghesche *a 4, 5, and 7, ed. A. Tillman Merritt, Recent Researches in the Music of the Renaissance, 42 (Madison, WI: A-R Editions, 1982), p. 40.*

The Greek mercenaries were not the only community parodied in verse and song. The "Moorish" style enacted as part of the public theater of the Venetian Carnival in 1572 represents yet another strand of community in the complex tapestry of European culture. The *moriscos* were originally Muslim converts to Christianity who remained in Spain after the conquest of Granada in 1492, which put an end to Islamic rule on the peninsula. Some of these so-called New Christians continued to practice their old cultural forms, including those of food and dress, but by 1567 King Philip II of Spain had decreed such practices illegal. He commanded that *morisco* children be surrendered to Christian authorities. Not surprisingly, some communities took up arms in response to these measures and were violently suppressed. Many *moriscos* fled to North Africa. Others were enslaved and sold to wealthy families in Spain and in the Spanish Kingdom of Naples. In fashionable houses across Europe they were prized as servants.

Like other minorities in Renaissance Europe, the *moriscos* were objects of both fascination and contempt. The Spanish writer Miguel de Cervantes, a veteran of the Battle of Lepanto, portrayed them in a sympathetic light in his satirical novel *Don Quixote* (1608). In theatrical works of the sixteenth century, *moriscos* often provide moments for masquerade and ridicule. As in the case of the *greghesche*, these theatrical encounters were echoed in poetry and music, since the plays frequently featured nonsense-syllable dance interludes that imitated the sounds of instruments. These verbal "dances" were in turn framed by outrageous bits of raunchy dialogue, animal sounds, and a barrage of insults among stock characters. The vocal genre known as the *moresca* (from the Italian form of *morisco*) enjoyed a particular vogue in the Spanish-ruled Kingdom of Naples during the 1550s. Printers in Rome and elsewhere exploited a niche market in printing polyphonic *moresche* alongside their arrangements of rustic villanelle and other humble texts.

We cannot help but be repulsed by the meanness of some of these burlesques, which dwell in a rough and bawdy world of prostitutes and fools whose unfortunate dealings are punctuated by frequent cries of "Alla" and other markers of "Moorish" heritage. The *moresca* also denoted a kind of exotic dance, often performed in costume or masquerade as part of Carnivals and other public festivals; it is the source of the English morris dance. In his *Orchésographie*, a treatise on dance published in 1588, the French cleric known as Thoinot Arbeau recalled having witnessed a young man perform the dance with a blackened face. The dance was later assimilated among an array of stylized dance types heard in instrumental music or as part of any kind of exotic theatrical pantomime (such as the *moresca* at the end of Monteverdi's *Orfeo* of 1607). It was also performed by professional dancers in courtly contexts.

The sixteenth-century musical landscape is dotted with similarly outrageous portrayals of outsiders, old lovers, and errant priests. As we saw in Chapter 10, composers like Orazio Vecchi (1550–1605) made a specialty of long, quasi-theatrical "madrigal comedies" dealing in these and other crude stereotypes drawn from the popular imagination and traditions like the improvisatory commedia dell'arte. (Orlando di Lasso himself took part in this kind of theatrical performance, which he first encountered during his time in Naples.) Vecchi's *L'Amfiparnaso* (Amphiparnassus, 1597) pokes fun at all the usual targets, including a hurtful scene in which Jewish pawnbrokers are unable to transact business on the Sabbath. Such scenes, enacted through polyphonic performance around a set of partbooks, were a kind of imaginary auditory theater. "The spectacle of which I speak," Vecchi wrote in the prologue to the work, "is beheld by the imagination which it penetrates through the ear, not through the eye." The comedies provided literate musicians with a way to lampoon cultural extremes from the safe distance of their drawing-room tables in a transgressive game of national "types" and social registers.

JEWS AND MUSIC, FROM ITALY TO ENGLAND

As Vecchi's repugnant caricature attests, the Jews endured a long history of scorn on the part of their Christian neighbors. Intolerance had its source in official policy. Like the *moriscos*, Jews in Spain were singled out for persecution during the fifteenth and sixteenth centuries. Many were forcibly converted to Christianity, then subjected to inquisition by church officials who policed religious conformance. Ecclesiastical archives record the brutal punishments meted out to those accused of secretly sustaining Jewish practices. Jews who did not convert were exempt from inquisition per se during the fifteenth century, but in 1492 they were expelled from the Spanish peninsula. They sought haven in North Africa, the Netherlands, and the Ottoman Empire (where they were welcomed). Some joined Jewish communities already in place in Venice, Mantua, and Rome. Here they were free to trade and practice certain professions, such as medicine and banking, but social contact with Gentiles was often limited, as Jews were obliged by local law to live in specific and enclosed neighborhoods known as ghettos. The one in Venice, the site of an old foundry, gave its name to countless communities of confinement instituted across Christian Europe during the next centuries.

Music served as a medium of cultural interaction among certain Jewish and Christian neighbors in these Italian communities. Choir schools and other ecclesiastical institutions were barred to Jews. But a select few—instrumentalists, dancers, and actors—managed to find privileged places at court, much as a tiny minority of Jewish advisors rose to positions of influence with elite rulers. The dancing-master Guglielmo Ebreo ("Hebrew") da Pesaro (ca. 1420–after 1484) created elaborate choreography for weddings and festivals at the courts of Milan, Urbino, and Florence during the second half of the fifteenth century. His teachings, articulated in a widely copied manuscript treatise, *De pratica seu arte tripudii vulgare opusculum* (A Work in the Vernacular on the Practice or Art of Dancing), combine Neoplatonic themes of the alignment of heavenly and bodily harmony with practical information on the courtly dances of the day. His ideas must have resonated nicely with the place of music in the humanist program of learning at courts like these.

Marsilio Ficino, the fifteenth-century Florentine philosopher-priest who was a key mediator of ancient and esoteric wisdom for Renaissance thinkers, certainly knew of this kabbalistic lore that melded Neoplatonic and Jewish wisdom. Jewish instrumentalists are also occasionally mentioned in archival sources from Italian courts. During the early decades of the sixteenth century, for instance, the lutenist Gian Maria Giudeo ("Jew") performed for dukes, cardinals, and popes in Rome (he later converted to Christianity and was ennobled by Pope Leo X). Abramo dall'Arpa, a prominent member of the Jewish community in Mantua and apparently a harpist of great skill, played the part of Pan in a dramatic production at the Gonzaga court theater in the 1540s. Several other members of his family also seem to have been harpists. His grandson Abramino was regularly on the household payroll of the Gonzagas during the 1570s and 1580s; he took part in public festivities at court, and served as a kind of music therapist to the ailing Duke Guglielmo Gonzaga.

Towns like the Gonzagas' Mantua seem to have been ripe with cultural contradictions. Even as Duke Guglielmo took solace in the sounds of Abramino's harp, and his courtiers were entertained by troupes of Jewish actors and instrumentalists, the duke instituted new and stringent rules for the local ghetto. He also made possible the continued work of the Inquisition and its search for banned books. The archives of this inquisitorial work yield some surprising information about the reading habits and musical tastes of at least some members of the Mantuan community. Most of the many thousands of books catalogued by Inquisitors among the households of their Jewish neighbors in 1595 are religious texts and commentaries in Hebrew or Aramaic. But there are many books in Latin and Italian, too, including works of history, philosophy, and current literature by Petrarch, Ariosto, and Tasso.

The music books are especially revealing: a Jew named Isaac Nortzi owned not only works by Dante, Terence, Virgil, and Pietro Bembo, but also music by Cipriano de Rore, the Roman composer Annibale Stabile, and the Venetian master Baldassare Donato. Since music was normally issued in partbooks, the obvious implication is that there were musical readers up to the task in the ghetto. Samuel Ariono owned a copy of the treatise Le istitutioni harmoniche (The Harmonic Foundations) by the Venetian chapel master, theorist, and composer Gioseffo Zarlino. It seems unlikely that books like these would have found their way into a library by chance, and less likely still that they were intended for private, silent reading. Their presence in the records of the Inquisition reminds us that music, like literary and philosophical ideas, could in the right circumstances cut across sharp lines of social demarcation.

THE BASSANO FAMILY

Perhaps nowhere are the bizarre contradictions of religious identity and musical opportunity played out more interestingly than in the story of the Bassanos, a family of instrument makers, performers, and composers active in Italy and England during the second half of the sixteenth century. Jeronimo (d. ca. 1550) and his six sons had long careers in and around Venice: They tuned the organs and worked as wind and brass players at San Marco and for the doge of Venice. Around 1540, at the invitation of King Henry VIII, Gaspare, Zuane, and Antonio Bassano emigrated to England (where they were known as Jaspar, John, and Anthony), serving as sackbut and recorder players and instrument makers to the court at various times during the sixteenth century.

There is strong circumstantial evidence that the Bassanos, although outwardly Christian, were secretly Jewish and probably descended from a New Christian family who originally converted in Spain or Portugal. Anthony, for instance, was posthumously identified as "Anthonius Moyses" by his friend Ambrose Lupo, a Milanese string player who served the English court until he was denounced as a "secret Jew" by the Inquisition. Anthony and several other instrumentalists at the English court were eventually exonerated and their positions restored. One historical tradition identifies another member of the family, Emilia (Bassano) Lanier, as the mysterious "Dark Lady" of Shakespeare's sonnets.

Some of the Bassanos returned periodically to Venice, where a separate branch of the family had successful musical careers in association with leading Catholic institutions of the day. Giovanni (1560/61–1617), second cousin to the Jeronimo whose sons moved to England, was already as a young man in the employ of the doge as an instrumentalist. He was a boy chorister at San Marco, a music teacher at the seminary there, and even directed the famous instrumental ensemble associated with the basilica. Augustinian friars asked him to supply a local convent with musical instruments. Giovanni was an accomplished composer of Latin church music in the grand polychoral style favored in Venice. He also wrote secular canzonette, as well as two important manuals on ornamentation and embellishment. (On Giovanni Bassano's place in the story of sixteenth-century embellishment, see Chapter 12.)

Given his long and close association with Christian institutions, it would seem unlikely that Giovanni identified himself as anything but Catholic, despite his apparently crypto-Jewish cousins. His ornamented version of *Susanne un jour* (see Chapter 12 and Anthology 23) seems to sum up the contradictory character of their lives, and the ways music can move between social or religious categories normally seen as mutually exclusive. As we learned in Chapter 11, the spiritual chanson by the poet Guillaume Guéroult and the musician Didier Lupi Second, both Protestants, retells the biblical story of Susanna and her resistance to the assaults of the elders. Orlando di Lasso's five-voice setting not only found a ready audience among French Protestants eager for chaste songs to sing at home, but also was widely reprinted and frequently arranged in new polyphonic guises by many leading composers, Catholic and Protestant alike. In short, a pious song by a Protestant poet and composer was first reworked by a Catholic composer and then transformed as a vehicle for virtuoso display by a Catholic instrumentalist who came from a long line of Jewish musicians.

FRENCH AND ENGLISH PROTESTANTS ABROAD

As waves of European explorers sailed off to claim new regions of the globe during the sixteenth century, they encountered alien civilizations with an amalgam of awe, curiosity, and miscomprehension. To judge from the chronicles they compiled, musical performance inspired a particularly intense fascination on the part of these cultural voyeurs, whose accounts typically mirrored European aims and assumptions. In the late 1550s, when the French Protestant missionary Jean de Léry visited coastal Brazil, he was deeply moved by what he called the "measured harmonies" of the assembled ceremonial voices of a shamanistic clan, the Caraïbes. "Whenever I remember it," he wrote in 1578, "my heart trembles; and it seems their voices are still in my ears." Léry marveled at the natural riches he saw and heard while wandering with native Tupinamba guides. "As I was passing with them through a great forest, contemplating so many different trees, grasses, and flowers, all green and fragrant, and hearing the songs of the countless birds warbling through the woods in the sunlight, I felt compelled to praise God, and feeling gay of heart, I began to sing aloud Psalm 104, 'Bless the Lord, O my soul.'"

Even more interesting than Léry's effusion, however, is the reaction of his three Tupi companions, who wondered at the sound of his voice ("for they understood nothing of the rest," he wrote). Pressed to explain the meaning of the song, Léry took the opportunity to deliver an evangelizing lesson. The psalm, he explained, served to praise God, "he alone who nourished all men and all animals" and indeed "the trees, fruits, and plants." It "had first been sung more than 10,000 moons ago (for that is their way of counting) by one of our great prophets, who left it to posterity in order to be used for the same end." Léry reported that his companions were "wonderfully attentive" and begged to be taught the secrets of the French. Yet the missionary must have faced a difficult dilemma: convinced that writing was the only way to approach knowledge of the divine, he was nevertheless forced to explain Scripture largely in oral terms. No wonder music became such an important medium of cultural exchange and inquiry for many of Léry's fellow explorers.

English travelers also saw and heard the New World in terms defined by European assumptions. Although some colonists grudgingly recognized the highly organized political and social systems in Native American communities, they often reserved special scorn for native religious practices. The preface to Capt. John Smith's *A True Relation* (1608) called upon would-be colonists to draw native peoples back from "the unknowne paths of Paganism, Idolatrie, and superstition." This was the same language that Protestant polemicists used to attack Catholic ceremony, with its veneration of saints and elaborate public rituals; the echoes of anti-Catholic sentiment were no doubt amplified by anxieties about the strong Spanish presence in the New World.

Many accounts by English colonists describe the songs and dances they heard as noise instead of music. In his *Historie of Travaile into Virginia Britannia* (ca. 1610), a memoir of the Jamestown expedition of 1609, William Strachey recalled how Algonquin voices made "such a terrible howling as would rather affright then [than] give pleasure to any man." He also claimed to have heard a "scorneful song they made of us" in which the natives told the story of the murder of several members of an English colonial party. As Strachey explained, successive stanzas of the song related how the English had been killed for their weapons, while the refrain imitated the Englishmen's cries upon hearing the fate of their comrades. For Léry, the natives' fascination with his psalm tune was evidence of their receptivity to Christianity. In Strachey's account, the Algonquins' musical imagination betokened their incivility. Lamentation had no place in their culture, he claimed; it was heard only as the mocking echo of European voices. No less than John Smith's exhortation to his countrymen, this would have been read by English audiences as an invitation to view the colonial enterprise as a civilizing process.

THE CATHOLIC MISSION IN NEW SPAIN

The implications for musical culture in the territories conquered, converted, and colonized by Spanish generals and missionaries during the early sixteenth century were no less profound than in those under Protestant rule. The fate of the great Aztec Empire and, in particular, of its capital, Tenochtitlán (upon which Mexico City was later founded), can stand as a case in point. Hernán Cortés was the general most directly responsible for the natives' defeat. Marching west from his coastal bastion at Vera Cruz, by 1521 he had captured the Aztec king Montezuma, subdued Tenochtitlán, and begun a harsh program to eradicate Aztec institutions. Spanish soldiers were soon joined by traders and monks. Like Protestant missionaries from France and England, the friars taught and preached among the Indians, frequently learning local languages and customs in the process.

The most astute of the Catholic friars sensed both the analogies and the differences between native and Spanish cultures, particularly when it came to music and religious practice. When the Franciscan monk Toribio de Benavente, known as Motolinia, wrote his *Memoranda* (1541) of his experiences in New Spain, he noted the many similarities between the old Aztec order and the conditions of church and state in Spain (see SR 77:495–99; 3/42:217–21). He described the royal musical household as a "chapel" whose trained singers carefully rehearsed before their public appearances in celebration of battles, coronations, and marriages. Aztec song, Motolinia observed, obeyed strict proprieties dictated by an elaborate liturgical calendar, much as plainsong did

Figure 13.2: *Bernardino de Sahagún, manuscript illustration of Aztec musicians, from an account of various Aztec crafts compiled during the sixteenth century.*

within the cloistered walls of traditional monastic life. He compared some of what he heard to the Christian Mass and likened the regulated movement of indigenous dancers to familiar Spanish forms. (See Figure 13.2 for a representation of Aztec musicians in performance, from a sixteenth-century manuscript compiled by a Spanish chronicler.)

Sound, it seems, was an important agent of conversion and enculturation from the very outset of the Spanish conquest of the New World. Already by the early 1520s, not long after the conquest of Tenochtitlán, a Flemish monk named Pedro de Gante (that is, Pieter of Ghent) and his colleagues began to train local boys in Latin and music, the traditional curriculum of the European choir school. Their first efforts were with the children of the Aztec nobility. "We take these children," Fray Martín de Valencia explained in a letter to Emperor Charles V in 1532, "in order that we may separate them from heathen influences by rearing and educating them in our monasteries. We devote much time to them, teaching them not only how to read and write, but also how to sing both plainchant and polyphonic music. We teach them how to sing the canonical hours and how to assist at Mass; and we strive to inculcate the highest standards of living and conduct."

We can hardly imagine that the coercive separation of children from their parents was as smooth as Martín would have Charles believe, particularly when he knew only too well how earnestly the Spanish monks and conquistadors had worked to destroy everything to do with the old religious order. The monks took the position that with the old temple and king swept aside, their native charges were something of a blank slate, ready to be written upon. According to the brothers, the young princes were exceptionally quick learners, easily memorizing the usual Latin catechisms of faith, repeating prayers like the *Ave Maria* and *Pater noster*, and quickly assimilating plainsong liturgy. Some became expert scribes and illustrators and, with their classmates, produced translations into Nahuatl, the ancient Aztec language, of the central texts of European philosophy and theology.

Sacred places and personalities familiar from the Aztec past were sometimes reinterpreted in Catholic contexts. According to stories recounted by a series of Christian Nahua chroniclers, in December 1531 a devout Aztec convert named Juan Diego saw a series of remarkable apparitions of a dark-haired woman surrounded by rays of light on a hillside at Tepeyac, outside Tenochtitlán. The woman identified herself, according to the story, as the mother of the true God and a source of protection for those who trusted her. The place of the miracle would hardly have surprised local folk: the site had long been a sacred spot where Aztecs worshipped the goddess Tonantzin ("Our Mother"). Faith in the healing power of the place and its protector has endured. In the 1990s, Juan Diego was canonized as a saint by Pope John Paul II, and the Church of Our Lady of Guadalupe in Tepeyac remains the largest pilgrimage site in the Americas.

SACRED MUSIC IN THE AMERICAS

Music was a crucial part of the process of cultural exchange. Some of this work involved the wholesale transplantation of European musical practices into the churches and monasteries of New Spain. Bishop Juan de Zumárraga, the first ecclesiastical authority in Mexico City, once pleaded with Emperor Charles V for funds to pay local singers; he returned from Spain with music books for them to use. By the second half of the sixteenth century, a small liturgical press had been set up in Mexico City, providing printed books for daily use in cathedrals and churches of the new territory. Meanwhile, books of polyphonic music by notable Spanish composers such as Cristóbal de Morales, Francisco Guerrero, and Tomás Luis de Victoria were brought from Europe. Some were later recopied for use in outlying centers. An early manuscript copy of a printed book of Morales's polyphonic masses, first issued in 1544, is preserved in the chapter archives of the cathedral at Puebla, Mexico; it is the earliest surviving manuscript of polyphonic music in the Americas.

Spanish missionaries saw their musical enterprise as a mirror of European sound and ritual. When Francisco Cervantes de Salazar described the elaborate ceremonies held at the monastery of San José in Mexico City in memory of Charles V, readers in Spain would probably have recognized a spectacle not unlike those they witnessed at home:

> The dignitaries having finally entered the Church of San José and having seated themselves (the procession itself lasted two full hours), the vigil proper began. Outside and inside the church stood a huge crowd of

onlookers. The cathedral choirmaster [Lázaro del Alamo] began by directing one of his choirs (his singers were divided into two antiphonal choirs) in the singing of the invitatory, *Circumdederunt me*, by Cristóbal de Morales; and then the other in the singing of the psalm, *Exultemus*, also by Morales. Both settings by Morales are polyphonic throughout, and the choirs sang them with the utmost sweetness. The vigil began then with a devotional fervor that elevated the minds of everyone present.

Some of the "huge crowd of onlookers" mentioned by Salazar must have been minor members of the Catholic clergy, Spanish and Aztec converts alike. But many more were members of the local population—Indian governors of various provinces in formal mourning attire, village dignitaries, plus thousands of gawkers who waited for the procession in the forecourt of the monastery and its nearby streets. "This tremendous Indian procession," Salazar continued, "was kept under control by interpreters who knew their languages and by peace officers from the local constabulary."

The need for translation extended to musical works, despite the insistence of many missionaries that music afforded a natural and immediate means of communicating religious devotion in new converts. Monks crafted Latin *contrafacta* of Indian melodies. Local interpreters translated important Catholic prayers for use by those unfamiliar with Latin. Mexico City choirmasters like Lázaro del Alamo produced polyphonic music for local use by the choirs that seemed to spring up in every church. Hernando Franco, a Spanish composer active in Mexico City around 1580, wrote a number of hymns and Magnificat settings for liturgical use by the cathedral choir. There are also songs and even a pair of polyphonic hymns in Nahuatl ascribed to Don Hernando Franco in the musical sources. (Although the composer of the Latin and Nahuatl pieces might appear to be one and the same, Don Hernando Franco was in all probability one of the Spanish musician's noble Aztec pupils.) At first glance, the text of one of these hymns seems indistinguishable from similar devotional texts heard in European churches for centuries, a prayer to the Virgin Mary to intercede with Jesus on behalf of the petitioner and his ancestors (Ex. 13.2):

Sancta maria yn ilhuicac cihuapille tinatzin dios yn titotenpantlatocantzin.
Ma huel tehuatzin topan ximotlatolti yn titlatlaconhuanimen.

Holy Mary, Queen of Heaven, Mother of God, thou art our mediator. Intercede ["speak thou well"] for us who are sinners.

It is difficult to say with certainty what Nahua Christians heard in compositions like these. For some, the work echoes the sound of flute and percussion orchestras known to have been a part of old Aztec temple rituals. Indeed, European

Example 13.2: *Don Hernando Franco, Sancta Maria yn ilhuicac, mm. 1–14. From Robert M. Stevenson,* Music in Aztec and Inca Territory *(Berkeley and Los Angeles: University of California Press, 1968), pp. 208–209.*

chroniclers of the day often worried about the instrumentalists who flocked to take part in Catholic services wherever they were instituted. They sought to limit what they heard as this sonic excess, much as they worried about participation by noisy town minstrels back in Europe.

MATTEO RICCI'S MUSICAL ENCOUNTERS IN CHINA

The religious order of the Society of Jesus, commonly called the Jesuits, played an important role in bringing Catholicism to Asia. Founded in the middle years of the sixteenth century under the guidance of St. Ignatius Loyola and promoted by Pope Paul III, the organization quickly established missions in Spanish and Portuguese centers such as Goa on the southwest coast of the Indian subcontinent, Manila in the Philippines, and Macao on the southeast coast of China. Education was a central part of the Jesuits' mission. In addition to founding the Collegium Romanum in Rome in 1571, they established rigorous schools wherever they worked. Books of emblems, impressive architecture, and religious drama were more important to the didactic efforts of the Jesuits than the creation of music or support of musical ensembles. Hence the prominent role of music in the Jesuit mission to the court of China undertaken by Matteo Ricci (1552–1610) and a few colleagues is noteworthy for various reasons.

Ricci was educated among the Jesuits of Rome during the 1570s, and was later sent by the order to Goa and Macao, where he learned Chinese. By 1601 he was invited to the Chinese imperial court at Beijing, where he remained until his death in 1610. Ricci was a specialist in natural philosophy, and his knowledge of everything from mathematics to rhetoric fascinated the Chinese scholars and literati he met. They were also drawn to his extensive collection of clocks, optical devices, and other instruments that often found their way into the luggage of diplomatic missions to the courts of Asia.

Ricci and his Jesuit sponsors recognized the need for a delicate approach to their work, particularly in light of the ejection of Christian missionaries from Japan not long before. Seeking out the correspondences between Christian and Confucian ethical teachings, Ricci made a careful study of Chinese courtly culture, adopting the dress of the literati, allowing converts to practice Confucian rites of ancestor worship, and loosely translating Christian concepts (such as the soul, for which there was no clear counterpart) into Chinese ideograms. As we'll soon discover, music played a surprisingly important role in this process of cultural mediation.

Ricci wrote extensively of his time at court, including treatises in Chinese on Christianity, geography, mathematics, and memory, all directed at local audiences. His chronicles in Italian were eventually brought back to Rome, where they were translated into Latin and published. Among the latter are various observations on the ceremonial music he heard in China and an account of the effort undertaken to introduce European music there. The Jesuits included a keyboard instrument—apparently a clavichord—among the various technical wonders they presented to the imperial court. The clavichord, portable and relatively easy to maintain, was better suited to private rehearsal and didactic work than to liturgical performance. Its intimate, perishable tone also made it the ideal medium for Ricci's larger project of religious instruction.

Ricci's reports of the reaction by court musicians to this instrument and their subsequent interactions around it are revealing of his insights about his Chinese friends and of his growing realization of the role that music might play in his missionary program. Fascinated by the clavichord, court officials sent four eunuchs for instruction on how to play it. Ricci reported that the Chinese displayed no less reverence for the instrument, which they treated "as if it had been a living thing," than for their teacher, Father Didaco (SR 80:507; 3/45:229). And they were careful to avoid making individual progress that might cause embarrassment to one of their classmates. Ricci's account was doubtless crafted for fellow Jesuits back in Europe looking for cultural insights about how to approach Chinese pupils of their own some day without trampling on local sensitivities.

The clavichord was also ideally suited to the acoustical tastes of the courtly literati, who were devoted to the Chinese zither (*qin*), an instrument with a tone every bit as intimate as the clavichord and similarly dependent on the careful touch of the player for convincing effect. In European contexts, the clavichord had no special repertory of its own, but could be used to play variations, dance tunes, and arrangements of vocal polyphony. *Qin* players, in contrast, had an extensive repertory of compositions written expressly for the instrument, often giving expression to a poem, story, or accompanying vocal part. Many of these works were on ethical or moral themes, both Taoist and Confucian.

When the eunuchs asked Ricci to provide their newly learned keyboard compositions with some appropriate Chinese words in order to make them suitable for performance at court, he crafted a set of eight poems designed to follow the structure of the musical works: "These were lyrics," Ricci tells us, "touching upon ethical subjects, teaching lessons of good morals and virtues, and aptly illustrated with quotations from Christian authors" (SR 80:508; 3/45:230). The poems soon became so prized at court that they were copied and eventually printed for wider circulation as *Eight Songs for the Western Instruments*. Unfortunately, the music of Ricci's devotional songs was not published along with the texts and is presumably lost. But after all, who among the Chinese would have been prepared to read European notation? And of what possible use would such notation have been without a clavichord or other European instrument upon which to play it? *Qin* players were highly literate, but their *dapu* notation was a tablature, quite different in its technical capabilities and conception from European mensural notation on a staff.

We may never know how well Ricci's *Eight Songs* captured either the sense or the structure of their models, much less what the eunuchs made of the results, particularly given the interdependence of meaning and inflection in tonal languages such as Chinese. However, in recognizing the complex interplay of words and their musical treatment, Ricci's recollection reminds us of the powerful claims on music in the several encounters we've traced in our brief survey of missionaries, colonists, and cultural voyeurs in the sixteenth century.

A MUSICAL PARLIAMENT OF NATIONS?

Like most colonial or imperial projects, the European encounter with new cultures in the Americas, Africa, and Asia was often violent and destructive, uncomprehending of the civilizations it found. Yet sound—and especially the power of song—remained for many of our travelers a profoundly effective means of communicating across these lines of difference, much as it had been a powerful medium of expression in the service of sacred and secular texts throughout the sixteenth century. For some colonists and missionaries, music provided evidence of the incivility of new peoples, even as it was a principal means to instill European ideas and beliefs in them. Might music also have been a medium uniquely capable of showing what was distinctive and even valuable about an alien culture? Given the biases inherent in so many of our sources, we may never know. But one European theorist and composer, himself attempting a characteristically humanistic reappraisal of the music of antiquity in terms that might be useful to musicians of the sixteenth century, seems to have had precisely this in mind.

In *L'antica musica ridotta alla moderna prattica* (Ancient Music Adapted to Modern Practice, 1555), Nicola Vicentino, hoping to transform the way composers approached their art, imagined all sorts of new musical horizons that might be opened through the study of the remote musical past. As part of his program, he designed a novel keyboard instrument called an archicembalo, which differed from conventional ones not only in its double keyboards and multiple ranks of keys, but also in its mechanical wizardry and extraordinary range of tunings. It was, in Vicentino's words, "the foremost and perfect instrument" on account of the exacting intonations these microtunings made possible.

Composers who used the archicembalo were at a distinct advantage, in Vicentino's view, when they tried to capture the distinctive inflections of different languages. "All nations," he observed,

> represent their own way of singing by means of the steps found in the division of my archicembalo. But with the music in use nowadays it is not possible to write French, German, Spanish, Hungarian, Turkish, or Hebrew songs—or songs of any other nation—because, when spoken in the mother tongue, the steps and leaps of the nations of the world proceed not only with the steps of the whole tone, natural semitone, and accidental semitone, but also with dieses [quarter tones] as well as enharmonic semitones, tones, and leaps. This is why I have devised my division, which allows all nations of the world to write with their own accents and to compose in as many voices as they like.

Vicentino put the expressive power of his ideas to the test in a few experimental madrigals and motets in which the humanist's passion for persuasion could press the old medieval tone system beyond its limits. His ideas were known to the most adventuresome musicians of the late sixteenth century, including Orlando di Lasso and Claude Le Jeune, who sought to restore ancient effects through modern means.

Whether the musical parliament of nations that Vicentino envisioned could ever have been successful is a matter of guesswork. But as we have seen, music was frequently the subject of intense interest on the part of the European explorers and missionaries who fanned out across new lands. Some, like Jean de Léry, experienced their new environments with a combination of awe and wonder. Others enlisted music in a vast project of cultural colonization, relying on the persuasive medium of sound to convert the communities they encountered. Music, with its power to transcend limits of language and place, was an ideal medium of exchange in this process, the echoes of which are still heard in the modern global marketplace of ideas and cultures.

FOR FURTHER READING

Bermudez, Egberto, "Urban Musical Life in the European Colonies: Examples from Spanish America, 1530–1650," in *Music and Musicians in Renaissance Cities and Towns*, ed. Fiona Kisby, pp. 167–80 (Cambridge: Cambridge University Press, 2001)

Bloechl, Olivia, "Protestant Imperialism and the Representation of Native American Song," *Musical Quarterly* 87 (2004): 44–86

Cummings, Anthony M., "Gian Maria Giudeo, Sonatore di Liuto, and the Medici," *Fontes artes musicae* 38 (1991): 312–18

Fenlon, Iain, "Magnificence as Civic Image: Music and Ceremonial Space in Early Modern Venice," in *Music and Musicians in Renaissance Cities and Towns*, ed. Fiona Kisby, pp. 28–44 (Cambridge: Cambridge University Press, 2001)

Lindell, Robert, "The Wedding of Archduke Charles and Maria of Bavaria in 1571," *Early Music* 18 (1990): 253–69

Lindorff, Joyce, "Missionaries, Keyboards and Musical Exchange in the Ming and Qing Courts," *Early Music* 32 (2004): 403–14

Prior, Roger, "Jewish Musicians at the Tudor Court," *Musical Quarterly* 69 (1983): 253–65

Woodfield, Ian, "The Keyboard Recital in Oriental Diplomacy, 1520–1620," *Journal of the Royal Musical Association* 115 (1990): 33–62

Ⓢ Additional resources available at wwnorton.com/studyspace

CHAPTER FOURTEEN

Tradition and Innovation around 1600

O ur encounter with music of the fifteenth and sixteenth centuries began with a pair of works that embodied remarkable changes in the craft of composition and the purposes of music during this period. Johannes Ciconia's polytextual motet *Doctorum principem* served ceremonial ends and was assembled in hierarchical layers according to a system of composition that had much in common with that of the thirteenth and fourteenth centuries. Luca Marenzio's madrigal *Liquide perle*, in contrast, hinged on variety, and on the power of music to represent the ideas, moods, and syntax of a literary text. In it, we were able to recognize an aesthetic impulse for music that was different in both purpose and means from music written in Ciconia's day. The rival claims of ritual and representation are also embodied in a set of compositions from the years around 1600. Through them, we will draw together the many threads of our study in ways that show the weight of tradition, and the promise of innovations in the years to follow.

A MADRIGAL BY CLAUDIO MONTEVERDI

Claudio Monteverdi's *Sfogava con le stelle* (Unburdening Himself to the Stars), from his *Fourth Book of Madrigals for Five Voices* of 1603, points in a number of significant directions (Anthology 26). Its poetic text is filled with striking images and changing perspectives. A narrator sets the scene for the lyrical outpouring of a man who calls on the stars to assuage a broken heart. The madrigal opens with a remarkable passage of choral recitative—in the original notation, each voice part has only held breves (equivalent to double whole notes). The singers are instructed to "freely declaim" long passages of the text in coordinated rhythmic unison. This effect points toward the *stile rappresentativo* (theatrical style), a kind of solo recitative, or speechlike singing, that can be heard in various experiments under way in Florentine academies of the 1590s in the works of Jacopo Peri, in the solo vocal monodies of the Roman singer-composer Giulio Caccini's *Le nuove musiche* (The New Musics, 1601), or in Monteverdi's first opera, *L'Orfeo* (Orpheus, 1607), written for a court wedding at Mantua. Indeed, the text of *Sfogava con le stelle* has been credited to Ottavio Rinuccini, a poet who also provided opera libretti to Peri for his own experimental opera on the Orpheus legend. Caccini later set *Sfogava con le stelle* as a solo song. (Wendy Heller discusses Monteverdi's madrigals and operas at greater length in *Music in the Baroque*.)

By the time Monteverdi (1567–1643) composed *Sfogava con le stelle* in the 1590s, he was aware of these new styles and their potential application to musical soliloquy and drama. The declamatory passages of this work, however, have more to do with the old liturgical recitative, falsobordone, an Italian version of the formulaic faburden and fauxbourdon traditions that we encountered in the fifteenth century (see Chapter 4), than with any operatic experiments. Falsobordone uses what to us sound like "root-position" triads, just as Monteverdi does here. In borrowing sounds from the world of religious music, Monteverdi may have meant to confer a spiritual quality on the scene set in the madrigal, as the narrator prepares us to hear the amorous "prayer" of the heartbroken lover asking the heavens to intercede on his behalf.

The worlds of erotic longing and religious devotion have often intersected in the music we have explored, from works like this one to settings from the Song of Songs by Dunstable or Lhéritier (see Chapters 4 and 11). We have also heard how Du Fay called on the spiritual sounds of fauxbourdon to frame a political motet, *Supremum est mortalibus*, with heavenly no less than worldly significance (see Chapter 4). In Monteverdi's madrigal, too, the ceremonial and the expressive (as well as the sacred and secular) draw close through sound.

Sfogava con le stelle is also unusual for the way it calls upon conventions of the serious and not-so-serious madrigal of the sixteenth century. Decorated melodic ornaments, with snappy repeating rhythms, recall the techniques of diminution we heard in both instrumental and vocal practice of the second half of the sixteenth century, from the lavish improvisations of Giovanni Bassano to the *concerto delle donne* of Ferrara (see Chapter 12). The reduction in texture from five voices to three reminds us that Marenzio and others borrowed from the light genres of the villanella and canzonetta to enhance the range of expressive possibilities in their madrigals.

Most remarkable of all are the many striking dissonances in the last section of *Sfogava con le stelle*. Dissonant suspensions had long been an important part of the expressive arsenal of sixteenth-century madrigal composers, from Arcadelt to Marenzio. But the use of dissonances without contrapuntal preparation, as we hear in the closing passages of Monteverdi's madrigal, defies the very logic of contrapuntal teaching as formulated by music theorists from Tinctoris to Zarlino. In the writings of these men, vertical intervals like seconds, fourths, and sevenths had to be approached smoothly and be carefully framed by the closest adjacent consonance, such as a third or sixth. Here Monteverdi brings the singers together on these intervals without preparation, as conservative musicians would complain. In a series of printed debates with the Bolognese cleric and music theorist Giovanni Maria Artusi about musical expression sparked by the publication of his *Fifth Book of Madrigals* in 1605, Monteverdi identified this liberal approach to dissonance as a hallmark of the *seconda prattica* (second practice). It represented an alternative to composition in which the expression of striking emotions and images in the text took precedence over the old claims of controlled counterpoint. This was the essence of the *seconda prattica*. In brief, Monteverdi's *Sfogava con le stelle* looks back to older traditions even as it anticipates some crucial innovations that held great importance for the seventeenth-century practice that Wendy Heller describes in *Music in the Baroque*.

The circumstances surrounding the publication of Monteverdi's *Fourth Book of Madrigals* likewise signify the coexistence of continuity and change in the world of musical patronage in the years around 1600. In 1603 Monteverdi was chapel master to Duke Vincenzo Gonzaga in Mantua, where he served for over two decades. But while his *Third Book* and *Fifth Book of Madrigals* (1592, 1605) were dedicated to Duke Vincenzo, the *Fourth Book* was directed toward nearby Ferrara. As Monteverdi explained, he had originally intended to present some of these madrigals to Duke Alfonso II d'Este, but the duke's death in 1597 made the gesture impossible. Monteverdi therefore combined the older madrigals with some new ones and dedicated them to an elite band of listeners, the newly formed Accademia degli Intrepidi (Academy of the Fearless Ones) of Ferrara: "Therefore may your most illustrious lordships deign to accept and receive this gift, though a small one, with that grandeur of mind that conforms to your talents, birth and profession, illuminating with the brightness of your names, and defending with your felicitous protection, these vocal pieces of mine."

In appealing to the "grandeur of mind" of his new patrons, Monteverdi's dedication reminds us of the enduring value of such markers of magnificence among Renaissance elites. We have encountered language not too different from this in our discussions of Castiglione's *Book of the Courtier* and at the fifteenth-century court of Burgundy. Monteverdi also hopes that his works will benefit from the "illuminating" glow and "felicitous protection" of his dedicatees. It was one thing to experiment in private with the idea of appealing to the rarefied tastes of Duke Alfonso II d'Este and his musical salon, which during the 1590s boasted composers like Giaches de Wert, poets like Torquato Tasso, and the famous singers of the *concerto delle donne*. But now that these works were about to circulate in public through the medium of the printed page, Monteverdi needed the security of prominent defenders.

The Accademia degli Intrepidi was exactly the right place to look for help. It was founded in 1601 by the Ferrarese nobleman Marquis Enzo Bentivoglio, a man of considerable learning and no less considerable diplomatic clout in Ferrara, Mantua, Rome, and other cities. Bentivoglio was devoted to court spectacle, public tournaments, and experiments with musical theater. Monteverdi was still in touch with him over two decades later. In all these ways, *Sfogava con le stelle* looks both back to aesthetic and social patterns we have seen before and ahead to developments of the seventeenth century, when music moved out of the courts, churches, and elite academies into the risky public spaces of the opera house and concert hall.

A MOTET BY CARLO GESUALDO

Composer, nobleman, madman, Carlo Gesualdo (ca. 1561–1613) wins the prize as the most notorious musician of his era. A member of a prominent family of Naples, he gruesomely murdered his first wife and her lover, the duke of Andria, before marrying Leonora d'Este at Ferrara in 1594. In the eyes of his contemporaries, Gesualdo's reputation as a composer was paradoxically enhanced by the honor killing, which was the legal right of a member of the nobility, and by his fitful melancholy "madness." Moreover, he was able to publish his music without incurring the taint of professionalism that was so often an anxiety of gentlemen interested in music.

Gesualdo was fortunate to have access to one of the most admired musical ensembles of the day, the *concerto delle donne* of the Ferrarese court (see Chapter 12). His virtuosic madrigals demand a high level of vocal ability to execute the tricky ornamentation, and also acute ears to handle the extreme chromaticism of his idiom. These madrigals, with their quirky changes of texture, fragmented approach to poetic texts, and hyperexpressive emotional palette, seem to align perfectly with Gesualdo's aberrant personality. His music represents a mannered extreme to which no other composer would actively respond for hundreds of years. The twentieth-century composer Igor Stravinsky was fascinated by Gesualdo's madrigals and in 1960 adapted three of them for orchestra under the title *Monumentum pro Gesualdo di Venosa (ad CD annum)* (Memorial for Gesualdo of Venosa [at 400 Years]). The modernist connection seems fitting for a Renaissance composer whose music was in many ways an anomaly in his time.

Gesualdo's *O vos omnes* (O All Ye), from his *Tenebrae for Holy Week* (1611), represents a lesser-known side of his musical output, although it shares in the extreme musical idiom of his madrigals (Anthology 27). The *Tenebrae* (literally, "shadows," a reference to the dimming light as candles are slowly extinguished in church) are not simply religious pieces; they are part of the liturgy of the last days of Lent, a period of great introspection and religious melancholy that ends at Easter. The gathering darkness reflects the somber spiritual mood commemorating the period between Jesus's death and his resurrection on Easter Sunday. Gesualdo's treatment of this cycle puts our assumptions about religious music of the years around 1600 to the test. Humanist clerics and the composers they guided were keen to put music to work in the service of the sacred. Practices varied from the restrained idiom of Palestrina's masses to the intensity of Byrd's liturgy for English crypto-Catholics to the bold statements of Lasso's motets. But we would be hard pressed to understand Gesualdo's approach to these liturgical texts as sharing the same range of musical possibilities, or even reflecting the same aims.

Many of the audacious musical combinations heard in *O vos omnes* can be traced to the innovations first put into practice in secular madrigals of the mid-sixteenth century. This vocabulary was highly expressive, and also self-consciously theorized by writers like Nicola Vicentino, who were keen to enlist music in the service of a humanist project that aimed to recover the persuasive effects of ancient music through the most modern musical means. We are thus prompted to wonder whether works like Gesualdo's inspire religious devotion or distract from it. The functional requirements of ritual have often dictated that music take a back seat to some other action. The humanistically inclined clerics of the Council of Trent sought sounds that would convey sacred texts with maximum intelligibility (see Chapter 11). The vibrant sounds of the *Tenebrae* do neither of these very easily; they demand our undivided attention and emotional involvement.

CLAUDE LE JEUNE'S *DODECACORDE:* THE MODES OF SOCIAL HARMONY

In 1598, about a half-century after Heinrich Glarean brought out his pioneering vision of a musical system of 12 modes to succeed the old ecclesiastical constellation of eight, the French composer Claude Le Jeune (1528/30–1600) issued a collection of psalm settings that echoed the title of the Swiss humanist's treatise *Dodecachordon* (The 12-String Lyre). Le Jeune's plan in the *Dodecacorde* was to select psalm melodies from the 150 tunes in the Calvinist hymnal, treating them polyphonically in ways that aligned with the system of 12 modes then gaining favor in French musical circles.

For centuries European choristers and composers had projected their music against the backdrop of the eight ecclesiastical modes. But first the demands of polyphonic harmony and later the expanding expressive possibilities of the chromatic musical scale worked to undermine those categories, as Gesualdo's *O vos omnes* demonstrates. By the mid-sixteenth century, Glarean and Gioseffo Zarlino imagined tone systems with room for modes centered on C and A, in addition to those on D, E, F, and G (see Chapter 2). These new categories seem in retrospect especially important, for they correspond to the major and minor modes that would eventually take hold in seventeenth- and eighteenth-century practice as the foundation of harmonic thought. As one of a number of musical collections influenced by this development, Le Jeune's cannot help but look forward to these new musical spaces. The *Dodecacorde* is a progressive project no less than a retrospective one.

The book is explicitly concerned with the 12 musical modes, their musical hallmarks, their expressive potential, and their powers of ethical persuasion. But strangely, while the title alludes to Glarean's publication of 1547, the sequence of modes that Le Jeune sets out follows the numbering scheme proposed by Zarlino in the revised 1573 edition of *Le istitutioni harmoniche* (The Harmonic Foundations). Surely the attempt to fuse the name of one system with the ordering of another cannot have been accidental: Le Jeune was scrupulous in seeking out among the dozens of tunes from the Geneva (French Protestant) Psalter those whose poetic conceits and language mirrored the emotional affects identified by Zarlino (and not Glarean) as emanating from the melodic mode at hand.

Faith in the expressive ethos of the musical modes was a frequent refrain in humanist discussions of music. It runs throughout the many speculative writings on music of the fifteenth and sixteenth centuries, from Franchinus Gaffurius to Marsilio Ficino to Glarean. Le Jeune's preface to the *Dodecacorde*, moreover, hints at a still wider goal for the 12 modes whose melodic and affective properties unfold across its pages. Ascribing to one's preference of musical mode a portent of individual emotional sensibility, Le Jeune invites "my companions to honor music of serious rationales, of serious notes and measures, in order to convince the most prudent of neighboring nations that our flightiness and changes have run their course; that a firm harmony is established in our hearts, and that the peace that is supported on our constancies is a lasting tranquility, not a temporary calm." Here music was imagined as a force for good that would exert its influence on society itself.

Le Jeune had good reason to think of music in such eloquently hopeful terms as a social salve. As a Protestant in the overwhelmingly Catholic kingdom of France, his career and even life were buffeted by the murderous mob violence that had ripped French cities apart for decades during the Wars of Religion. Indeed, during the early seventeenth century the French music theorist and friar Marin Mersenne repeated the story of how the only manuscript of the

Dodecacorde had been saved from the flames of anti-Protestant rioting in 1590 by Le Jeune's Catholic colleague Jacques Mauduit. Under the rule of the tolerant King Henry IV in 1598, Le Jeune apparently felt that social harmony seemed at least possible. As his preface explains, the *Dodecacorde* aimed to promote not the *expression* of emotions, but their *moderation*, in this instance through the balanced array of all the modes as they gave voice to biblical songs of praise.

All of this suggests that for Le Jeune and the earliest readers of the *Dodecacorde*, the framing system of modality was not a set of abstract musical types, or even a collection of intrinsic emotional states. Instead, it was a kind of musical "grid" on which humanity itself might be oriented. The book serves as measured space where the familiar sounds and texts of the Genevan psalm tunes were inscribed in the balanced music spaces of the Renaissance tone system and its correspondence in an idealized social harmony. The centuries-old cantus-firmus tradition that stretched back through Josquin des Prez, Guillaume Du Fay, and Johannes Ciconia to the very roots of polyphonic practice in Europe was here interpreted in a new, progressive light.

LAST WORDS

Like the many other musical works we have encountered throughout this study, the pieces by Monteverdi, Gesualdo, and Le Jeune look back to earlier traditions even as they break new ground. Music history often works in more than one direction at once, with the result that we must train our ears to listen for the old alongside the new. Stravinsky might have found a kindred musical spirit in Gesualdo's pungent chromaticism and his apparent independence from the strict rules of modal counterpoint. The *Tenebrae*, however, are no less noteworthy for their strict adherence to the requirements of Holy Week liturgies.

Monteverdi's striking capacity to represent the feelings, images, and even the declamatory profile of his chosen poetic texts anticipates some important developments of the seventeenth century. Yet his madrigals depend on both familiar traditions of melodic embellishment and the old order of aristocratic patronage. Le Jeune's psalm cycle similarly seems at once modern and antique. It recapitulates ancient teachings on the ethical effects of music. It uses old cantus-firmus technique, in this case drawing on the congregational psalm tunes of the Calvinist hymnal. Yet it assimilates these teachings and melodies to new systems of modal thought that emerged in the middle years of the sixteenth century, including categories that seventeenth- and eighteenth-century listeners would hear as "major" and "minor."

Throughout this book we have traced a number of persistent themes, both cultural and musical. Le Jeune's use of cantus-firmus technique, for instance, reminds us of the central role played by musical borrowings in Renaissance music, above all in the motets and tenor masses of the fifteenth century. These hierarchical textures were supplanted around 1500 by musical structures, both declamatory and imitative, built around the units of text these textures served to set off. But the principle of borrowing persisted, manifest in Palestrina's *Missa Nigra sum*, Le Jeune's *Dodecacorde*, and many other works.

Over the course of the fifteenth century, as composers sought new means to give vivid expression to literary and sacred texts, they explored an ever-increasing set of contrapuntal and harmonic possibilities heard in music from Josquin's day down to the edgy experiments of Gesualdo and Monteverdi. The latters' pieces also remind us of the fluidity of musical forms and genres, as high and low, written and unwritten, sacred and secular were recombined by composers and performers in a dizzying mix. This profoundly open and inventive approach to musical language is as evident in Du Fay's use of faux-bourdon in the political motet *Supremum est mortalibus* as it is in Marenzio's appropriation of the textures drawn from villanelle in his many madrigals. Instrumentalists like Giovanni Bassano and Diego Ortiz elaborated all manner of vocal music, even as composers of polyphonic works learned from virtuosic players and singers.

We have also traced the place of music in the wider cultural landscape. Music played a central role in changing patterns of court life, particularly under the twin influences of Aristotle's "magnificence" and Castiglione's *sprezzatura*. Both prince and courtier sought to demonstrate their status in sound, whether by acts of patronage or by carefully staged performances. For musical thinkers like Tinctoris or Ficino, the origins, purposes, and workings of music remained subjects of intense speculation and debate. In keeping with ancient Pythagorean doctrines, music was often identified with the enduring, rational structure of the cosmos.

Alongside this intellectual thread we have examined a set of new ideas that sought to align music with language rather than with number, and above all with the humanistic arts of eloquence, oratory, and persuasion. It was here that new sounds—and new combinations of old sounds—were put to work in the expression of literary and sacred texts. The possibilities for combining text and tone are endlessly rich, from the intricate courtly rondeaux of Beatrice's chansonnier to the vivid images and feelings heard in madrigals by Jacques Arcadelt, Luca Marenzio, or John Wilbye. For composers of religious music, too, the relationship between text and tone was an irresistible attraction, as we have heard in the moving works of Josquin, Lasso, Byrd, and others.

The comparatively new technology of music printing figured centrally in many of these developments. It was through print that music moved beyond the narrow confines of the court and church, inaugurating new publics for music across wide geographical and social divides. There were new roles for amateurs as collectors and performers, and new roles for women no less than for men. It was through print that unwritten routines of counterpoint, ornamentation, and embellishment were taught and widely disseminated. It was through printed tablatures and arrangements that amateur instrumentalists were able to experiment with all manner of vocal genres, sacred as well as secular. Finally, it was through print technology that the roles of composer and interpreter became increasingly differentiated, giving rise to a new consciousness about the status of musical works themselves.

This was neither the first nor the last time that new technologies, from notation to sound recording, exerted profound effects on the uses and means of music-making. But in music, as in many other areas of European culture, print accelerated change. It also encouraged the rapid movement of the formerly perishable medium of music across huge gulfs of experience, as Europeans came into contact with other cultures at home and abroad. The music of the fifteenth and sixteenth centuries cannot help but sound as foreign to us as the music of these distant communities must have sounded to the men and women of the Renaissance. Whether such cross-cultural or transhistorical listening is possible remains an open question. But through this book and the scores, we may begin to approach the musical ideas of Du Fay, Tinctoris, Josquin, Castiglione, Willaert, Zarlino, Palestrina, and Marenzio from their vantage point as well as ours.

FOR FURTHER READING

Tomlinson, Gary, *Monteverdi and the End of the Renaissance* (Berkeley and Los Angeles: University of California Press, 1987)

Van Orden, Kate, *Music, Discipline, and Arms in Early Modern France* (Chicago: University of Chicago Press, 2005)

Watkins, Glenn, *The Gesualdo Hex: Music, Myth, and Memory* (New York: W. W. Norton, 2010)

◎ Additional resources available at wwnorton.com/studyspace

GLOSSARY

Agnus Dei (Latin, "Lamb of God") Fifth of the five sections of the mass.

altus (Latin, "high") In Renaissance music, vocal part in range between tenor and superius. Originally, *contratenor altus*.

antiphon A chant sung as a refrain to the verses of a psalm; also, a polyphonic setting of an antiphon.

authentic mode A mode in which the final tone is at the bottom of the range. Compare with *plagal mode*.

bas (French, "low") Designation of quiet instruments such as harp, lute, and recorder; compare with *haut*.

basse danse (French, "low dance") Type of stately couple dance of the fifteenth and early sixteenth centuries, often with a slow-moving melodic line and other lines improvised above.

basso ostinato (Italian, "persistent bass") Also called *ground bass*; a continuously repeating bass pattern, over which the melody changes in the form of variations.

bassus (Latin, "low") The lowest vocal part; originally *contratenor bassus*.

breve (from Latin *brevis*, "short") In medieval and Renaissance notation, the rhythmic value between the long and the semibreve, equal to two or three semibreves.

cadence Close of a musical phrase.

canon (Latin, "rule") A polyphonic compositional technique in which a rule or set of rules is applied to a single voice to derive an additional voice or voices; such rules might include singing the melody backwards, in mirror form, at different pitch, or at a different speed.

cantus (Latin, "melody") In Renaissance music, the highest voice, especially the texted voice in a polyphonic song. In some pieces, this role is also called *superius*.

cantus firmus (Latin, "fixed melody") A plainchant or other existing melody that is used for the basis of a polyphonic work, in which it is often presented in long time values.

cantus-firmus mass A mass in which each move ment is based on the same cantus firmus, usually in the tenor.

canzonetta (Italian, "little song") Polyphonic song genre of the sixteenth century in a light, homorhythmic style.

carol Popular song of England with a religious subject, generally with multiple verses or a verse-and-refrain structure.

chanson (French, "song") Secular song with French poetic text, especially one with a polyphonic setting.

chansonnier (French, "songbook") Manuscript collection of monophonic or polyphonic French secular songs.

chant See *plainchant*.

chapel Group of musicians and clerics employed to officiate and provide music at the private chapel of a patron.

choir Vocal ensemble, particularly one used to perform in religious services.

choirbook Manuscript book from which choir members read, with vocal parts written individually on the same page.

church mode See *mode* (1).

concerto delle donne Professional virtuosic vocal ensemble of women, particularly associated with the court at Ferrara in the late sixteenth century.

consonance Interval or sonority that is considered stable or harmonious. Compare with *dissonance*.

contrafactum (Latin, "counterfeit"; pl. *contrafacta*) A musical work in which a new text, sometimes in a different language, has been substituted for the old.

contrapuntal Employing counterpoint.

contratenor (Latin, "against the tenor") Originally, a vocal part composed as counterpoint to a tenor, in the same range; by the later Renaissance, equivalent to *contratenor altus*.

contratenor altus ("high countertenor") Contratenor part written somewhat higher than the tenor; often written *altus*.

contratenor bassus Contratenor part written somewhat lower than the tenor; often written *bassus*.

counterpoint The compositional practice or method of combining melodic lines, resulting in polyphony.

courtly love Idealized love between man and woman, celebrated in the songs of troubadours and trouvères.

Credo (Latin, "I believe") Third of the five sections of a mass, containing the creed or statement of faith.

cross-relation The occurrence, simultaneously or in quick succession, of two different chromatic forms of a note (e.g., F and F-sharp) in two different voices; also called *false relation*.

cycle A general term for a group of related works that can be thought of as a whole, as for example madrigal cycles or masses.

descant See *discant*.

diminution In the sixteenth and seventeenth centuries, a type of improvisation or ornamentation in which the notes of the melody are subdivided into smaller values using scales and other melodic figures.

discant (Latin, "singing apart") (1) In the late Middle Ages, improvised singing above a plainchant. (2) See *superius*.

dissonance Interval or sonority that is considered unstable or harsh, requiring resolution to a consonance.

division See *diminution*.

faburden English style of fauxbourdon in which the liturgical melody is in the middle voice, with the additional voices added a perfect fourth above and a third below (but moving to a fifth below at structural points).

false relation See *cross-relation*.

fantasia (Italian, "fantasy"), **fantasy** Instrumental composition that is improvisatory in style, often employing imitative techniques.

fauxbourdon Parallel harmonizing technique encountered in fifteenth-century continental music, in which the liturgical melody is harmonized below in parallel sixths that cadence to octaves, with a third voice added in parallel perfect fourths below the top voice.

folia (Italian, "madness") A contrapuntal scheme originating from a dance and popular as the basis for instrumental variations in the late Renaissance and Baroque.

forme fixe (French, "fixed forms") Type of musical-poetic form such as a rondeau or virelai based on patterns of repetition, popular in late medieval and fifteenth-century French chansons.

frottola (pl. *frottole*) Italian genre of secular polyphonic song of the late fifteenth and early sixteenth centuries, tending to be homorhythmic and syllabic, often with light or witty text.

galliard Sixteenth-century dance in fast triple meter and commonly with three repeated sections, often written to follow a pavane.

gamut In the musical system of the Middle Ages and Renaissance, the full range of sung pitches from low ("gamma") to high ("ut").

Gloria (Latin, "Glory") Second of the five sections of a mass.

Gregorian chant The repertory of plainchant used in the Roman Catholic Church.

ground bass See *basso ostinato*.

harpsichord Keyboard instrument, popular throughout the Renaissance and Baroque, in which strings are plucked.

haut (French, "high") Designation for loud instruments such as trumpet, shawm, and sackbut. Compare with *bas*.

heterophony Musical texture that results when two or more voices or instruments perform a melodic line together but in different ways, as with different embellishments.

hexachord (from Greek, "six strings") In medieval and Renaissance music solmization and theory, the organization of the gamut into overlapping series of six pitches, *ut, re, mi, fa, sol, la*, starting on C, F, or G; the semitone is defined as between *mi* and *fa*.

homorhythmic Relating to a texture with voices or instruments moving in the same rhythm.

Hours of the Divine Office See *Office*.

imitation A device in polyphonic music in which one voice or musical line repeats a melodic segment of another voice, immediately after and sometimes overlapping, at the same or a different pitch.

imitation mass Mass in which the polyphony of all five movements makes use of the voices of a polyphonic chanson or other model. Also called *parody mass*.

imitative counterpoint Technique of contrapuntal composition employing imitation.

imperfect division In medieval and Renaissance notation, the relation of one to two between two levels of time units; see *mode, time, and prolation*.

improvisation Spontaneous invention or elaboration of music while performing, including devising *diminutions* and *ornamentation*.

intabulation Arrangement of a polyphonic vocal composition for lute or other solo instrument, often written in tablature.

just intonation Tuning of pitches according to their natural harmonic ratios; according to this system, some thirds and fifths of a scale are perfectly in tune, while others are somewhat or even extremely out of tune. Compare with *temperament*.

Kyrie (Greek, "Lord") First of the five sections of a mass, with a short, three-part Greek text.

Leise German devotional song.

lira da braccio Bowed instrument of Renaissance Italy, with about seven strings, including pair of octave drone strings. Held like a violin, and often used to improvise accompaniments to sung poetry.

liturgy The prescribed body of texts to be spoken or sung and ritual actions to be performed in a religious service.

long In medieval and Renaissance notation, the longest time value, equal to two or three breves.

lute Pear-shaped string instrument with a wide fretted neck, a single treble string, and five or more additional pairs of strings; in the Renaissance it was plucked with fingertips and was commonly used for polyphonic music.

lute song Solo song with lute accompaniment, popular in Renaissance England.

madrigal (Italian *madrigale*, "song in the mother tongue") Setting of secular poetry as a polyphonic vocal work, often featuring elaborate musical depiction of the text, and popular in sixteenth-century Italy and Elizabethan England.

madrigal comedy, madrigal cycle A work of the late Renaissance consisting of a series of madrigals in succession, presenting a plot or series of connected scenes.

major scale Scale with a major third and major seventh above the keynote.

Mass (from Latin *missa*, "dismissed") (1) (*capitalized*) Main service of the Roman Catholic service. (2) Musical setting of the texts of the Ordinary of the Mass, usually the Kyrie, Gloria, Credo, Sanctus, and Agnus Dei.

mean-tone temperament A type of temperament used widely for keyboard instruments of the Renaissance, making fifths narrow (flat) in order to favor major thirds.

melisma A segment of melody in which many notes are sung to a single syllable of text.

melismatic Using many melismas; compare with *syllabic*.

mensuration canon A canon in which the same music is sung by different voices according to different mensuration signs.

mensuration sign In late medieval and Renaissance music, sign used to indicate mode, time, and prolation; predecessor of time signature.

meter Regular pattern of strong and weak beats.

metrical psalm Psalm that has been translated into metrical, rhymed verses in the vernacular and set with the same music for each verse.

minim In late medieval and Renaissance music notation, the note value equal to half or a third of a semibreve.

minor scale Scale with a minor third, sixth, and seventh above the keynote.

mode (1) A scale or melody type, identified by the particular intervallic relationships among the pitches; in particular one of the eight (later twelve) scale or melody types recognized by church musicians and theorists beginning in the Middle Ages (and often termed *church mode*), distinguished from one another by the arrangement whole and half steps in relation to the final tone. (2) Mode, time, and prolation.

mode, time, and prolation (Latin *modus, tempus, prolatio*) The three levels of division in the rhythmic notation of the Renaissance, indicated by mensuration signs; mode defines the triple (perfect) or duple (imperfect) relationship of long to breve; time of breve to semibreve, and prolation of semibreve to minim.

monophony Music or musical texture consisting of unaccompanied melody.

motet (from French *mot*, "word") (1) In the late Middle Ages, polyphonic vocal composition based on a tenor, in which other, usually faster-moving, vocal lines are added, each with its own text, in Latin or vernacular and not necessarily related. (2) In the Renaissance, a name used generally for a polyphonic setting of a sacred text (other than the mass).

musica ficta (Latin, "false music") (1) Musical tones outside the gamut. (2) In medieval and Renaissance polyphonic music, practice in which musicians perform a written tone with an alteration (a semitone higher or lower) according to their knowledge of counterpoint.

musica humana In the scheme of medieval theorist Boethius, the "music" that harmonizes the human body and soul.

musica instrumentalis According to medieval theorist Boethius, music in the common sense, as produced by instruments and voices.

musica mundana In the scheme of medieval theorist Boethius, the "music" that is the result of numerical relationships in the stars, seasons, and other nonhuman aspects of the physical world.

musica secreta Name for the highly expert, virtuosic, expressive music of sixteenth-century chapel music, particularly in courts such as Ferrara.

noël French strophic devotional song.

Office (from Latin *officium*, "obligation" or "ceremony") A series of eight prayer services celebrated at specified times of the day, especially in Roman Catholic monasteries and convents. Also known as the *Hours of the Divine Office*.

Ordinary (from Latin *ordinarium*, "usual") The portions of the Mass whose text is unchanging through the liturgical year, as compared with the Proper. See *mass* (2).

ornament A brief elaboration applied to a melodic line, often improvised by the performer.

ornamentation The practice of embellishing an instrumental or vocal part, whether notated by the composer or improvised by the performer.

paraphrase Reworking of a chant or other melodic line with changes to rhythm or added notes, and set polyphonically.

parody mass See *imitation mass*.

partbook An alternative to the choirbook format made practical by the invention of music printing, in which each vocal or instrumental part is bound separately or, in some cases, with two parts on facing pages.

pavane (pavan) Sixteenth-century dance in slow duple meter, commonly with three repeated sections. Often paired with a galliard.

perfect division In medieval and Renaissance notation, the relation of one to three between two levels of time units; see *mode, time, and prolation*.

Phrygian cadence Cadence in which the bottom voice moves down by a semitone and upper voices move up a whole tone to form a fifth and octave.

Phrygian tetrachord Tetrachord (or four-note scalar pattern) with a semitone between the lowest two pitches.

plagal mode A mode in which the final tone is in the middle of the range. Compare with *authentic mode*.

plainchant, plainsong A monophonic setting of liturgy.

points of imitation Musical texture in which successive text phrases are set imitatively in all voices of a polyphonic composition.

polyphony Musical texture consisting of two or more independent melodic lines, combined according to the practice of counterpoint.

prima prattica (Italian, "first practice") Claudio Monteverdi's term for the style and practice of sixteenth-century polyphony, characterized by strict adherence to contrapuntal rules for approaching and leaving dissonances. Compare with *seconda prattica*.

prolation See *mode, time, and prolation*.

psalm A poem of praise to God, one of 150 in the Book of Psalms in the Hebrew Scriptures (the Christian Old Testament). Singing psalms was a central part of Jewish, Christian, Catholic, and Protestant worship.

psalter A published collection of metrical psalms.

Pythagorean intonation A system of tuning the notes of a scale in use in the Middle Ages, in which fifths, but not thirds, are based on their natural harmonic ratios; compare with *just intonation* and *temperament*.

quinto, quintus (Latin, "fifth") In vocal or instrumental polyphonic music, the name often used for an additional part in five-part writing, often but not necessarily a middle part.

recorder End-blown wind instrument with a whistle mouthpiece, usually made of wood.

refrain A recurring verse in a poem or text which, in song, is set to a recurring melody.

Renaissance (French, "rebirth") Period approximately defined by the fifteenth and sixteenth centuries, which in arts were particularly characterized by an emphasis on humanism, individual expression, and a revival of ideas from ancient Greece.

res facta (Latin, "something made") Written musical composition, which is required to follow principles of counterpoint, as opposed to improvised counterpoint.

respond A refrain that is used as a response, traditionally sung by a group in response to solo verses of a psalm.

responsorial Pertaining to a manner of performing or a type of plainchant, such as a psalm or hymn, with a soloist and group alternating.

retrograde Statement of a melodic line beginning with the last note and proceeding backwards.

ricercar, ricercare (Italian, "to seek out" or "to attempt") Instrumental work in improvisatory style, or, starting in the late Renaissance, involving imitation.

romanesca A contrapuntal pattern that was popular as the basis for dance and instrumental variations in the late Renaissance.

rondeau (pl. *rondeaux*) A one-stanza poetic forme fixe that begins and ends with a refrain, with verses and a partial refrain between.

sackbut Early trombone, popular in the Renaissance.

Sanctus (Latin, "Holy") Fourth of the five sections of a mass, beginning with the invocation "Holy, holy, holy" from Isaiah 6:3.

scale The arrangement in ascending or descending order of the pitches used as the basis of a melody or musical composition.

seconda prattica (Italian, "second practice") Claudio Monteverdi's term for compositional practice that places expression of text above rules of counterpoint, particularly with regard to dissonances, which he contrasted with the prima prattica prevalent in the sixteenth century.

semibreve In medieval and Renaissance notation, the time value equal to half or a third of a breve, and to two or three minims.

semiminim In late medieval and Renaissance music notation, the note value equal to half of a minim.

shawm Double-reed instrument used in the late Middle Ages through the early seventeenth century, precursor of the oboe.

solmization A method of singing using assigned syllables (especially *ut, re, mi, fa, so, la*; see *hexachord*).

superius (Latin, "highest") In Renaissance music, the highest vocal part, eventually equivalent to soprano.

syllabic Using a musical setting of one note per syllable of text. Compare with *melismatic*.

tablature A system of notating music for lute or other fretted instruments according to placement of fingers rather than identification of pitch.

temperament Any system of tuning that compromises (tempers) just intonation in order to avoid extremely out-of-tune intervals; the result is that most intervals are very slightly out of tune.

tenor (from Latin *tenere*, "to hold") (1) Fundamental voice of polyphonic music, a slow-moving plainchant (or other borrowed melody) around which other voices were composed. (2) By the late Renaissance, a vocal part lying between bassus and altus.

tenor mass See *cantus-firmus mass*.

tetrachord (from Greek, "four strings") In Greek and medieval music theory, a series of four pitches arranged by step and spanning a perfect fourth.

time See *mode, time, and prolation*.

time signature Sign or numerical proportion placed at the beginning of a musical composition to indicate notated meter.

transcription Arrangement of a piece from one medium to another, for example of a polyphonic vocal piece for lute solo.

troubadour Poet-composer of monophonic songs of the twelfth and thirteenth centuries, writing in the language of southern French (*langue d'oc*), especially on the topic of courtly love.

trouvère Poet-composer of monophonic songs of the twelfth and thirteenth centuries, writing in the language of northern France (*langue d'oïl*), especially on the topic of courtly love.

variations Type of compositional form, usually structured by a cantus firmus, ground bass, or other material that is repeated, each time with different elaborations.

vihuela Guitar-like instrument of Renaissance Spain, generally with six pairs of strings.

villanella (pl. *villanelle*) Secular polyphonic song, generally in a simple three-voiced homorhythmic texture.

viol (viola da gamba) Bowed instrument with a fretted neck and six or seven strings, resting on or between the legs (*gamba*, leg), in wide use in the Renaissance and Baroque.

viola da braccio Bowed string instrument held on the shoulder (*braccio*, arm) like a violin.

virelai Musical-poetic forme fixe with a recurring refrain and stanzas in an **aab** form.

virtuoso Expert singer or instrumentalist who displays a very high level of technical ability.

ENDNOTES

CHAPTER 1

5. "Divide them into four segments": translation by Richard Taruskin, from *Music in the Western World: A History in Documents*, ed. Piero Weiss and Richard Taruskin, 2nd ed. (New York: Schirmer, 2008), p. 57.

5. "dispose your musicke": Thomas Morley, *A Plaine and Easie Introduction to Practicall Musicke* (London: P. Short, 1597), p. 177–78. Morley's treatise is also available in two online versions, from Indiana University's *Texts on Music in English* database (a transcription of the print of 1597) and from the University of North Texas Digital Library (a facsimile of an edition from 1771).

6. "If therefore you will compose in this kind": Morley, *A Plaine and Easie Introduction to Practicall Musicke*, p. 180.

13. SR 57:366; 3/22:88: Throughout the text, these citations refer to *Strunk's Source Readings in Music History*, Leo Treitler, general editor (New York: W. W. Norton, 1998). The first reference is to selection and page number in the one-volume edition. The second is to the volume in the seven-volume set, with selection and page number: in this case, volume 3 (*The Renaissance*, ed. Gary Tomlinson), selection 22, page 88.

CHAPTER 2

18. "But I refusing and pretending ignorance": Thomas Morley, *A Plaine and Easie Introduction to Practicall Musicke* (London: P. Short, 1597), p. 1.

18. "Begin at the verie beginning": Morley, *A Plaine and Easie Introduction to Practicall Musicke*, p. 2.

23. "Here be some following of two parts": Morley, *A Plaine and Easie Introduction to Practicall Musicke*, p. 55.

24. "Through these examples": Sebald Heyden, *De arte canendi*, trans. Clement Miller, Musicological Studies and Documents, 26 (n.p.: American Institute of Musicology, 1972), p. 40.

24. "art that is suited for princes and noblemen": Ihan Gero, *Il primo libro de' madrigali italiani et canzoni francese a due voci*, ed. Lawrence Bernstein and James Haar, Masters and Monuments of the Renaissance, 1 (New York: Broude Bros., 1980), p. xxiii.

24. "I have gone through your 'Letatus sum'": *A Correspondence of Renaissance Musicians*, ed. Bonnie J. Blackburn, Edward E. Lowinsky, and Clement A. Miller (Oxford: Clarendon Press, 1991), p. 443.

25. *Novae aliquot . . . ad duas voces cantiones*: See Orlando di Lasso, *Liber mottetarum trium*

vocum; novae aliquot, ad duas voces cantiones, ed. Peter Bergquist, Orlando di Lasso: The Complete Motets, 11, Recent Researches in the Music of the Renaissance, 103 (Madison, WI: A-R Editions, 1995).

26. "for it must proceede only of the judgement of the composer": Morley, A Plaine and Easie Introduction to Practicall Musicke, p. 147.

26. "Just as I predicted, it came out without order and truth": A Correspondence of Renaissance Musicians, ed. Blackburn et al., p. 376.

28. "each mode was capable of including different passions": Gioseffo Zarlino, On the Modes: Part Four of Le istitutioni harmoniche, 1558, trans. Vered Cohen, ed. Claude V. Palisca (New Haven: Yale University Press, 1983), p. 20.

28. "some claiming one thing and others another": Zarlino, On the Modes: Part Four of Le istitutioni harmoniche, 1558, p. 26.

28. "Excellent musitions have discontinued it": Morley, A Plaine and Easie Introduction to Practicall Musicke, p. 121.

29. "counterpoint" as second in importance only to the study of liturgical plainsong: see the excerpt from Gerson's regulations in Craig Wright, Music and Ceremony at Notre Dame of Paris, 500–1550 (Cambridge and New York: Cambridge University Press, 1989), p. 167.

30. rules for "syngers or makers or techers": Sanford B. Meech, "Three Musical Treatises in English from a Fifteenth-Century Manuscript," Speculum 10 (1935): 242.

31. "Those who are more doltish than really learned in music": Clement A. Miller, "Erasmus on Music," Musical Quarterly 52 (1966): 339.

31. "I have known not even one man": Johannes Tinctoris, The Art of Counterpoint, trans. Albert Seay (n.p.: American Institute of Musicology, 1961), p. 141.

32. "A method of singing counterpoint is rare in Germany": Adrianus Petit Coclico, Musical Compendium, trans. Albert Seay (Colorado Springs, CO: University of Colorado Press, 1973), p. 21.

32. "here is how we ought to use them": Adrianus Petit Coclico, Musical Compendium, p. 23.

33. Polyphonic music "requireth most art": Morley, A Plaine and Easie Introduction to Practicall Musicke, p. 179.

CHAPTER 3

40. "Monday, the 8th day of the said month": Jean Le Févre, Chronique de Jean Le Févre, Seigneur de Saint-Remy, ed. François Morand, 2 vols. (Paris: Librairie Renouard, 1876–81), 2:293.

41. "and before the tables came knights, squires, trumpeters, and minstrels": Le Févre, Chronique de Jean Le Févre, Seigneur de Saint-Remy, 2:293–94.

43. "Magnificence is an attribute of expenditures of the kind which we call honourable": Aristotle, Nicomachean Ethics, 1122^b. Cited in The Complete Works of Aristotle: The Revised Oxford Translation, 2 vols., ed. Jonathan Barnes (Princeton: Princeton University Press, 1984), 2:1772.

46. "Since we have decided to make a chapel": Paul Merkley and Lora L. M. Merkley, Music and Patronage in the Sforza Court (Turnhout: Brepols, 1999), p. 42.

50. "O virgin worthy of God's throne": Translation from Leeman L. Perkins and Howard Garey, The Mellon Chansonnier, 2 vols. (New Haven: Yale University Press, 1979), 2:424.

50. "Fair Welcome, the servant of Love": Translation from Perkins and Garey, The Mellon Chansonnier, 2:188–89.

53. "Little Snubnose, you've put me to death": Translation from Perkins and Garey, The Mellon Chansonnier, 2:201.

55. "some teams will take the treble part of any piece you care to give them": Anthony Baines, "Fifteenth-Century Instruments in Tinctoris's De Inventione et Usu Musicae," Galpin Society Journal 3 (1950): 24.

CHAPTER 4

59. "First, for the instruction of simple people": Cited in Michael Baxandall, Painting and Experience in Fifteenth-Century Italy: A Primer in the Social History of Pictorial Style (New York: Oxford University Press, 1972), p. 41.

63. "earns the companionship of the angels": Gilles Carlier and Johannes Tinctoris, On the Dignity & the Effects of Music: Two Fifteenth-Century Treatises, trans. and ed. J. Donald Cullington and Reinhard Strohm (London:

Institute of Advanced Musical Studies, King's College London, 1996), p. 29.

63. "If at the death of certain saints": Carlier and Tinctoris, *On the Dignity & the Effects of Music*, p. 30.

64. "Have mercy on your dying Du Fay": Translation by Allan W. Atlas, *Anthology of Renaissance Music: Music in Western Europe, 1400–1600* (New York: W. W. Norton, 1998), p. 489.

66–67. On Obrecht's *Missa de Sancto Donatiano*: M. Jennifer Bloxam, "Saint Donatian Mass: Jacob Obrecht," http://obrechtmass.com.

67. "How lovely and wonderful you are, most beloved": translation by Allan W. Atlas, *Anthology of Renaissance Music: Music in Western Europe, 1400–1600* (New York: W. W. Norton, 1998), p. 487.

72. "There is no rose of such virtue": Modern English translation by Lawrence Rosenwald and members of Anonymous 4 vocal ensemble, from *On Yoolis Night* (Harmonia mundi 907099, [1993]), pp. 70–72.

74. The entire assembly turned through the gate: Reinhard Strohm, *Music in Late Medieval Bruges*, rev. ed. (Oxford: Clarendon Press, 1990), pp. 80–83.

75. Perhaps the idea was prompted by a reference to the "psalm-like" sound of streams: Idea suggested by Willem Elders, "Guillaume Du Fay's Concept of Faux-Bourdon," *Revue belge de Musicologie/Belgisch Tijdschrift voor Muziekwetenschap* 43 (1989): 179.

CHAPTER 5

81. Musical actions embedded in these compositions: Anne Walters Robertson, "The Savior, the Woman, and the Head of the Dragon in the *Caput* Masses and Motet," *Journal of the American Musicological Society* 59 (2006): 537–630.

84. "L'homme armé doibt on doubter": quoted from Anthoine Busnoys, *Collected Works: The Latin-Texts Works*, ed. Richard Taruskin, Monuments and Masters of the Renaissance 5 (New York: Broude Brothers Trust, 1990), Part 3, p. 26. My translation.

84. "Cancer eat plenus sed redeat medius": Reinhard Strohm, *The Rise of European Music, 1380–1500* (Cambridge and New York: Cambridge University Press, 1993), p. 467.

84. "a rule showing the purpose of the composer": Johannes Tinctoris, *Dictionary of Musical Terms: An English Translation of Terminorum musicae diffinitorium*, trans. Carl Parrish (New York: Da Capo Press, 1978), pp. 12–13. A digital edition of Latin text is available online in Indiana University's *Thesaurus Musicarum Latinarum* database.

85. "enjoyment which truly refreshes the hearing": Henricus Glareanus, *Dodecachordon*, 2 vols., trans. Clement A. Miller (n.p.: American Institute of Musicology, 1965), 2:274.

87. A theological premise underlying the musical plan: Willem Elders, "Symbolism in the Sacred Music of Josquin," in *The Josquin Companion*, ed. Richard Sherr (Oxford: Oxford University Press, 2000), pp. 535–36.

87. Archetypes of moral rather than real combat: Craig Wright, *The Maze and the Warrior: Symbols in Architecture, Theology, and Music* (Cambridge, MA: Harvard University Press, 2001).

CHAPTER 6

97. "music has as its principles those of natural philosophy and those of number": Gioseffo Zarlino, *Le istitutioni harmoniche* (1573) (Ridgewood, NJ: Gregg Press, 1966), p. 38 (ch. 20).

98. "An octave was heard": Martin Agricola, *The "Musica Instrumentalis Deudsch" of Martin Agricola: A Treatise on Musical Instruments, 1529 and 1545*, trans. William E. Hettrick (Cambridge and New York: Cambridge University Press, 1994), p. 127.

98. "useful for all organ makers": Agricola, *The "Musica Instrumentalis Deudsch" of Martin Agricola*, p. 134.

100. "In order to have perfect knowledge concerning music": Gioseffo Zarlino, *On the Modes: Part Four of Le Istitutioni Harmoniche, 1558*, trans. Vered Cohen, ed. Claude V. Palisca (New Haven: Yale University Press, 1983), p. 106.

101. "Music itself comes together in our birth": Franchinus Gaffurius, *The Theory of Music*, trans. and ed. Walter Kurt Kreyszig (New Haven: Yale University Press, 1993), p. 37.

103. "The true melancholic": André Du Laurens, *Discours de la conservation de la veue. Des maladies mélancholiques des catarrhes, et de la vieilesse* (Rouen: Claude Le Villain, 1600), pp. 112–13.

104. A persistent melodic marker: Peter Holman, *Dowland Lachrimae (1604)* (New York and Cambridge: Cambridge University Press, 1999), p. 40.

106. "Many men are melancholy by hearing musicke": Robert Burton, *The Anatomy of Melancholy* (Oxford: John Lichfield and James Short, 1621), p. 375 [from Part 2 ("Cure of Melancholy"), Subsection 3 ("Musicke a Remedy")].

107. "I felt ravished by a celestial harmony": Pontus de Tyard, *Oeuvres: Solitaire premier*, ed. Silvio Baridon (Geneva: Droz, 1950), p. 5, lines 15–16.

107. "divine furor, or what the Greeks term Enthusiasm": de Tyard, *Oeuvres: Solitaire premier*, p. 10, lines 174–76.

111. "Why is it that all those who have become eminent": Pseudo-Aristotle, *Problems*, Book 30, Section 953a. Cited in Aristotle, *The Complete Works of Aristotle: The Revised Oxford Translation*, 2 vols., ed. Jonathan Barnes (Princeton: Princeton University Press, 1984), 2:1498–99.

CHAPTER 7

114. "Should he stray from the path of his forebears": Baldassarre Castiglione, *The Book of the Courtier: The Singleton Translation, an Authoritative Text Criticism*, ed. Daniel Javitch (New York: W. W. Norton, 2002), Book I, Section 14. All further references are to book and section numbers.

116. "collected many very excellent and rare books in Greek, Latin, and Hebrew": Castiglione, *The Book of the Courtier*, I.2.

117. "Whenever the Courtier chances to be engaged in a skirmish": Castiglione, *The Book of the Courtier*, II.8.

117. "Whether in word or deed": Castiglione, *The Book of the Courtier*, I.26.

117. "cool ease": Castiglione, *The Book of the Courtier*, I.26.

117. "in showing no concern, and in seeming to have one's thoughts elsewhere": Castiglione, *The Book of the Courtier*, I.27.

117. the term "recklessness": "a certain Reckelesness," cited in *The courtyer of Count Baldessar Castilio diuided into foure bookes. Very necessary and profitable for yonge gentilmen and gentilwomen abiding in court, palaice or place, done into English by Thomas Hoby* (London: William Seres, 1561), fol. E ii recto. Also in modern edition as *The Book of the Courtier, from the Italian of Count Baldassare Castiglione, done into English by Sir Thomas Hoby anno 1561* (London: David Nutt, 1900), p. 59.

117. "And although he may know and understand what he does": Castiglione, *The Book of the Courtier*, II.12.

118. "so that it seems that they have put in an appearance": Castiglione, *The Book of the Courtier*, II.12. For the Hoby translation of this passage, see SR 45:325–29; 3/10:47–51.

118. "we note and follow the fine style and the melody": Castiglione, *The Book of the Courtier*, II.13.

118. "It is especially appropriate when ladies are present": Castiglione, *The Book of the Courtier*, II.13.

118. "the moste noble and melodious instrument of Musicke": quoted in Adrian Le Roy, *A briefe and plaine instruction to set all musicke of eight divers tunes in tableture for the lute* (London: James Rowbothome, 1574), p. 5. Available as a digital facsimile at Early English Books Online.

121. "In a manner serene and full of plaintive sweetness": Castiglione, *The Book of the Courtier*, I.37.

121. "the world is made up of music": Castiglione, *The Book of the Courtier*, I.47.

123. "ignorance and self-conceit": Castiglione, *The Book of the Courtier*, IV.6.

123. "famous captains and other excellent men": Castiglione, *The Book of the Courtier*, IV.9.

123. "mind continually occupied with worthy pleasures": Castiglione, *The Book of the Courtier*, IV.10.

124. "of whose admirable virtues": Castiglione, *The Book of the Courtier*, III.36.

125. "virtues of mind": Castiglione, *The Book of the Courtier*, III.5.

125. "have knowledge of letters, of music, of painting": Castiglione, *The Book of the Courtier*, III.9.

125. "And so when she dances": Castiglione, *The Book of the Courtier*, III.8.

127. "Signor Guilio Cesare said very angrily": Richard Wistreich, *Warrior, Courtier, Singer: Giulio Cesare Brancaccio and the Performance of Identity in the Late Renaissance* (Aldershot and Burlington, VT: Ashgate, 2007), p. 250, from a letter of 28 July 1583, from Alessandro Lombardini to Cardinal Luigi d'Este, Alfonso's brother.

128. "disdained the pursuit of this profession": From Rolando Pico, *Appendice di vari soggetti parmigiani* (Parma, 1642), [p. 192], quoted in *Neapolitan Lute Music: Fabrizio Dentice, Giulio Severino, Giovanni Antonio Severino, Francesco Cardone*, ed. John Griffiths and Dinko Fabris, Recent Researches in the Music of the Renaissance, 140 (Middleton, WI: A-R Editions, 2004), p. xii.

128. "But when after manie excuses, I protested": Morley, *A Plaine and Easie Introduction to Practicall Musicke*, p. 1.

CHAPTER 8

131. "an already perfect art": Henricus Glareanus, *Dodecachordon*, 2 vols., trans. Clement A. Miller (n.p.: American Institute of Musicology, 1965), 2:248.

133. "My Lord, I believe that there is neither lord nor king": Lewis Lockwood, "Josquin at Ferrara: New Documents and Letters," in *Josquin Des Prez: Proceedings of the International Josquin Festival-Conference Held at the Juilliard School at Lincoln Center in New York City, 21–25 June 1971*, ed. Edward E. Lowinsky (London and New York: Oxford University Press, 1976), p. 131.

134. "To me he seems well suited": Lockwood, "Josquin at Ferrara: New Documents and Letters," p. 133.

137. "It is not long ago that certain verses": Baldassarre Castiglione, *The Book of the Courtier: The Singleton Translation, an Authoritative Text Criticism*, ed. Daniel Javitch (New York: W. W. Norton, 2002), Book II, Section 35.

137. Johannes Ghiselin "is sending a new work": Lockwood, "Josquin at Ferrara: New Documents and Letters," p. 110.

138. Petrucci meant the book as a public tribute: Stanley Boorman, *Ottaviano Petrucci: Catalogue Raisonné* (New York: Oxford University Press, 2006), p. 284.

138. "All will easily recognize JOSQUIN": Stephanie P. Schlagel, "The *Liber Selectarum Cantionum* and the 'German Josquin Renaissance,'" *Journal of Musicology* 19 (2002): 590.

139. Georg Forster recalled "that a certain famous man said": Translation from Rob C. Wegman, "Who Was Josquin," in *The Josquin Companion*, ed. Richard Sherr (Oxford: Oxford University Press, 2000), p. 27. Latin original in Helmuth Osthoff, *Josquin Desprez*, 2 vols. (Tützing: G. Olms, 1962–65), 2:9.

140. when Willaert "pointed out that it was in fact his own": Gioseffo Zarlino, *On the Modes: Part Four of* Le Istitutioni Harmoniche, *1558*, trans. Vered Cohen, ed. Claude V. Palisca (New Haven: Yale University Press, 1983), chapter 36. Translation from Wegman, "Who Was Josquin," p. 25.

143. Some startling revisions in recent years: See the Selected Readings for references.

145. "I was entrusted to the protection of the most noble musician Josquin": Adrianus Petit Coclico, *Musical Compendium*, trans. Albert Seay (Colorado Springs: University of Colorado Press, 1973), p. 7.

145. "My teacher, Josquin des Prez": Coclico, *Musical Compendium*, p. 16.

146. "No creative individual can be seen as totally distinct": Wegman, "Who Was Josquin," p. 38.

147. "in compositions of this kind, to say frankly what I believe": Glareanus, *Dodecachordon*, 2:274.

147. "If the knowledge of twelve modes and of a true musical system": Glareanus, *Dodecachordon*, 2:264.

CHAPTER 9

163. "Each of you, benign readers, knows": Thomas Whitney Bridges, "The Publishing of Arcadelt's First Book of Madrigals" (Ph.D. diss., Harvard University, 1982), p. 205.

163. A copy was presented to him or her by the composer or printer: For a typical presentation text, see the dedication of Palestrina's mass book of 1567, in SR 60: 373–74; 3/25:95–96.

164. The personal library of Jean de Badonvillier: François Lesure, "Un amateur de musique au début du XVIᵉ siècle, Jean De Bandonvillier," in *Musique et musiciens français du XVIᵉsiècle* (Geneva: Slatkine, 1976), pp. 79–81.

CHAPTER 10

177. "Mille regrets de vous abandoner": translation by Frank Dobbins, *The Oxford Book of French Chansons* (Oxford: Oxford University Press, 1987), p. 329.

178. "Martin menoit son pourceau au marché": translation by Dobbins, *Oxford Book of French Chanson*, p. 330.

180. "If therefore you will compose in this kind": Thomas Morley, *A Plaine and Easie Introduction to Practicall Musicke* (London: P. Short, 1597), p. 179.

181. "Il bianco e dolce cigno": translation by Alan Atlas, *Anthology of Renaissance Music*, p. 494.

183. "Madonna mia famme bon'offerta": translation from Adrian Willaert et al., *Canzone villanesche alla napolitana and villotte*, ed. Donna G. Cardamone, Recent Researches in the Music of the Renaissance, 30 (Madison, WI: A-R Editions, 1978), pp. xxvii–xxviii.

186. "Ancor che col partire": texts and translations by Derek Yeld, from Vecchi, *L'amfiparnaso*, performed by Ensemble Clément Janequin, dir. Dominique Visse (Harmonia mundi 901461, 1993), pp. 38–39. Modern edition of the parody madrigal in Orazio Vecchi, *L'amfiparnaso: A New Edition of the Music with Historical and Analytic Essays*, ed. Cecil Adkins (Chapel Hill: University of North Carolina Press, 1977), pp. 70–73.

189. "Liquide perle Amor da gl'occhi sparse": translation from Marco Bizzarini, *Luca Marenzio: The Career of a Musician between the Renaissance and the Counter-Reformation*, trans. James Chater (Aldershot: Ashgate, 2003), p. 142.

CHAPTER 11

195. "most strange effects in the hearer": Thomas Morley, *A Plaine and Easie Introduction to Practicall Musicke* (London: P. Short, 1597), p. 179.

196. "In the very sentences there is such hidden and concealed power": William Byrd, *The Byrd Edition*, 17 vols. (London: Stainer & Bell, 1976), 5, ed. Philip Brett, p. xvii. For a slightly different translation see SR 63: 378; 3/28:100.

197. Byrd meant to keep the Eucharist more clearly before our eyes: Joseph Kerman, *The Masses and Motets of William Byrd* (London and Boston: Faber and Faber, 1981), p. 288.

198. "in accordance with the decree of the sacred Council of Trent": Lewis Lockwood, *The Counter-Reformation and the Masses of Vincenzo Ruffo* ([Vienna]: Universal Edition, 1970), p. 99.

199. "Therefore I have both already labored on those poems": Oliver Strunk, *Source Readings in Music History from Classical Antiquity through the Romantic Era* (New York: W. W. Norton, 1950), pp. 323–24 (not in SR).

207. "Do not be eager to become a papist priest": Martin Agricola, *The "Musica Instrumentalis Deudsch" of Martin Agricola: A Treatise on Musical Instruments, 1529 and 1545*, ed. William E. Hettrick (Cambridge and New York: Cambridge University Press, 1994), p. 73.

208. "as agreeable as it was marvelous": from Adrian Le Roy's letter to Orlando di Lasso in 1574, cited in Richard Freedman, "How a Printer Shaped Musical Tastes: Orlando di Lasso, Adrian Le Roy, and Listeners at the Royal Court of France," in *Die Münchner Hofkapelle des 16. Jahrhunderts in europäischen Kontext* (Munich: Bayerische Akademie der Wissenschaften, 2007), p. 149.

209. "The tenor of these partes be for the people when they will syng alone": from the preface to Matthew Parker, *The Whole Psalter*

Translated into English Metre, Which Contayneth a Hundreth and Fifty Psalmes (London: John Daye, 1567).

209. "to make the art of singing as easy and expeditious as possible": Sebald Heyden, *De arte Canendi*, trans. Clement A. Miller (n.p.: American Institute of Musicology, 1972), p. 22.

212. "But when learning is added to all this": Martin Luther, *Luther's Works*, ed. Ulrich S. Leupold and Helmut T. Lehmann, 55 vols. (Philadelphia: Fortress Press, 1955–86), 53:324.

213. "joined with serious texts and removed from all impurity": translated from the editor's preface to *Recueil du Mellange d'Orlande de Lassus, contenant plusieurs chansons tant en vers latins qu'en ryme francoyse, a quatre, et cinq parties* (London: Thomas Vautrollier, 1570).

228. "The *fantasía* one cannot demonstrate": Diego Ortiz, *Trattado de Glosas: New Edition in Four Languages of the Original Spanish and Italian Editions, Rome 1553*, trans. Annette Otterstedt and Hans Reiners (Kassel and New York: Bärenreiter, 2003), p. 73.

229. "upon a subject": from Part III, ch. 63 of Gioseffo Zarlino, *Le istitutioni harmoniche (1573)* (Ridgewood, NJ: Gregg Press, 1966), p. 302.

229. "a point [of imitation] at his pleasure": Thomas Morley, *A Plaine and Easie Introduction to Practicall Musicke* (London: P. Short, 1597), p. 181.

229. "in the sense that it only proceeds from the fantasy and industry of the author": Luis Milán, *El Maestro*, trans. Charles Jacobs (University Park: Pennsylvania State University Press, 1971), p. 296.

CHAPTER 12

217. "the little experience I have acquired while I was conversing in houses": Vincenzo Giustiniani, *Discorso sopra la musica*, trans. Carol MacClintock (n.p.: American Institute of Musicology, 1962), p. 67; this passage is not in SR.

219. "the marvels, art, character, voice, grace, disposition, memory, and the other abundant and rare qualities": Carol MacClintock, *Giaches de Wert (1535–1596): Life and Works*, Musicological Studies and Documents, 17 (Rome: American Institute of Musicology, 1966), p. 236.

220. "O verdi selve, o dolci fonti, o rivi": text and translation from Luca Marenzio, *Il Sesto libro de madrigali a sei voci (1595)*, ed. Patricia Myers, Luca Marenzio: The Secular Works, 6 (New York: The Broude Trust, 1983), p. xxxv.

223. "First, they embellish the composition or enhance the counterpoint": Silvestro Ganassi, *Regola Rubertina. First and Second Part. A Manual of Playing the Viola da gamba and of Playing the Lute. Venice 1542 and 1543*, ed. Hildemarie Peter, trans. Daphne and Stephen Silvester (Berlin: Robert Lineau, 1977), p. 9.

225. "diminution always causes the loss of numerous consonances": Nicola Vicentino, *Ancient Music Adapted to Modern Practice*, trans. Maria Rika Maniates (New Haven: Yale University Press, 1996), p. 300.

CHAPTER 13

235. "After glorious ordeals": translation quoted from Andrea Gabrieli, *Complete Madrigals 2: Madrigals a 4, Greghesche a 4, 5, and 7*, ed. A. Tillman Merritt, Recent Researches in the Music of the Renaissance, 42 (Madison, WI: A-R Editions, 1981), p. xiii.

236. A young man performing the dance with a blackened face: Thoinot Arbeau, *Orchesography* (New York: Dover Publications, 1967), p. 177.

237. "The spectacle of which I speak is beheld by the imagination": Orazio Vecchi, *L'amfiparnaso. A New Edition of the Music with Historical and Analytic Essays*, ed. Cecil Adkins (Chapel Hill: University of North Carolina Press, 1977), p. 17.

238. Samuel Ariono owned a copy of the treatise *Le istitutioni harmoniche*: Shlomo Simonsohn, "Sefarim v'seferot shel y'hudi mantova, 1595," *Kiryat sefer* 37 (1962): 108 and 112.

240. "Whenever I remember it my heart trembles": Jean de Léry, *History of a Voyage to the Land of Brazil, Otherwise Called America*, trans. Janet Whatley (Berkeley: University of California Press, 1990), p. 144.

240. "As I was passing with them through a great forest": Jean de Léry, *History of a Voyage to the Land of Brazil*, p. 149.

240. "first been sung more than 10,000 moons ago": de Léry, *History of a Voyage to the Land of Brazil*, p. 149.

240. "the unknowne paths of Paganism, Idolatrie, and superstition": John Smith, *A True Relation of Such Occurrences and Accidents of Noate as Hath Hapned in Virginia since the First Planting of That Collony* (London: Printed for I. Tappe, 1608), p. 3.

241. "such a terrible howling": From Strachey, *Historie of Travaile into Virginia Britannia* (London, ca. 1610), quoted in Andrew Hadfield, *Amazons, Savages, and Machiavels: Travel and Colonial Writing in English, 1550–1630: An Anthology* (Oxford and New York: Oxford University Press, 2001), pp. 300–301.

242. "We take these children in order that we may separate them from heathen influences": Robert Stevenson, *Music in Mexico, a Historical Survey* (New York: Crowell, 1952), p. 54.

243. "The dignitaries having finally entered the Church of San José": Stevenson, *Music in Mexico*, p. 89.

244. "Sancta maria yn ilhuicac cihuapille tinatzin dios yn titotenpantlatocantzin": text, translation, and transcription from Robert Stevenson, *Music in Aztec and Inca Territory* (Berkeley and Los Angeles: University of California Press, 1968), p. 206.

246. Various observations on the ceremonial music Ricci heard in China: see excerpts from Ricci's *Journal* in SR 80:505–8; note, however, that the English translation from the 1940s used there is flawed in a number of respects.

247. *Eight Songs for the Western Instruments*: examples in Jonathan D. Spence, *The Memory Palace of Matteo Ricci* (New York, NY: Viking Penguin, 1984), and via a web resource compiled by guqin scholar and performer John Thompson, www.silkqin.com.

248. "the foremost and perfect instrument": Nicola Vicentino, *Ancient Music Adapted to Modern Practice*, trans. Maria Rika Maniates (New Haven: Yale University Press, 1996), p. 315.

248. "All nations represent their own way of singing": Vicentino, *Ancient Music Adapted to Modern Practice*, p. 270.

CHAPTER 14

252. "Therefore may your most illustrious lordships deign to accept and receive this gift": translation by Stanley Appelbaum, from *Claudio Monteverdi Madrigals Books IV and V* (New York: Dover Publications, 1986), p. vii.

255. "to honor music of serious rationales, of serious notes and measures": quoted in Claude Le Jeune, *Dodecacorde, Comprising Twelve Psalms of David Set to Music According to the Twelve Modes*, 3 vols., ed. Anne Harrington Heider, Recent Researches in the Music of the Renaissance, 74–76 (Madison, WI: A-R Editions, 1988), 1:xvi–xvii.

PHOTOGRAPHS

MUSICAL EXAMPLES

INDEX

Note: Page numbers in *italics* indicate illustrations or musical examples.